The Church Can Change the World

Living from the Inside Out

Jimmy Seibert

This book is dedicated to:

Laura, my faithful, loyal, and loving wife – you are the perfect one for me.

Abby, Lauren, Caleb and Daniel - you are truly the greatest gifts I could ever have; and the entire Antioch family - your love and faithfulness have changed our lives.

With special thanks to Rebecca Herndon, who tirelessly compiled, edited, and partnered with me to write this story. Rebecca, thank you for your gifts, your skills, and your heart of love to Jesus. Most of all thank you for "carrying us through."

Contents

Preface

Dear Antioch family,

Over twenty years ago, Laura and I set out on a journey to love Jesus with all of our hearts, choosing to follow and obey Him wherever He would lead us. We never had the intention to be in full-time vocational ministry but simply to hear and respond to His call in our lives.

As we look back, we have seen God do above and beyond all that we could ask or think. Not only have we personally experienced His love, presence, and power, but God has brought us into a family of believers who have changed our lives and taken part in impacting the world around us.

Laura and I are so thankful for the mothers and fathers that God has brought to us, our kids, and to the whole movement. You have been the pillars we have needed as we have grown.

We are also thankful for the deep friendships that God has brought along the way: men and women to walk with who have encouraged us, spurred us on, and allowed us to be a part of something greater than ourselves.

To our sons and daughters in the faith, you have taken the vision and the values, in many instances, farther than we have. You started out as sons and daughters and now have become mothers and fathers yourselves, not only in the natural but also in the spiritual. We look forward to co-laboring with you for His glory until our last breath.

Laura and I are grateful for generation after generation of disciples, men and women who continue to be raised up in our midst. We are astounded at the love and faith, the community and desire to have a passion for Jesus and His purposes in the earth.

I remember having a conversation several years ago with a couple of leaders in the body of Christ. They commented that many people they had observed to be fruitful and successful had spent 20 to 25 years of their journey in one location. Our intention was not necessarily to be in Waco for 20 plus years, but that is where God has led us. And, as we look back, we are forever grateful. God has taken simple people from a small town in Texas and allowed us to see His hand at work all over the world. Archimedes said, "Give me but one firm spot on which to stand and I will move the earth." Truly, with this family, we have begun to see the first fruits of that statement come to pass.

In the following pages, we tell the stories that have shaped and directed us through the years. There is no possible way to mention everyone and the ways they have specifically impacted us, but we tried to capture key events along the way that shaped and directed us. Our hope is that it will not simply be a recounting of the "good ol' days," but that it will be a revisiting of the key places from which God launched us forward and would cause us all to reevaluate if we are still living as radically and freely as we did in the beginning.

Psalm 78:6-7 says, *"That the generation to come might know, even the children yet to be born, that they may arise and tell them to their children, that they should put their confidence in God and not forget the works of God, but keep His commandments."* This book is all about not forgetting what God has done and looking to the future from this place of remembrance.

As Laura and I begin to make the transition of our oldest daughter Abby going to college, we realize that the best is yet to come. Because our children have been raised differently in a community of people who radically love Jesus, they are not only surviving the ministry but are going to be stronger and purer than we ever thought. I completely concur with the old African proverb that says, "It takes a village to raise a child."

Thank you, thank you, thank you that you have changed our world and have been responsible for changing thousands of peoples' lives as well. For those who have been with us on this journey, we hope that as you read these stories you will be reminded of God's goodness and faithfulness. As we have been with you, Laura and I have fallen more in love with Jesus and have experienced more of His heart for the world. We pray that this is your testimony as well.

For those of you who are just connecting with our community, we pray that these pages will point you to Jesus and to the simple life of loving Him and loving those who are before you with all your heart.

To all of you, our family in the Lord, may you be stirred again to give all that you are to all that He is.

In His Strength & Love,
Jimmy

Introduction

A passion for Jesus and His purposes in the earth...

A few years ago, a group of pastors from a large church in the Midwest visited us at Antioch Community Church. As we took them on the tour around our modest facilities, we peeked into the Antioch Training School. We listened in as one of our church-planting couples shared about their experiences of serving in Mongolia and the Himalayas – loving Jesus in the midst of their journey, investing in people, and seeing lives changed.

When we finished the tour, I said to our guests, "Well, guys, that's it. It's nothing fancy; we are fairly simple people. In fact, we have chosen to spend our time and energy on just a few things: we seek to love Jesus with all of our hearts and to know Him every day; we intentionally invest in people's lives so that they can invest in others; and, we are committed to reaching the lost, whether it is here or around the world. Every year we learn more about these three things, and that is where most of our fruit comes from."

As we walked back across the street to our offices, I saw tears roll down the lead pastor's cheek. He said to me, "You know, I used to be good at those things, too. But 15 years and several thousand people later, I find that I am good at everything except those things."

It is stories like these that make me aware that our journey of simplicity and devotion to Jesus has tremendous power. We are not doing anything new; everything that we want to be is from Scripture, straightforward and clear. Maybe what is unique about Antioch though is that we are committed to giving everyone the opportunity to love God, invest in people's lives, and see the lost come to Christ.

God has called us, His church, to love Him with all of our heart, soul, mind, and strength. He has called us to love one another. He has called us to love people who do not know Him. And He has called us to celebrate all of these things in community. At Antioch, we believe this kind of church is the most exciting and powerful thing happening on the planet.

Two thousand years ago, Jesus stepped into a world that looked a lot like today's world: oppressive political powers, a religion of rules and not relationship, the rich refusing to distribute the goodness of God to the poor, and multitudes of people distressed and downcast. Jesus showed up to right all of these wrongs. By coming to earth Himself, God showed the world who He really is and set His redemptive plan into motion.

Proclaiming the message of a new Kingdom, Jesus shocked people because it was so radical. This Kingdom wasn't about "do's and don'ts" but about love, healing, and forgiveness. It was about doing what was right because you have a relationship with the One who is right. It had everything to do with a God who wanted to connect with people instead of a God who wanted to distance Himself.

And with that radical message, Jesus extended a radical invitation: Follow Me. Though some rejected Him, others left everything in order to follow Him. That radical response allowed them to become Jesus' most intimate friends - fishermen, tax collectors, harlots, people from every walk of life. As they interacted with Him day after day, He taught them about His Kingdom and invested in them so they could one day take His message to the world. Jesus even prophesied that He would build His church and that the gates of hell would not prevail against it.

Perhaps the hardest thing for His followers to grasp was Jesus' teaching about His own death. He told them that unless He died, unless He shed His blood, unless He gave His life on a cross, they would not be able to enter into all that He had for them. No matter how hard they tried to be good enough for God, it would never be enough. They needed a sacrifice. Jesus was that sacrifice. He hung on that cross even as these friends denied Him and ran away. He suffered tremendous pain and shame, and with His final breath, He asked God to forgive those who killed Him.

It didn't end there though. Three days later, He rose from the dead. And when He did, it proved once and for all that death would never have power over anyone who would believe. Jesus went back to His friends, the very ones who had failed Him just a few days earlier, and restored them. He reminded them about His Kingdom. And, finally, it made sense to them. Before it had just been cool to hang out with Jesus, but they never fully understood what He was talking about until He rose from the dead.

The reality of the Kingdom, of everything Jesus had ever said to them, so transformed them that they were willing to give their own lives for Jesus' message. Jesus' friends and followers became His value carriers, carrying the values He had imparted to them and reproducing them in the next generation.

Just before Jesus ascended into heaven, He told His followers, "...but you will receive power when the Holy Spirit has come upon you; and you shall be My witnesses both in Jerusalem, and in all Judea and Samaria, and even to the uttermost parts of the earth" (Acts 1:8). With faith, 120 of them gathered to pray and wait for Jesus' promise.

On Pentecost, the power of God came so heavily that it shook the place they were in. Each one of the 120 was filled with the Holy Spirit and went out to the streets prophesying and speaking in the different languages of the people in the city. They told of the glory of God and the goodness of His heart toward men. Peter jumped up and preached a phenomenal message. Those listening were amazed, and their hearts were cut to the quick. "What must we do?" they cried out. Peter told them to repent and be baptized...3,000 of them did (Acts 2:1-41).

In one day the church was born. Jesus had spoken of this: the ingathering of the people of God rightly living together in communion with Him and community with one another so that His life could be reproduced all over the world for His glory. Those disciples who had walked with Jesus remembered that He had said, "I will build My church; and the gates of Hades will not overpower it" (Matthew 16:18). They were seeing the first fruits of Jesus' prophecy.

Jesus loves His church...He died for it. And as we see through the rest of the book of Acts, the church loved Him too. They were on fire for Him. Having heard His radical message, they responded radically and became His church. I love to read in the pages of the New Testament about who the church is and what it looks like. In one day, by the gospel of Jesus Christ and the power of the Holy Spirit, God gathered to Himself a people who were, and today continue to be, the fullness of Christ (Ephesians 1:23), the body of Christ (Acts 9:4-6), a spiritual house made up of living stones (1 Peter 2:4-5), the family of God (Ephesians 3:14-19), the bride of Christ (Ephesians 5:25-31), the administration of Christ (Ephesians 3:8-9), the army of God (Joel 2:11), the pillar and supporter of the truth (1 Timothy 3:15), the eternal purpose of God in Christ (Ephesians 3:10-11), and so much more.

What we see in Acts 2 is huge. By empowering His followers with His Spirit, Jesus established His church so that He could walk in close relationship with them, so that they could live in tight community with one another, and so that He could draw the whole world to Himself. Over the years, I've fallen in love with Jesus and His church; you can't have one without the other. You can't say that you love Jesus but not His people and purposes – they are not separate.

Once those first 120 were multiplied to 3000, Peter and the apostles immediately gathered them from house-to-house so that they could learn how to follow Jesus as the church. Acts 2:42-47 describes what the early days of the church looked like:

They were continually devoting themselves to the apostles' teaching and to fellowship, to the breaking of bread and to prayer. Everyone kept feeling a sense of awe; and many wonders and signs were taking place through the apostles. And all those who had believed were together and had all things in common; and they began selling their property and possessions and were sharing them with all, as anyone might have need. Day by day continuing with one mind in the temple, and breaking bread from house to house, they were taking their meals together with gladness and sincerity of heart, praising God and having favor with all the people. And the Lord was adding to their number day by day those who were being saved.

These people who had said "yes" to the message of the Kingdom were beginning to experience the reality of the Kingdom. What the church is and should be is this: believers gathering house to house, praying, studying the Word, experiencing a sense of equality and humility, seeing signs and wonders, feeling the awe of God, and adding to their number day by day.

In those early days, as they lived out the values of the Kingdom before the whole city, they gained a reputation in Jerusalem. Acts 4:13 says, "Now as they observed the confidence of Peter and John and understood that they were uneducated and untrained men, they were amazed, and began to recognize them as having been with Jesus." The first church was known simply as a people who had been with Jesus. Day by day, they experienced Him and walked out His life together, and the world around them took notice.

Peter and the Acts 2 church were having a great time together in Jerusalem, so much so that they forgot Judea, Samaria, and the uttermost parts of the earth that Jesus had mentioned before He ascended into heaven. So, in His mercy, God allowed a little persecution to come to help them move on with His purposes.

The church at Jerusalem was threatened, Christians were imprisoned, and some were even killed. The believers prayed about how to respond, and by the will and direction of God, some stayed in Jerusalem to see the church grow to 10,000, but others left. These did not flee simply because they were scared but because God led them.

As they went, they preached the same message they had heard in Jerusalem, the message of the Kingdom. And no matter where they traveled, they lived out the same Acts 2 church community they had lived out in Jerusalem, house-to-house fellowship, worship, prayer, experiencing God, and seeing Him move powerfully in their midst. Because they faithfully carried the values of the Kingdom everywhere they went, they saw the church spread to Judea and Samaria and all over Asia.

Throughout the book of Acts, we see churches becoming hubs where laborers were released, received back, refueled, and sent out again. This movement was so effective that in Acts 19:10, it says that all of Asia had heard the gospel. And they had not just heard about Jesus but about Jesus and His church - people on fire for God, embodying the values of the Kingdom, and corporately expressing those values to rightfully distribute the gospel. This is the way that the world will be won today, by the church being the church, carrying and imparting Kingdom values.

For the original disciples, it was the simple values of knowing Jesus and making Him known that allowed them to endure persecution, to have joy in suffering, to experience power in their ministry, and to see the world changed. John said, "What was from the beginning, what we have *heard*, what we have *seen* with our eyes, what we have looked at and *touched* with our hands, concerning the Word of Life...we proclaim to you also, so that you too may have fellowship with us" (1 John 1:1-3). This wasn't a religion of dead works, but a people who had experienced the real God with their hands, eyes, and ears.

More than a great desire to see the world won to Christ, our focus at Antioch has always been to live from the inside out. What we have seen, heard, and touched are the things that we proclaim to you and to the world. Because we have met Jesus and found the life-giving power of His Kingdom, we want to reproduce His values in the lives of people everywhere so that they too can know Him and make Him known...until the whole world hears and knows. And just like the early disciples, we desire to be known as a people who have been with Jesus.

When God was first gathering us and establishing His work in our midst in the late 1980s, I asked God, *"Who are we? How do I describe what you are doing in our midst?"*

In a time of prayer, God spoke a phrase to me, "A passion for Jesus and His purposes in the earth."

"Yes," I thought, *"That is who we are! God, You have called us to be a people who are passionately pursuing You with all of our hearts and are deeply committed to Your purposes."* God doesn't just want to change what we do but to change who we are. The doing will flow out of the being. Our desire is not just to be, and it is not just to do. We want a life of obedience and faith that flows out of a deep place of intimacy with Jesus. Learning to love Him in a world that desperately needs Him is how we can be a part of God's plan to change this world.

My prayer is the same for you. As you read these pages, I don't want you to get caught up in our story. I want you to be caught up with a God who loves you passionately. May you find Jesus and His love and never lose it. May you be absorbed in Him so that you are encouraged to love Him more with a desire to see His purposes fulfilled in and through your life. As you walk through these pages, look for Jesus and ask Him how you can partner with Him to change the world.

If there is anything you get out of this book, I pray that you will get a vision for your life. Yes, God has worked through a few people in Waco, Texas, but that is not the message we want you to hear. We want you to know that you too can love Jesus with all your heart. You too can experience Him personally in a way that others will see Him in your life. You too can join with Jesus' church to proclaim Him to the uttermost parts of the earth.

Chapter 1

Little to Much

"Therefore if anyone is in Christ, he is a new creature;
the old things passed away; behold, new things have come."
2 Corinthians 5:17

When I turned on the radio one day, I didn't know Heather Mercer and Dayna Curry were the guests on James Dobson's radio program. Heather and Dayna are two young women from Antioch Community Church who were imprisoned in Afghanistan by the Taliban for 104 days because they were telling their Afghan friends about Jesus. Dr. Dobson invited Heather and Dayna to share their story with his radio audience.

On the air, as they spoke about what it was like to be in jail, they told a story about hearing a man being beaten in the prison next to theirs. Not knowing how else to respond to this heinous act, they sat in their own cells and began singing the song by Martin Smith, *There is a Light*. James Dobson was so touched by this particular story that he asked them to sing the song live on the radio.

He cried as they sang, and when they were finished, he asked them a very telling question: "Are you all aware that when you say the word Jesus, the name Jesus, you say it in a different way than many other people do? You say it in a way that shows deep, deep love and appreciation and compassion and respect. Are you aware of that? It shows through not just in the way you say Jesus' name but in what you've done with your lives."

I did not listen to the rest of the interview. After Dr. Dobson's remark, I turned off the radio and prayed aloud, "Thank You, Jesus! I know a thousand more just like them."

West Bank – Love Greater than Fear
2003

In 2003, the situation in the West Bank was dangerous. Several times a week, there were exchanges between Palestinians and Israelis, and as the Israeli army moved in to squelch the unrest, they began shooting rockets from helicopters, booby-trapping telephone booths, and placing snipers in the mountains. Sometimes, these attempts would go awry, injuring and even killing innocent bystanders.

Antioch had a team living in Nablus, West Bank at that time. The two families, Chris and Rebekah and their four children and Micah and Cara and their two children, lived a few streets away from each other in the midst of this crisis. Things had gotten so bad that all of the other mission agencies were pulling their people out of the West Bank.

Technically, we had the authority to tell our guys to leave the country, and had we done so, I know they would have respected our decision. But we wanted to honor them and their commitment to the Palestinians. They loved the people of Nablus and had given their hearts and lives for them. We asked the team to seek God about whether or not they should stay.

After they prayed, they felt led to stay in the West Bank. We agreed to let them stay under one condition: any time they walked out the door, they first had to pray and be in agreement that the Spirit of God was leading them to go out. I told them that the voice of the Lord might be the only difference between walking into an assassination attempt or safely reaching their destination.

The team had no problem with this condition. In fact, to honor it wholeheartedly, they put a big sign over their door saying "Stop and Pray" to remind them of their commitment to seek the Lord with every step.

For three weeks, they lived with constant threats. God protected them and answered their prayers for guidance as they came and went. In the end, because they had stayed, the people of Nablus opened their hearts and welcomed them into their lives.

Waco, Texas – An Overcoming Faith
2005

Sara came to Baylor and immediately got involved in a Lifegroup at Antioch. She dove in with all her heart, living with people she met at church and eventually even leading her own Lifegroup.

During her sophomore year, Sara's sister Shelly transferred to Baylor as well. Shelly had been making disastrous choices with partying, drugs, and alcohol, but she hoped that moving to Waco would help her start a new life. However, shortly after transferring to Baylor, she found her life headed in the same old direction. Although she met many of Sara's Lifegroup friends, this didn't keep her from a lifestyle that was leading her towards destruction.

Sara's heart broke for her sister, as did the hearts of many friends in her community. At one point, some of the Lifegroup community felt like the Holy Spirit was impressing them that Shelly was in a very dangerous time, that she was actually at the crossroads of making a decision between a journey that would lead her to death or to choose life in Jesus. They decided to call a corporate fast on Shelly's behalf.

Things definitely did not look hopeful when Shelly showed up at the Lifegroup leader's apartment and, in a very belligerent and scornful manner, said that she would never accept Jesus. In fact, Shelly even told Sara that she knew she was going to hell, and she was fine with that.

Although broken-hearted, Sara and the Lifegroup community continued to believe for Shelly's life. Shelly seemed to take a turn for the worse when her boyfriend broke up with her. She threw herself fully into drugs, stopped eating, stopped sleeping, and was seemingly trying to destroy her life through partying.

It was during this time that Shelly, while on a drug high with another friend, mysteriously began talking about Jesus. Although it was very contradictory to the state she was in, she found herself talking about how Jesus was the only way to heaven. The more she talked, the more she became convinced. Finally she looked at her friend and said, "God is giving me another chance. I would be a fool not to accept His offer of a changed life."

Shelly left the apartment where she was doing drugs and went straight to her sister's place. Sara opened the door, shocked to find Shelly broken and tender, telling her that she wanted to give her life to the Lord. The Lifegroup celebrated that night as word got around that God had miraculously intervened at a time when things seemed the most hopeless.

The next week at Dwelling Place, our college service, the celebration was equal to a football team winning a national championship. People screamed and cheered. Shelly had invited many friends to come because she wanted to share with them what God was doing in her life. For the ones who didn't want to change, though, she made sure that she distanced herself so not to be influenced by them into more trouble.

Shelly's parents were so touched by her transformation that they began coming to Antioch even though they lived out of town. They had a heart to do mission work and decided that Antioch was the community that they wanted to be a part of. After going through the training school, they joined the staff and are now preparing to join a church-planting team. Sara also went through the training school and is deeply involved in serving with the urban ministries at Antioch.

Today, Shelly is a Lifegroup leader, discipling other girls. She spent a summer in Peru where she was able to lead many people to the Lord, boldly sharing her testimony of God's deliverance from drugs and a destructive lifestyle. Now Shelly and her whole family are being used powerfully by God to see lives transformed as they serve Him with all their hearts, reconciled to each other, and fully in love with Jesus.

Waco, Texas – A Life Laid Down
2004/2005

Ruth Reese was my assistant and one of my closest confidants for 13 years. She was an intercessor, a mother, a discipler, and a trusted friend.

When Ruth reached her forties, she realized that she was probably not going to be married. Though that was a painful thought, she began to pursue the idea of taking in foster kids. One by one, she brought children into her home and life. She allowed us all to take part in caring for them as she would help them to get adopted into wonderful Christian homes.

After several kids had come through Ruth's home and then had been adopted by other Christian families, God brought an 18-month-old boy named Eric into Ruth's life. Not only did she love Eric like she had the rest of them, but there was something special with him. She prayed about adopting Eric, and after a long 18-month process, Eric became her son.

Shortly after the adoption, Ruth was diagnosed with cancer. The Antioch community rallied around her with love and support. Her family was very concerned and involved in her life, so we also began to take opportunities to minister to them. Ruth loved her family and had prayed for them for years that God would take hold of their hearts. She had a strong desire for those who were not Christians to be saved and for the others who were already saved to live wholeheartedly devoted to Jesus.

Ruth and Eric Reese

During her ten-month battle and struggle with cancer, we saw signs of remission and hope, as well as painful signs of deterioration. Eventually though, the battle was over, and Ruth went home to be with Jesus. But through the process, God began to answer Ruth's prayers.

Her brother Scott was so touched by what God was doing in and around Ruth that he made a commitment to Christ and invited his wife Carrie to join him in being involved in a church and Bible study. Her other brother Wes turned from a life of drugs to follow Christ and was radically transformed. Ruth's mother, who had always stood by her side, experienced a revived heart and life through her relationship with Christ. She adopted Eric and continues to live in community with friends who are helping to raise this young man.

Ruth's life is a testimony of what God can do through one woman whose heart is wholly His.

Waco, Texas – An Invested Inheritance
2001

Noel and Amy, a young couple at Antioch Community Church, felt called by the Lord to serve with our church-planting team in Germany. The only problem was they had to pay off their financial debt before they could go. As Noel and Amy put their dream on hold, they had faith that God would provide so that they could fulfill the call He had put in their hearts.

In 2001, when our church was in the midst of a season of sacrificial giving toward the restoration of our building, another couple in the church received an inheritance. This family was not rich. Though they had enough to pay the monthly bills, they did not have savings or extra money. Wanting to be obedient with their inheritance, they prayed about what they should do with it.

After praying, they came to me and said, "Jimmy, we know that the church body is giving towards this building, but as we pray, we feel led to give this money anonymously to Noel and Amy. We want to give them $20,000 to pay off their debt."

Wow! I thought that was awesome. It was clear to this precious couple that sowing into the Kingdom is the best investment they could make with their money and their lives. God had led them to give so that He could provide a way for others to share His love in Germany.

When Sunday came around, a Sunday set aside for giving toward the building, everyone gave as the Lord had led, and we celebrated how God was providing for us. Before we were finished with the service, I announced, "Oh, one more thing. Noel and Amy, I just want you to know that your debt is paid in full. You have been given an anonymous gift of $20,000!" Boy, did they rejoice and the whole crowd with them. We were all thrilled over what God had done for them.

Waco, Texas – Grateful Service
1997

Joe did not grow up in an ideal family. His mother was married and divorced three times to abusive, alcoholic men. Living barely above the poverty line, Joe suffered at home with his siblings until he moved out at age 16.

While on his own as a high school drop out, Joe began a lifestyle of drug and alcohol abuse. Eventually, he was reduced to only the clothes on his back, living in a city-condemned house. Three Christian students befriended Joe and offered him a place to live, but he was too proud to accept their offer. All he knew of God was that He was far away and had never intervened in all of his years of misery.

Hopelessness finally led to a suicide attempt. But as Joe sat cutting his wrists with a pair of scissors, he heard a voice speak to his heart: "Stop what you are doing. Go to the phone and call your Christian friends." That Sunday, Joe went to church and gave his life to the voice who had spoken to him, Jesus Christ.

Joe at World Mandate

When Joe's life radically changed, all of his old friends rejected him. He would spend his lonely nights reading and learning to practice what he understood from the Bible. His new Christian friends convinced him to move in with a family for refuge. Dr. Peter Leininger and Pete Jr. (who later became our church-plant leader in Mainz, Germany) welcomed Joe into their lives and treated him like a son and a brother. Joe's time in the Leininger home was pivotal as he continued his education and was even able to achieve a far-fetched dream of attending Baylor University.

During his college years, Joe got involved in our college Lifegroups. The teaching and discipleship he received radically impacted his life, as he experienced increasing grace and healing over childhood wounds. He started walking in deeper relationship with Jesus and living in the freedom he found. It was also in this community that he met his wife Jessica. Together, they were equipped to serve, love, and lead others as God gave them increasing vision and passion for Christ.

When Joe finished his years at Baylor, he asked Dr. Leininger how he could repay him for all he had done. His response was simply, "Joe, I don't want anything from you. All I ask is that you do the same for someone else." That set Joe and Jessica on a journey of simply loving Jesus and always looking for that "someone else" to serve and love, no matter where they were.

Joe and Jessica went through the Antioch Training School and served on the church- planting team in Mongolia. After that, they gathered a team of men and women, and along with their beautiful daughters headed to northeast Africa to reach Muslims for Jesus.

Afghanistan – Stepping into Darkness
May 2001

It was 5:15 a.m., May 2001, when Kurt heard a loud clanging at the gate in his home in Afghanistan. Instinctively, he knew something was wrong. By the time he got to the door, his Afghan friend, Andrew (his alias name), had already opened the gate.

Just behind Andrew stood a crowd with black turbans and eyeliner to highlight the fierceness of their gaze. One man had a curved sword pulled out. The other two had rods, like barbed wire covered with leather.

"Allah is not pleased, Andrew," they said. "You did not come to pre-dawn prayers at the mosque. We will subject you to the punishment. First, we will beat you with these rods and then we will shave your head and take you to the prison run by the religious police for 13 days of forced prayer and teaching at the feet of the mullah. Then you will know how to obey Allah."

At that point, they saw Kurt, though at first they didn't know he was a foreigner because he wore the local clothing. "Sirs," Kurt said in their language, "Andrew was my guest last night. He was making me tea this morning. It is my fault that he didn't go to the mosque."

Kurt went on to say to them, "If you are going to beat anyone, here," as he placed his arms out, "I am the one."

They dropped their rods, the man put his sword back in its sheath, they lowered their heads and walked away...the Taliban walked away.

Andrew shut the gate and looked at Kurt with wide eyes and said, "Why did you step into our darkness? Why did you offer to take my beating? You are a guest in this country. You didn't need to do that."

Kurt responded in simple humility, "Andrew, I am only doing what was done for me. I deserve the beating. I deserve punishment. I am only doing what Jesus did for me. He took my place."

Waco, Texas – Something Bigger
2007

These people's individual stories are powerful, but they are also part of something so much bigger. I recently received an email from a pastor at another church in Waco who had encountered a group of people from Antioch. He wrote,

My family and I were eating lunch...Sunday afternoon, and this group of four guys and two girls...walked in. They placed their order, and one of the young men stood up in the restaurant and said to everyone listening, 'I just want to share something with you real quick. I am a Christian and believe in Jesus...He can heal you and make you complete. If there is anyone that has a prayer request, we would like to pray for you.' Then, he went on to say, after no one spoke up, that if anyone would like to receive Jesus as their Savior, or have any questions about who Jesus is, they are here to help. It was one of the most amazing things I have ever seen a young man do and was a great thing for my children to see. Someone was boldly proclaiming Jesus and His Kingdom. I had him come over to my table and asked him what church he attends. First, he asked if I knew Jesus and I assured him that I did. Then, he said that he went to [Antioch]. He told us about his missionary trip to Juarez, Mexico, and how that affected him and that there are people in Waco that need God just as much as in Juarez. It was amazing to see them step out and do that.

They did have the opportunity to pray with some people in the restaurant.
I just wanted to say what a great job the family of [Antioch] is doing...
God bless you and the family of [Antioch].

Each testimony that comes out of Antioch grows out of a collective community of people who are walking together in the simple values of the Kingdom: loving Jesus with all their hearts, intentionally investing in one another's lives, and loving those who don't know Him. These truths not only brought us together, but they have changed all of our lives.

Our journey started 20 years ago with me, my wife Laura and the people around us saying, "We love You, Jesus, and we want to do all that is in Your heart."

Chapter 2

Beaumont to Baylor
1981-1985

"But seek first His kingdom and His righteousness,
and all these things will be added to you."
Matthew 6:33

As a junior in high school in Beaumont, Texas, I began to realize that friends, athletics, and partying were not meeting the deep need in my heart. On Sunday mornings, I would sit in the back of churches, many times after being out most of the night, hoping to hear something about God that would make God real to me. Sadly, the two or three places I visited were not able to communicate to me clearly how I could know God. By the third visit, I decided to put it out of my mind.

But God saw the longing in my heart, and He divinely stepped in to meet my heart's longing with the reality of the gospel.

Beaumont, Texas – Encountering God
April 1981

In April of 1981, while I was still a junior in high school, a friend shared some tapes with me about the end times that included a clear presentation of the gospel. I had heard that Jesus loves everyone and that He died on a cross, but never before had I heard that I needed to respond to this message. I didn't know that I could know Him personally. Through this man's simple testimony and explanation, I realized that I needed to make a decision.

That evening when I went home, my older brother David was there. It was strange for him to be home because it was the middle of the week and usually he was in Waco where he was a student at Baylor. I knew that David experienced God in college, though I wasn't exactly sure what had happened to him. All I knew was that when he was home and prayed for the meals, it was different.

In retrospect, I have to laugh at some of his prayers. In his attempt to share the gospel with us one Thanksgiving, he prayed something like this: "Lord Jesus, I thank You for loving us and having a perfect plan for our lives. All of us are sinners and have fallen short of Your glory, but if we repent and turn to You, Jesus, then You will save us and make us new creatures. Thank You for this family and for this food. Amen." At the time, I knew he was trying to say something, but I wasn't sure what it was.

When I came home after listening to that tape, I went to David and explained to him what I had heard that evening. I told him what I understood about the gospel and asked him what he thought about it. Wisely, he asked, "Well, what do you think about it?"

I responded, "I realize this is a big commitment. I'll have to live life differently, and I don't know if I am ready."

David said, "Do you believe that Jesus is who He says He is and that He has eternal life for us?"

"Yes."

"Well," he challenged, "what are you waiting for?"

When he said that, I realized that God was answering my heart's cry. He was inviting me into the divine relationship that He had made me for. I prayed a simple prayer with my brother that night: "Lord Jesus, I need you in my life. I have sinned against you and others. I want you, and I need you in my life." An incredible peace filled my heart; a peace I had never known before. Up to that point, I had been running from party to party and from achievement to achievement to try to be somebody and feel like I was worth something. But, in that moment of simple response to Jesus, I realized I was somebody...I was His son.

My brother left Beaumont the next morning to go back to Baylor. Before he left, he told me to read the Bible, pray every day, and to tell everyone I knew about Jesus. He also gave me a Christian tape by BJ Thomas called "Happy Man." With that crash course in discipleship, I was ready to go. I started to read my Bible, talk to God, and tried to share my faith.

What no one told me was that people didn't like it when you shared your faith. A couple of weeks after my decision to follow Christ, I was with a few friends at our annual spring break beach getaway. We were sitting around fishing and drinking beer as we always had, but Clint, the guy who had shared the tape with me, and I had agreed to be different. We went around from person to person, asking them what they thought about God and what they knew about Jesus. The leader of our group began to ask, "Hey, what's your deal, guys? Why are you trying to ruin our time talking about God? We are just trying to have a good time here. Have you guys gotten weird or religious?"

Clint and I fumbled around and said nothing in response. We were not ready for that kind of pushback. The rest of the week, we backed off and went with the flow as if nothing had changed in our lives.

For the rest of my junior and senior year of high school, I did not grow much because I didn't have regular Christian community or discipleship. I kept the same friends, and my days slipped back into their normal routine. It was in the midst of this season that God spoke to me in a very unique way, a way I had never experienced before. God spoke to me in a dream:

As I stood in a windy wheat field, a white fence ran in front of me, through the middle of the field as far as I could see. A voice spoke to me, saying, "I am coming to separate the wheat from the chaff and no longer will people be able to ride the fence, for they will either be for Me or against Me."

I had never had a spiritual dream, nor did I know that other people did. All I knew was that somehow God was trying to speak to me. Unsure of what to do about it, I simply went on with my life. Before long, this dream became very significant.

Waco, Texas – Baylor University
1982-1984

In the fall of 1982, I enrolled as a student at Baylor University. My career ambition was to become an influential person who changed the world through business, law, or politics. One of the main reasons I chose Baylor was because I had heard that there were people there who loved and knew Jesus, and I wanted to learn how to do that, too. I showed up on campus with all of these desires in my heart.

In orientation, they used a diagram called the Welcome Week Wheel to illustrate the concept of living holistically. This wheel had Jesus Christ in the middle with four surrounding spokes: social, physical, spiritual, and intellectual. They all looked great to me, so I dove in with all my heart.

Physically, I began working out and getting into shape. Spiritually, I joined Bible studies and went to church. Socially, I made dating and hanging out top priorities. Intellectually, I worked hard enough to make B's, but I also honored the words of my mom, who had told me before I left home, "Remember, college is about more than good grades."

Over those first two years, I got involved in a fraternity, leadership opportunities, and service projects. I was on the fast track to be somebody. It wasn't that I was a bad guy; I was just doing what I saw around me. My basic understanding was that God loved me no matter what, and as long as I didn't do anything super bad, I would be just fine. I could pursue all my ambitions as long as I added the little phrase; "I want to do all this for God." Though it sounded good, I knew in my own heart that I was living a double life.

Towards the end of my sophomore year, it was apparent to me that I was missing something. By that time I had heard the saying, "You are not really living for Jesus. You are just riding the fence." My dream about the wheat field and the white fence came back to me, and I realized that fence was the dividing line for God. I couldn't live on the fence; I was either going to be for Him or against Him. He was coming to separate the wheat from the chaff, and I wanted to live in the fruitfulness of God. With that connection, I began to say, "God, I want to follow you with all my heart."

34

I was dating a girl at the time who was a young believer like me, and we really started searching Scripture together, trying to better understand the Christian life. But as God drew me closer to Himself through His Word, my girlfriend began to drift away from me. At the end of the school year, I went to visit her at her home in San Antonio. It was there that she officially broke up with me. I was shocked and devastated because I had really begun to believe that she might be the woman I was supposed to marry.

Just after our defining conversation, I went jogging. Running down the street, crying out for help in my pain, I realized that I had a choice to make. Pain is inevitable, and as humans, we react to painful experiences, but with every heartbreak comes a choice beyond the initial reaction. We can either respond by drawing near to God or by pulling away from Him. This was an opportunity for me to draw near. That one decision, as much as any decision I have made, changed the course of my life.

Beaumont, Texas – Three Months
Summer of 1984

As I drove down Interstate 10 from San Antonio to my home in Beaumont, it became clear to me that I hadn't given God all my heart. So, I began asking Him to help me. "God," I prayed, "I'll give you three months to show me who you really are."

I realized that there were distractions, things in my life that were not going to help me know Him. So, I began to respond. First, I took my Beechnut chewing tobacco and threw it out the window; it had been a habit since the seventh grade. Then, I took my secular cassette tapes and threw them out the window as well. I didn't want anything to distract me from pursuing God with all my heart. I made a decision not to watch TV or movies for three months because I realized that I was living my life vicariously through other people. When I would see someone on the screen, I wanted to be like him or her instead of looking at Jesus and wanting to be like Him. As I categorically went through my life, I made decisions for that three-month window to make sure that I would connect with God with all my heart.

In Beaumont, I had a job lined up working at a chemical plant eight hours a day. My daily routine for the summer involved seeking

God and working. I made a commitment, starting with the book of Matthew, to read a chapter of the Bible every day and to do exactly what it said. In the morning I would read, and then I went to work. I talked to God throughout the day, and whatever I could remember from the words and life of Jesus that I had read that morning, I would apply.

Let me tell you, doing exactly what the Bible says is harder than it sounds. By the end of Matthew 6, I had given away almost everything I had and had forgiven everyone I hadn't planned on forgiving. By the time I got all the way through the book of Matthew, my whole worldview had changed.

Somewhere in the middle of the summer, I thought to myself, *Oh my goodness, I'm turning into a weirdo! All I do is read the Bible and pray.* But the more I thought about it, the more I realized that I had never before sensed God's presence, love, and peace the way I was experiencing them then. *Oh well,* I concluded. *If that's what a weirdo is, then that is okay with me. I want to be wholly His.*

On the morning I was to return to Baylor, I woke up at 6:00 a.m. and began to weep uncontrollably. This was not normal for me; I am not an overly emotional person. At the breakfast table, I could not hold back the tears. My parents were obviously concerned and said, "Son, do we need to get you a psychologist? What's wrong with you? It seems that you are falling apart." Though they did not understand my spiritual journey at that time, I still knew that they loved me.

I didn't know why I was crying, and so I just responded, "No, I just love you guys. That's all it is." Somehow I convinced them that I was fine, and they reluctantly let me leave.

Driving back to Baylor, I continued to cry for another hour. I asked God what was wrong with me, and He spoke to my heart: "You asked me to show you I am real, and I have." In that moment, I realized that everything I had wanted, God had given. That summer, the Kingdom became so real that it shaped the rest of my life, and I was forever changed.

Baylor University – A Different College Experience
Fall of 1984

Because I had changed so much over the summer, my final two years at Baylor looked remarkably different than my first two years. When I first returned to Waco, I found a group of guys who had dynamically encountered Jesus over the summer. We began meeting in our apartment in the evenings, and God would show up as we worshipped, prayed for one another, and shared our hearts with one another.

For the first time in my life, I understood the reality of Acts 2 where it says, "Everyone kept feeling a sense of awe" (Acts 2:43). There was something about those times that was powerful. Though some would make fun and ridicule, others were drawn and changed by the presence of the Lord.

One day after class, my roommate and I were hanging out at our apartment, and we decided to pray together. As we were on our knees, seeking the Lord, I told him that I was seeing a picture in my mind. He said he was seeing one too. I explained that I saw a road with Jesus walking down the middle. There were people in the ditches on both the right and left sides. It seemed to me that we were to walk down the middle with Jesus. He told me he was seeing the same thing.

As we began to pray and talk about this, we realized that this picture had to do with a common debate in the church at that time regarding conservative versus charismatic theology. We felt like Jesus was telling us that people had fallen to the right and to the left, but if we would just follow Him, we would always be on the right path. This experience has marked both of our walks with the Lord ever since. We learned that we were never to get caught up in one side or the other, but simply to follow Jesus.

Waco, Texas – A Heart for the Nations
Fall of 1984

Within the first couple of weeks after returning to school, my buddy Kyle and I went on a bike ride. So many great things were going on that I asked him, "Hey, man, what do we do with all of this that is happening in our lives?"

He said, "Have you ever heard of missions?"

"No," I responded.

"Missions is where you go tell people about Jesus in other nations," he explained.

"Wow, it sounds great to me. Do you know anybody that knows anything about it?"

"I don't know," he said. "But why don't we pray and ask God to show us."

The next morning, Kyle and I went to Sunday School at Highland Baptist Church with some friends. As we broke up into classes, they said that there was a missionary from Thailand who was going to talk about God's call to missions. Kyle and I looked at each other and said, "Let's go."

The missionary spoke on Matthew 28:19-20 about God's call to the church to share Jesus with the nations. Well, having just learned how to apply the words of Jesus that I had read in Matthew that summer, I was impressed with this missionary's message and life. I wanted to encourage him that he was doing a great job of preaching exactly what the Bible said.

After his talk, Kyle and I, along with our friends Bill and Susan, went to affirm him. I am sure I came across naïve and maybe even ignorant as I told him what a great job he was doing, but he was very gracious to us. He explained that he had a friend in Papua New Guinea who looks for lost tribes who have never heard the gospel. "He would love to have students join him next summer if you guys are interested."

Immediately we said, "Yes, that would be great!" Bill, Susan, and I went to lunch and dreamed about the adventure. Over the next few months, we saw God move powerfully as we prepared to go and eventually found ourselves in the jungles of New Guinea in the summer of 1985.

Waco, Texas – A Cry for the Holy Spirit *1984-1985*

I remember seeing Laura Mielke sitting in the back of a Campus Crusade meeting and thinking, "Hey, she sure is good looking. I wonder if she would go to New Guinea." I went home that night and asked my roommate if he thought Laura would go to New Guinea. His opinion was that Laura loved Jesus and would probably do whatever He wanted her to do. I decided to ask her out, and we went on our first date in October.

Today I am struck by how much I had changed in six months. The previous year, I would have asked out Laura simply because she was beautiful. After those six intense months with Jesus though, the question in my mind changed. What had become more important to me was how much she loved Jesus.

Laura and I had gone out a few times, building our friendship, before I went to Mountain Ministries in Almont, Colorado. Bob and Becky Stuplich had vision for a ministry much like Francis Schaeffer's L'Abri ("the shelter") in Switzerland. Francis Schaeffer had discipled Bob through challenging years in the 1960s and 70s, and Bob had come out of that experience with a desire to do the same for others.

Those few days with the Stuplich family were life changing as we talked about the claims of Christ and what it meant to live wholeheartedly for Him. As I would listen to the teaching and talk with Bob and Becky, I realized that God was speaking directly to me regarding issues in my life, specifically being self-centered and impatient. Every day while I was there, I read 1 Corinthians 13 and realized how much help I really needed. My specific prayer that week was, "*God, teach me how to be a patient and loving man.*" Little did I know that when you pray prayers like that, God is committed to answering them.

Within a week of returning to school in January of 1985, I realized that something was wrong with Laura. We had just eaten dinner, and I was walking back to my room when the Lord spoke to me, "She's in trouble!" Startled, I looked around and wondered if I had imagined it. The thought kept running through my mind, though, and I felt led to ask my roommate about it. He told me that his cousin had anorexia nervosa and that Laura was showing signs of having it, too. It seemed like everywhere I turned the next few days, people were coming to me with concern for Laura. After a day of seeking the Lord, I felt that I had to confront her.

I went to her and said, "Laura, it seems to me that you have a problem with anorexia and that you need to deal with it. Whether you love me or hate me, I am committed to standing with you to work through this problem."

That night was the beginning of a long journey for Laura and me. I discovered that she had fallen into this eating disorder because she had struggled with feelings of self-worth. Baylor is a great place with a lot of incredibly gifted people. In that environment, it is hard to feel unique and special. Laura was already wrestling with these issues when she discovered how easily she could lose weight and control her appearance. Before long, she was trapped in the pain and lies of anorexia.

Over the next several months, God broke both Laura and me as we sought freedom from this stronghold. I gained 15 pounds because when we would go out to eat, I would get three times as much and say, "That's not much on your plate!" There were times when she hated me and times when she loved me, but I stayed the course God had called me to. I was to walk with her through this season and in the process learn patience and love. God used Laura's battle to teach me that He is the strong one, not me. No matter how much I wanted to fix Laura's circumstances, I couldn't...but God could. My patience and love for Laura had to come out of total reliance upon God to move in a powerful way in her life.

Around spring break, I was talking to a counselor friend about Laura's situation. Reminding me that our battle was not with flesh and blood, but with a spiritual enemy, he suggested that we fast and pray for a spiritual breakthrough. My first reaction was, "Yeah, right. That's exactly what she would want: to not eat. Starving herself is the problem, not the solution." What God had to teach me, though, was the difference between spiritual fasting and not eating. We decided to take the counselor's advice and seek God's power through fasting.

After the fast, I realized that we were in the midst of a spiritual battle, not a physical one. I had been trying to convince Laura with words, out-eat her at restaurants, and do everything I could in my natural strength to make her change, but it wasn't working. Because Laura's problem was spiritual, crying out to God through prayer and fasting put her on a path to deliverance.

As I watched the power of the Spirit work miracles in her life, I became increasingly aware of my need for that same power. At the time, we were attending Highland Baptist Church, and the people there were experiencing God's presence in a way I had never before encountered. The Holy Spirit was alive and well in their midst. They were telling me that He wanted to empower us to obtain victory in every area of our lives. Now, I loved Jesus, I was saved, and I knew the Holy Spirit was within me, but these people had something, knew something, that I didn't.

In my desperation to see spiritual breakthrough in Laura's life, I drove out to the lake in Waco one night and cried out, "Holy Spirit, if You're real, I have to have You!" It wasn't a theological request but an earnest need of the heart. I knew I needed all of the power that God had in order to help Laura. God loves to answer genuine prayers like that. Heart prayers connect with His heart, and He does not turn away from them.

After that experience, I began to believe that God would meet me in my weakness. Reading through the book of Acts, I would look for places where the Holy Spirit would show up. In whatever way He had manifested there, I would ask Him to show up in the same way in my life. By the time I got to chapter 4, I noticed that the people who received the filling of the Holy Spirit in Acts 2 needed that same filling in Acts 4 in order to have boldness to preach the gospel. Getting somewhat frustrated, I told God I would not leave my room until He fell on me like He had fallen on them. I resolved to stay there until God showed up in some way like He had in the book of Acts.

As I began to pray and worship, God met me. Joy bubbled up inside, and He spoke mysteries to me that not even my mind could understand. It was life changing, not a one-time experience, but a catalyst into daily reliance upon the Holy Spirit in everything I do. Since then, I know I can only accomplish God's will for my life through the powerful person of the Holy Spirit working in me.

During this time, Laura also had a powerful encounter with the Holy Spirit that was so profound that she would wake in the middle of the night and journal about what God was speaking to her heart. She said she knew she had experienced the power of God when she walked in her house where her roommates were watching her favorite soap opera and it turned her stomach. She has never watched a soap opera since.

In these months, God gave me a verse from Leviticus and told me that He would break the bars of Laura's prison. When the power of

God came on her in one of her prayer times, she had a picture of a little girl in a cage. God came and bent the bars of the cage, calling her out. As Laura experienced progressively greater freedom from the prison of anorexia, I saw her beauty multiply as she grew in the knowledge and understanding of a big, loving God. She has never been the same since that time. I watched her fall in love with her Savior, the One who rescued her from an otherwise inescapable lifestyle of deception and defeat. Most people diagnosed with anorexia struggle with it their entire lives. They may learn healthy life habits, but the battle remains within. Laura, however, was totally set free. Hers is a testimony of the awesome power of God breaking through to accomplish what was impossible in her own strength.

Those early experiences in college were an incredible journey into the Kingdom of God, giving Laura and me a clear understanding of His plan and purpose. I am so grateful that He heard our hearts' cries and brought circumstances, situations, people, and plans to set our hearts free.

Remembering back to the dream God had given me as a new believer of separating the wheat from the chaff, I saw that in those few short years, its prophecy was beginning to come to pass in my life. God didn't want me to ride the fence. He wanted me to be wholly His.

God had set a standard before me in that dream. Would I be for Him or against Him? Through the journey of the previous five years, I realized that being wholly His was not only right, but it was satisfying.

In Your presence is fullness of joy
In Your right hand there are pleasures forever.
(Psalm 16:11)

I was experiencing both joy and pleasure in His presence, and I would never turn back.

Chapter 3

Baylor to Papua New Guinea 1985

*"Go therefore and make disciples of all the nations...
and lo, I am with you always, even to the end of the age."*
Matthew 28:19-20

I have always been a dreamer who wants to live life to its fullest. When I read the words of Jesus and the stories of the people of God through the book of Acts, it makes me believe that all of us can be a part of this incredible journey and adventure. In our lifetime, we can see the same kind of things happen just by believing and stepping out in faith.

It is encouraging to see how most of the people that God used in the New Testament were initially either fearful and unsure of themselves or prideful and arrogant. When they finally encountered Christ face-to-face, they were transformed and willing to risk their lives for what they believed in.

These examples helped me and others begin to take the initial steps of faith over our fears. Whether they were steps toward looking for lost tribes in the jungles of New Guinea or steps toward trusting God with our finances, these risks turned out to be the places where we encountered God the most. I was born a chicken, but somewhere along the way I decided I would rather risk my life on God and His word than stand by and do nothing. These risks and steps of faith have borne the most fruit in my life and have allowed me to know God more.

Hebrews 11:1-2 says, "Now faith is the assurance of things hoped for, the conviction of things not seen. For by it the men of old gained approval." We have to reach out beyond what our eyes can see, knowing that our faith is pleasing to God. Even when we miss it, if our faith and hearts are bent towards Jesus, we can trust Him to take care of us and restore us because we have pleased Him by stepping out in faith.

As Bill, Susan, and I began our trek toward New Guinea, we had no idea just how much our faith would be challenged.

Waco, Texas – Give and it will be Given
Spring of 1985

During the summer of 1984, I had worked hard and made more money than I ever had in my entire life. At the same time though, I was reading through Matthew, determined to obey no matter the cost. In Matthew 5:42, Jesus said, "Give to him who asks you, and from him who wants to borrow from you do not turn away." So, even though I had earned much, I had given away over half of it. As the finances dwindled, I had to believe that God would take care of me when I obeyed His Word.

With the summer of 1985 quickly approaching, Bill, Susan, and I ran into a major financial obstacle in trying to get to New Guinea. A month before we were supposed to leave, our college pastor came to us and said there was only enough money for two of us to go or for all of us to go for a shorter period of time. Bottom line, we needed to come up with $3,000 to make the whole trip happen.

Bill had faith and proclaimed, "If God told us to go, then He will provide the money!" We left that meeting encouraged, but we also wondered whether we were to go for a shorter amount of time since God hadn't provided all the resources yet.

The following Wednesday night at church, I only had one dollar to my name. Someone came up to me and gave me $20 that they had owed me, bringing my total net worth up to $21. Later in the service, when they passed the offering plate, I felt God telling me to put it all in. In that moment, there was no logical reason why I should give that $21. But I had learned that the only logic that matters is following the lead of Jesus without question. So, I put it all in.

My mother called a few days later and told me that I was $54 short on rent money that month...just what I needed to hear. At church on

Sunday, the pastor said that he felt led to take up an offering for people who had needs. God gave him a specific revelation that someone was there who needed about $50 to help pay rent. Now, I'd never accepted money from anyone and wasn't going to tell anyone about my need. However, after the service, we were talking to the pastor about our upcoming trip to New Guinea, and I felt convicted to confess that the rent money might be for me.

The pastor phoned the associate pastor and found out that no one had been given the rent money yet. A few moments later, the associate pastor knocked on the door of the office and walked in. The pastor asked what he thought we should do and he replied, "God told me that the rent was $54, but that I should give you $21 extra. Here's $75." Wow! God knew. Not only did He know who I was, but He knew the intimate needs of my life.

It boosted our faith over the next few weeks to see incredible provision pour in. The first of it came a few days later when a gentleman gave us $2,200 towards our trip. The next day I found a $100 bill in my locked car in the cassette deck. We were well on our way towards our goal of $3,000.

The next week, when finals were over and school had ended for the semester, I sold all of my books, paid all of my bills, and ended up with $14 and a quarter tank of gas. I was planning on driving to Houston to spend a few days with Laura before I left for New Guinea. I know what you are thinking: a quarter tank of gas and $14 doesn't go a long way. But I had already resolved in my mind that I would drive as far as I could. If I ran out of gas, I would either walk, or God would provide a miracle somehow.

At the last Sunday evening service at Highland before I was to leave for Houston, Susan, Bill, and I were supposed to present our remaining financial need for New Guinea to the church. When I stepped out of my car to go into the service, the Holy Spirit spoke to me and said, "Go get your wallet." I immediately thought, *but I only have $14.* I knew, however, that I had heard the voice of Jesus, so I grabbed my wallet and went in. When they passed the offering plate, I gave that $14. For the first time in my life, I stood up in worship when no one else was standing; I raised my hands, and with tears flowing, I said, "Oh God, I surrender all," because I knew I had nothing.

On that particular Sunday night, the wife of Nate Saint, one of the five famous missionaries who were killed among the Auca Indians in South America, spoke at the service. She asked people to contribute to build water wells in Africa where her son was currently working. Everyone responded enthusiastically, and we took up over $3,000.

Then the pastor mentioned that there was another missionary with us from France named Francois. After he shared, we took another offering to help with the work there. As the congregation sang the benediction song, we thought that we were sunk. The pastor had forgotten us.

But at the last minute, as he was saying good-bye, the pastor remembered. "Oh yeah, there are three college students going to New Guinea this summer. If anybody wants to help out, they are over here."

God is so faithful. The first person to walk up to us that evening gave us three tickets to Los Angeles, the first leg of our trip. Then others gave us cash and checks. My Bible had been sitting next to me the whole time, and as best as I knew, it was untouched by anyone. As we rejoiced over God's provision, I opened my Bible and saw two crisp $100 bills. I was amazed. It was as if God had personally pulled out cash and said, "Here, son, this is for you."

I told my teammates that God had miraculously given us $200 more towards our trip. After meeting with the pastor, I found out that we had $1,500 more than we needed. Susan said she felt the Holy Spirit telling her that the $200 in my Bible was meant for me, to meet my personal needs and not for our trip. Right away, I went to the gas station, filled up, and headed to see Laura. We had a wonderful three days together before I left for the summer.

Within a year of learning that all I had was the Lord's and should be given to those who ask, I also learned the truth of Luke 6:38: *"Give and it will be given to you..."* I would rather give away everything I own so that God can provide all my needs than to cling to the measly wealth I accumulate in order to take care of myself.

As Bill, Susan, and I were on the plane headed for New Guinea, I asked the Lord for a Scripture for the summer. He led me to Matthew 28:19-20:

Go therefore and make disciples of all the nations, baptizing them in the name of the Father and of the Son and of the Holy Spirit, teaching them to observe all things that I have commanded you; and lo, I am with you always, even to the end of the age.

God highlighted that very last part of verse 20 for me, "...and lo, I am with you always, even to the end of the age." He spoke to me, "If you will simply go, I will always be with you."

Papua New Guinea with David Sitton – Indiana Jones for Jesus Summer of 1985

I have met some amazing missionaries in my day, but I will never forget the first one I was privileged to work with: David Sitton. He was like an Indiana Jones for Jesus, trekking through the New Guinea mountains at any cost to share the gospel.

Our first journey into the jungle with David to reach lost tribes was quite eventful. We took the four-wheel drive truck as far as it would go through the jungle roads and then hiked the rest of the way to the river. There, we met local Papuans straight from the pages of National Geographic, bones through their noses, loincloths, the whole works. These men were our guides to take us upriver to a village that had not yet heard the gospel.

As we sat in our hand-dugout canoes going up the Sepik River, I realized what we had done. I thought to myself, "You're stupid...you are crazy. What in the world have you gotten into? You are going to die out here in the middle of the jungle." As we went under the tributaries, the rain

Papua, 1984

started falling and darkness set in. As I stared into the red eyes of the crocodiles swimming around us, making sure to keep my hands inside the boat, I became keenly aware of our need for God. This was not all fun and games...the adventure had become reality, and it was serious. We were going to have to find God on another level.

When we docked, the villagers extended a plank to get us ashore. Bill and I carried a generator across, but when I reached the top, the plank broke in half and all six feet two inches and 230 pounds of Bill fell into the crocodile-infested river. I had never seen anyone walk on water, nor have I since. But within seconds, Bill was out of the water and running past me on the bank!

As we pitched our tents that night to go to bed, we were wondering if it was worth it. The next morning though, we found out that it was. Because local folklore taught the villagers of a creator god and a great flood, we started our presentation of truth with a slide show of creation and the flood. We then explained that the God they had been trying to appease for years was not a God of terror, but one of love. That first morning in the village, we saw 19 people give their hearts to the Lord. Over the ensuing days, much of the rest of the village did so as well.

The night before we left this area, a man sent for us. Suffering from cancer, he had laid on his mat for two months unable to get up. He explained that he wanted God either to heal him or to end his misery and let him die. We shared the gospel with him, and he gladly accepted Christ as his Savior. Then, we prayed for his healing but did not see any immediate result. The next morning as we were packing up to leave, one of the villagers ran to us and said, "The old man is up! The old man is up! He is fixing breakfast for you. He has been healed."

David took us on many adventures in the mountains of New Guinea. Those were exciting and terrifying days, taking the gospel to places it had never before been proclaimed. I remember one particular journey where we had been dropped off on a grass airstrip with the pilot's assurance to return within a week. What a comforting promise to a group of missionaries looking for the last cannibal tribes!

Before the week was up, David contracted black water malaria. His only chance of survival was to return home immediately for medicine and recuperation. However, we had told the next village that we would come to them. David suggested that Bill and I continue on with the local guides while he and Susan went back to radio for the airplane to come pick us up the next day. He warned us that it was imperative to return by nightfall so as not to miss our flight off the mountain the next morning.

Bill and I went on to the village and saw more people saved. As the day grew long, we realized that we had to get back as David had instructed. The people urged us to stay the night, but we insisted that we had to go.

Our guides explained that the only way to get back in time was to take a treacherous shortcut. Of course, all Bill and I heard was "shortcut," and we were all for it. The guides warned us, "I don't think you want to take *this* shortcut," they said.

We were young and arrogant and replied to these small but tough mountain men, "Come on. What's wrong with you guys?" Humoring us, they gave in.

I am so thankful for those guides. By the time we got down one side of the mountain, they were carrying our backpacks. As we continued up the other side of the mountain, we had to stop frequently because of utter exhaustion, but they helped us along, and we made it back to the village just as full darkness set in.

Jimmy with Papuan guide

God was so faithful during those days with David. God protected us from harm and disease. He provided through the kindness of locals. He guided our steps and strengthened us when we were at the end of ourselves. Most amazingly though, He allowed us to step into the adventure of sharing with those living in the furthest reaches of the world.

Papua New Guinea with Fred Piepman –
Overcoming a Spirit of Fear
Summer of 1985

If David were an Indiana Jones for Jesus, Fred Piepman was like the apostles Peter and Paul rolled up into one. After being on the mission field for about ten years, Fred had seen people healed and raised from the dead. He had established more than 60 churches that were led by Papuan men whom he had personally discipled. The power of God was on Fred's life and ministry, and the people of New Guinea were changed because of it. After spending some time with David, we joined Fred's ministry for the rest of our trip.

I remember sitting at Fred's feet for hours, learning from him. He possessed a wealth of knowledge of the things of God. Fortunately for me, Bill, and so many Papuans, he believed in "on-the-job training" when it came to discipleship and church planting. He invested in us with his words, but then let us experience face-to-face the realities of what he had taught.

Fred decided to utilize our team in an area known as Benna. While some regions Fred had worked in were very responsive to the gospel, Benna had been very resistant. The villagers had run the last missionary away by burning down his house. They also tried to burn the church, but it wouldn't burn, proving to them that there was a God who was real.

The night before we went into Benna, we spent time praying with Fred and his wife Darlene. As we waited on God to speak to us, Darlene said, "I feel specifically that we should pray for their safety." While we appreciated the prayers, she could have kept that concern to herself. To say the least, we were scared to death.

Even before Darlene's prayerful concern, we were struggling with fear. The previous night, I was awoken by a sense of being choked by something that I could not see. It was as if the Devil himself was in the room! (I'm sure it was just a wimpy demon, but to me it seemed like the Devil himself.) Through struggling and choking and saying the name of Jesus, I eventually gained just enough strength to lie awake scared for the rest of the night.

After praying with Fred and Darlene, Bill and I were still afraid. When we confessed this to Fred, he explained that we were being attacked by the spirit of fear. He told us that if we didn't deal with it, it would chase us for the rest of our lives.

Unfamiliar with the reality of the demonic and spiritual realms, we asked Fred how we could get rid of this spirit of fear. I will never forget the picture he painted for us that night:

If a mangy, rabid dog came into my house and went after my children, what would I do? Would I sit around and shoo him, hoping he went away? No! I would chase him out of my house, beating and kicking him...whatever it took! That is what you do with the spirit of fear. Use the Word of God and the Spirit of God until you chase that spirit out of your house.

Bill and I stayed up for hours praying, rebuking the spirit of fear, singing, reading the Word, doing anything that would help us to see the power of God overcome our fear. By God's mercy and our weariness, we were finally able to fall asleep at about 4:00 a.m.

Before we left for Benna the next morning, we prayed with the men who had been trained by Fred. As we drove the Land Cruiser through the coffee fields, we would pass groups of people along the road and would slow down to look at them. The men with us would either nod "yes" or "no," indicating whether we should stop. Later, Bill and I realized that these men had visions of certain people in their prayers that morning. As we paused to look at the crowds, they were seeing if these were the ones God had revealed to them during that prayer time.

I was asked to preach to the first group of people at our first stop. I felt like God wanted me to preach about the realities of heaven and hell. This scared me because I knew there were witchdoctors in the crowd, and I wasn't interested in upsetting them. But I remembered Fred's charge to preach the gospel boldly, no matter the consequences. So that is exactly what I did.

As I spoke openly about the Devil and a good God combating for the souls of men, I heard a demonic voice coming from a man behind me in the bushes. My hair stood straight up on end. As I kept preaching, the voice eventually subsided. Despite my fear and because of the powerful draw of the Holy Spirit, many people came to Christ that day.

The next day, Bill was sick and Fred had planned for us to go to a village he had never been to before. As I was explaining to Fred that we wouldn't be going on the trip because of Bill's condition, Fred looked me in the eye, and said, "I have promised them that we will be there, and I never break my promise," which meant I was going.

This particular village was home to a group of believers led by a man who had been discipled by Fred. When this man met Christ, he was passionate and knew he had been called to pastor and preach. The only problem was he couldn't read. Fred had laid hands on this man and prayed, "Oh, God, let him read Your Holy Word!" Miraculously, he began to read...but he could only read the Bible, nothing else. After this encounter with the power of God, he returned to his village and led most of them to the Lord.

We drove through the countryside as far as the Land Cruiser would take us and then hiked up the side of a mountain. As we entered the village, it seemed that the love of God overwhelmed us. The people ran toward us and embraced us like we'd known each other for a lifetime. Though I didn't know the language, somehow the language of God communicated for us. We ate a meal together, a feast that they call a moo-moo.

After this time of fellowship, the group asked me to preach. At that point in my life, I only knew a couple of Scripture passages by memory...one of which I had learned the night before: "For God has not given us a spirit of fear, but of power and of love and of a sound mind" (2 Timothy 1:7). Since it was so fresh on my mind, I thought it was a good place to start preaching.

We sang a few songs in the local language, Tok Pisin, and then through two translators, I preached. As I spoke, I began to cry. Then they began to cry. The presence of God filled the meeting place, and we worshipped together for the next few hours. When I would open my eyes and look around, it seemed to me that the walls were shaking. I was reminded of Acts 4 where it says, "...the place where they had gathered together was shaken, and they were all filled with the Holy Spirit and began to speak the word of God with boldness" (Acts 4:31).

The book of Acts came alive that day. No matter what the debates were back home about expressions of worship and spiritual gifts, I had experienced reality - the reality of Christ among a humble people who loved Him with all of their hearts. These people were contriving absolutely nothing. They had simply met a Savior and were living out the reality of the Kingdom by loving Him with all of their hearts. This picture still sticks in my mind as I yearn and hunger for the same thing to happen in communities here in our own nation.

Almont, Colorado – Fathers in the Faith
Spring of 1985

The spring before I went to New Guinea, I spent more time with Bob Stuplich at Mountain Ministries in Colorado. He took me to a Rotary Club meeting in Crested Butte where his pastor was sharing about the power and influence of men in our lives. He went around the room and asked us to name an influential man in our lives. As they got closer to me, I didn't know what I was going to say. I was trying to think of a man who had influenced me significantly outside of my own family, but I couldn't come up with anybody. Before they landed on me, I decided to name Bob because my few days with him had been highly impacting. However, the group ran out of time before I had to share.

Even though I didn't have to answer the question at the meeting, my inability to come up with one man who had invested in my life really bothered me. I wondered, *Am I that prideful?* I told Bob what was bothering me and asked him if he thought I was prideful. His answer was, "Well, maybe, but I think it is more of an indictment to my generation because we didn't value investing in those coming up behind us. We climbed the ladder of success but never took the time or made it a priority to invest in younger men's lives. Why don't you pray and ask God to bring men into your life? I think He will do that."

I prayed that prayer in the spring of 1985. Since that time, God has provided many fathers and mothers in the Lord who have profoundly affected who I am and how I live my life. Fred Piepman, the missionary we worked with in New Guinea, was among the first answers to that prayer. He was a true father in the faith. He taught me how to hear from God, to believe in the supernatural, to learn by doing, to trust God completely with my finances, and to be a godly man who loves his wife and family and not just the work of the ministry. The list could go on and on.

I came out of New Guinea with an even firmer conviction of life-on-life ministry. To me, that means that discipleship is the way that Jesus raised up His leaders and the way that they raised up their leaders. Paul said to Timothy, "The things which you have heard from me in the presence of many witnesses, entrust these to faithful men who will be able to teach others also" (2 Timothy 2:2). This is the way that lives are changed.

Fred Piepman had 10 or more one-room huts on his property where men would live with their wives and children. Fred invested in them and then sent them out to plant churches. He and his wife shared their lives with these people and that life-on-life ministry produced incredible and powerful fruit. No matter how many different types of ministries there are, when it is all said and done, the way the world will be won is through life-on-life ministry.

My time with David, Fred, Bill, and Susan that summer changed my life forever. Just as the book of Matthew had come alive to me the previous summer, shaping my understanding of Jesus and His Kingdom, the book of Acts jumped off the pages as we traveled through New Guinea, profoundly changing my perspective of God's power and the church.

We encountered the intense battle between darkness and light. If God's power was not greater than the pervading evil in the villages of New Guinea, then the gospel was not what they needed. But the reality is, God is more powerful, and His gospel is enough to save and deliver from darkness. My experience with the believers there will forever mark my view of what the church can be, not just in those small villages, but in America, Europe, or anywhere in the world.

People can argue about the validity of signs and wonders, but what I experienced in those jungles became my reality for the rest of my days. Never again would I question whether God's power through miracles was for today. He still leads people to the throne of grace just as He did in Acts, helping, healing and restoring. All over the world, believers who love and trust Jesus with abandonment are experiencing the supernatural power of God in astounding ways. God's power is not a thing of the past...it is available to us today.

Chapter 4

Papua New Guinea to Waco 1985-1986

" 'For I know the plans that I have for you,' declares the Lord, 'plans for welfare and not for calamity to give you a future and a hope. Then you will call upon Me and come and pray to Me, and I will listen to you. You will seek Me and find Me when you search for Me with all your heart.' "
Jeremiah 29:11-13

So many times in life, we get confused in the journey. The delight of God is to simplify complexity. In Genesis 1 and 2, we see a perfect world where God and man interacted with joy and freedom. Adam and Eve were not complex people; they were simple. They had a deep, heartfelt connection with God and each other, and they had a clear purpose for their lives. They were at peace and rest.

In Genesis 3, when sin entered the world, life got complex. Suddenly, they didn't understand God any more. They didn't trust one another, and they lost the clarity of their purpose.

I am so thankful for the simple statements of Jesus because I realize that human internal complexity is a result of sin, not the way God intended to communicate with His people. One particular statement of Jesus in Matthew 22:35-40 has given me joyful clarification time and again:

'You shall love the Lord your God with all your heart, and with all your soul, and with all your mind.' This is the great and foremost commandment. The second is like it, 'You shall love your neighbor as

yourself.' On these two commandments depend the whole Law and the Prophets.

This truth saves my life when things get too complex. These simple words of Jesus have brought peace in my journey.

Waco, Texas – Back to "Normal" Life
Fall of 1985

Upon returning from New Guinea, I was confronted with two deep challenges. The first was culture shock. I had lived in an isolated foreign culture for a summer and had seen the deeds of God in a powerful way. I had become sensitized to the Holy Spirit and had caught a vision for the Kingdom and would never look at life the same. But coming home, I also did not know how to relate to my own Bible-belt culture.

Susan and Bill were the only ones I could relate to. No one else had been there, not my roommates, not Laura, not anyone. Having tasted the goodness of God, I knew I should continue to pursue Him wholeheartedly, but I often felt misunderstood by those around me. Life in the U.S. had gone on ordinarily while we had experienced the extraordinary in New Guinea.

Laura had stayed in Waco that summer to attend classes at Baylor. We had been dating for almost a year when I returned, and I was asking God whether she should be my wife. Her life still revolved around Baylor at a time when I was being drawn further away from the college lifestyle.

My change of worldview rattled Laura's and my relationship. She was deciding on her priorities in life and how she would live out her relationship with Jesus and His plan for her life. Now, I had come home wanting to live in the jungles instead of going down a more normal path that we were both accustomed to.

This personal struggle for Laura ended up being a place of great victory where she resolved in her heart that following Jesus wherever He may lead is the only way to go. I am so thankful that over and over again she settled on wholehearted devotion to Jesus as her heart's only desire.

The second crisis I faced when I came back to Waco was that the pastor at Highland Baptist Church resigned after confessing his involvement in sexual sin. This caused heartbreak and crisis for hundreds of people. Some like-hearted friends and I had just started a discipleship house, wanting to live out our newfound faith in community. The falling of this pastor caused some in our house to reevaluate and pull back from the gifts and power of the Spirit because they could not resolve how he, a pastor who had taught and moved in these spiritual gifts, could have lived in such sin. This conflict in their hearts and minds caused them to doubt the reality of these gifts.

These two challenges, culture shock and the crisis of our pastor's sin, made it extremely frustrating for me to apply the things I had learned over the summer. One day while driving home from school, I was so confused about what was real and what was not that I threw a stack of tracts out the window and screamed, "Lord, You save them. I don't know how to share the gospel. I am not even sure about my own salvation."

In the midst of that turmoil, God spoke to me so profoundly that I will never be the same. As I stood there in my driveway evaluating what it meant to follow and trust Jesus, God asked me a few simple questions that brought me back to simple truth.

First, He asked me, "Jimmy, who is someone that you know who really loves Me?" I immediately thought of my friend Chris.

"What is it about Chris that shows you he loves Me?" the Lord asked. As I thought about it, I realized that Chris loved Jesus with all his heart, soul, mind, and strength. Then the Lord asked me, "Jimmy, can you try to do that?"

"Yes, Lord, I can," I replied.

Then He asked me, "What else do you notice about Chris?" I knew what made Chris special was not only his love for God but also his love for others. The Spirit spoke once again and asked, "Do you think you can do that too? Can you love the people in front of you?"

"Yes, Lord, I think I can do that," I said.

"The whole Law is wrapped up in that simple statement," He reminded me. "You are to love Me with everything you have, and you are to love your neighbor as yourself. As long as you do that, you are always free. You don't have to worry about all the unanswered questions. Simply live out that life of love."

This truth has anchored me through the years. When I have questioned different theological or doctrinal perspectives on my own journey, I always come back to the simplicity of loving God and loving people. I am always right in the center of God's will when I am doing these two things.

Waco, Texas – No Matter What
Spring of 1986

After years of working with young people in relationships, I have learned that well-meaning believers will often get married without a clear sense of vision or focus. Being called to walk the "narrow way" is many times cast aside when it comes to love, romance, and relationship. I knew in my own journey with the Lord, despite my weaknesses and bumbling, I had to feel that I could to do whatever God was saying on any given day. Whomever I married would have to say the same thing, and we would have to be committed to honoring Him every step of the way.

Laura and I were still dating through my senior year at Baylor and getting more serious all the time. As we began to talk about marriage, I knew that we would have to discuss how we would live our lives together. It scared me a little bit to go to this place because I didn't want to lose her, but I knew that if we couldn't agree on God's leadership, then we couldn't be married.

So, I made a simple statement: "Laura, if we choose to get married, there are a few things we have to agree on. Number one is that no matter what, we will listen and obey God every day of our lives. Whether I like it or you like it, whether my parents or your parents like it, whether our friends like or dislike it, it doesn't matter. I have to know that together we can listen and obey Him no matter what."

I'm so thankful for Laura's tender heart to Jesus and her desire to always say "yes" to Him. She responded to me, "That is what I want to do." Within a couple of months, in March of 1986, I asked Laura Mielke to marry me.

Houston, Texas
Summer of 1986

Our first chance to say "yes" to God came before we were even married. My plans were to go to seminary so that we could go into ministry. The morning I was walking to the mailbox to mail my completed application to Fuller Theological Seminary, the Lord intercepted me so strongly that I doubled over in the driveway. I was not supposed to go to seminary.

Though I was confused, I knew God was speaking to me, so I walked back in the house and threw the application away. "What do you have for me, Lord?" I asked. He didn't answer me right away.

As I sat down to study for a finance test though, He spoke to me and said, "I want you to go into business."

"But God, I gave all that up," I protested. "When you said, 'Follow Me,' I gave up my pursuit of business and chose to follow You."

Immediately I heard Him say, "Trust Me, and I'll lead you the right way."

Laura and I had already committed to say "yes" to Jesus no matter what, so I began looking for business opportunities. One opened up in Houston for a medical supply company. After graduation, I packed up and moved to Houston while Laura stayed in Waco to finish school.

For me, there was only one goal for my time in Houston: learn to love God more than ever by learning to abide in Him. Every morning I would read and meditate on John 15:1-15. I would think and pray through these verses and do everything I could to adapt them to my life. Before I went to work, I focused on the words of John 15:5: "I am the vine, you are the branches; he who abides in Me and I in him, he bears much fruit, for apart from Me you can do nothing." The phrase that repeated over and over in my mind through the day was, "...apart from You, I can do nothing."

Out of that simple abiding relationship, I saw God move powerfully while I worked in business. By listening and talking to people, I had opportunities to share Christ, see people healed, and see lives redirected. I found God's presence so near that it seemed moment by moment I tangibly knew He was with me. Some of my fondest memories of walking intimately with the Lord are from those days. No one had talked to me about how to be a Christian business man; it just happened because I simply wanted to follow Jesus. I learned that wherever God puts me vocationally, the answer to bearing fruit in that place is simply to listen and obey God.

One day, I overslept and had to rush out the door without the chance to meditate on John 15. Though I tried to quote Scripture throughout the day, it just seemed like I wasn't in sync with the Lord. That evening, I went to a friend's church where they opened up the altar at the end of the service to come and pray. I got on my knees and started to sob uncontrollably. I thought, *God, what is happening?* I found these words coming out of my mouth: "I miss You! I miss You! I miss You!" You see, I had grown so accustomed to abiding and living in His presence, that when I didn't connect with Him first thing in the morning, I missed Him as the day went on.

That summer I got so addicted to Jesus, to abiding in Him, that I found it was too difficult to live life apart from Him. Truly for me, apart from Him, I can do nothing.

After a few months of working in Houston, my general manager came to me and asked me what God had for my life. I poured my heart out to him, sharing the depths of my burden for missions and God's work around the world. He suggested that I take a few days off to pray with Laura about what God wanted us to do. I agreed and set off to Waco again to seek the Lord's direction.

On my way, the Lord spoke both revelation and direction to me. First, He told me that when I went to Waco for college, I was seeking reputation. This time, He was going to bring me back to lose my reputation. Second, He wanted to teach me to love Laura as Christ loved the church.

Waco, Texas – "Called" to Ministry
Fall of 1986

I've never thought of myself as a pastor...I know that sounds strange. I mean, I've never thought of my position as a vocational move, a call, or a career. My thought process has always been *What is Jesus saying, and am I doing that?* If I am being obedient to what He is saying, then I know I am fulfilling my "calling."

When I returned from New Guinea, I thought I had found what I wanted to do with the rest of my life. Then God told me to go into business, so I thought I was to live for Jesus in the business world. In my heart, however, I knew leading and pastoring people was what I wanted to do even though I had never been specifically "called" to it.

Not having an official "calling," I was confused about what God wanted from me. I went to the elders at Highland for counsel. After I tried to describe to them what I thought God was saying to me, they simply asked me what I wanted to do. Well, there was nothing more I wanted to do than to serve Jesus with all my heart all the time, leading people to Christ, building them up, strengthening them in their faith, and seeing God's glory in the earth.

The response from Charles Davis, the pastor at Highland, gave me such peace. He used this illustration: "I have four boys. If one of my sons came to me and said, 'Dad, more than anything in the world I want to be a pastor,' I would get excited about that. To me, that would be a sign of the way God had made him. To me God-given passions and desires are as much of a calling as feeling some emotional draw toward a 'calling.' I believe my son could live with passion and desire for the rest of his life and be content with that being his calling. So many times, our calling is around that thing that God has made us to be."

Since that day, Laura and I have never looked back. God has visited us in key times and led us clearly to what we were to do at specific times. However, the general understanding that God had created us a certain way and placed specific desires in our hearts is all the "calling" we have needed to pursue those things. There was no point in time when God distinctly spoke to us about our calling as much as He just opened our eyes to how He had created us and then freed us to pursue our passions.

Robert Ewing – Watch Me Build My Church

The first Wednesday evening after returning to Waco to be with Laura, I went to the evening service at Highland. There, God spoke to me more clearly than maybe I've ever heard. He said, "I want you to stay and watch Me build My church from the bottom up." I really had no idea what that meant, nor did I have any position to do that from my perspective, but I knew that God had spoken. His words to me were especially significant because they confirmed something He had planted in my heart more than a year earlier.

Robert Ewing is one of my spiritual fathers. He and his family had been a part of the charismatic renewal in Waco in the late 1940s, and Robert had developed a deep love for the Church. Along with his ministry team, Robert was an overseer of 80 churches around the world.

Robert opened his life to me, teaching and mentoring me in the faith. I loved going to his house for lunch and hearing his stories of dramatic healings, miracles, and testimonies of smuggling Bibles into closed countries. His work inspired me to believe God for the impossible. He would talk for hours about the Church. He was convinced that it was God's instrument to change the world. As he would talk about the different scripture passages that speak about God's design and desire to see the Church be all that it is called to be, my heart was set afire. This was the dream that I was willing to live and die for: that God would be glorified in the earth through His Church. If we could learn to be the Church and reproduce the Church around the world, then the glory of God could be seen in every tribe, tongue, people, and nation. Those days deeply shaped who I am today and my love for the Church.

The season surrounding my time with Robert was also a season of great brokenness. When I wasn't working, I would spend hours at Robert's house in a room by myself seeking God. It was there that I had an experience that I call "meeting authority," realizing that God is in charge of the world and not me. I realized that, at best, I am the worst sinner who has ever lived. One day in particular, I remember grabbing my shirt, throwing myself to the ground, weeping, and crying out, "Lord, everything in me is sinful. If there is anything you can do with my life, pick me up off this ground and blow me where you will."

A few days later, I was at home when the same feeling of inadequacies over my own sinfulness came over me. I grabbed the leg of the bed, saying, "uncle!" (When I was a boy, my brothers would hold me down until I cried out "uncle" in surrender.) What I was saying was, "God, You've got me. I'm Yours. Whatever You want to do, whether I sweep streets or lead a large church, I just want to be Yours fully and completely." God has been so faithful to answer that prayer along the way.

More than a year later, God told me that He wanted me to stay and watch Him build His Church from the bottom up. Since this came after my season of brokenness, I was no longer thinking about plans of grandeur and all that God would do as much as I was just glad to be alive and to be His. I continually prayed, "God, I just want to be wholly Yours, to walk with a people who are wholly Yours, and to see You get glory through the Church."

A friend told me once, "The brokenness of one brings blessing to millions." I don't know if I will ever touch millions, but I do know that brokenness brings great grace for whatever God has for us.

Ron Higgins – Call to Faithfulness
Fall of 1986

Robert's church needed host homes for some of the visiting missionaries attending a conference. I opened up our apartment, and God brought a man into my life named Ron Higgins. Ron had been used mightily by God in India and Pakistan, preaching at massive crusades where thousands of people were saved and healed. More than anything, though, Ron was a humble and tender man.

When Ron stayed with my roommate and me, I asked him if I could spend time with him. He said, "Sure, why don't you meet me at 5:00 a.m. tomorrow morning." I thought, *5:00 a.m.!? What are we going to do...go fishing?*

The first morning we met, Ron told me that the first hour of the day was for prayer. *Awesome*, I thought. *What a great idea to pray for the first hour of the day.* Ron went to his corner, and I went to mine. I said a few prayers and then fell asleep.

An hour later, Ron woke me up and told me it was time to study the Word. *Wonderful,* I thought, *I love the Bible!* I began reading and soon started meditating as well. Meditating, as you may know, is a dangerous practice when you are tired. As you might guess, I fell asleep. Again, Ron awakened me, this time with drool leaking onto the open pages of my Bible. We ended our morning by praying together for our day. Ron asked God to fill us with the Spirit so that we could see every divine appointment He had for us.

I followed Ron for four days, driving him around and sticking as close to his side as time allowed. Everyone he met soon discovered that he knew Jesus. He would either pray for them, love on them, or encourage them in some way. Often times, he would be bold and share the gospel with them on the spot. It was awesome to witness such a lifestyle of love.

When we had time alone in the car or at night, I would ask Ron to tell his stories of seeing God's power in India and Pakistan. But instead, he would turn around and ask to hear my stories. Over those four days, Ron began digging into my life to test the authenticity of my walk with the Lord.

On the fifth morning we were together, we sat at the breakfast table discussing the great things of God. We spoke of nations coming to faith and God revealing Himself mightily in power. The presence of God was so tangible that you could feel it. It seemed as if Jesus Himself were sitting at the table with us.

In this awesome atmosphere, Ron put his hand on my shoulder and said, "Brother Jimmy, I have a word for you." He began proclaiming an incredible prophecy over my life. It was one of those intense times when your hair stands on end because God is in your midst. I was overwhelmed by the amazing words Ron spoke and was thinking, *This is awesome. Finally, the hour of God's anointed power on my life has come. I've read about things like this and now it is happening to me!*

By the time he was finished, visions of worldwide revival danced in my head, and I saw myself standing on stage leading a hundred thousand to Christ. As we got up off the floor, wiped the snot from our noses, and gathered our composure, I asked Ron, "So, what now? Where do I go from here?"

Ron simply replied, "Jimmy, I've been living across the hall from you for a week now, and your room is a mess."

Confused, I thought, *Well, I hope it didn't bother you...* Then I asked again, "Okay, but what are we going to do about the world-wide revival, Ron?"

"I don't think you understand, Jimmy," Ron went on to explain. "Unless you learn to make your bed, you will never be able to administrate the great things of God that were just spoken over you."

Immediately, I went from the prophetic mountaintop to a sobering valley of reality. Ron quoted Jesus, "He who is faithful in a very little thing is faithful also in much" (Luke 16:10).

"How is your prayer life?" Ron asked. I told him I was into praying an hour a day. "How often do you do that, Jimmy?" he probed some more. God's presence lingered heavy in the room, and I remembered what happened to people who lied in the presence of God, so I opted for honesty…only a couple times a week. Ron challenged me to be faithful in prayer. He suggested I start with five or ten minutes a day, get that down seven days a week, 365 days a year, and then go to 15 minutes. His encouragement was to make prayer the first priority in the morning as an act of the will to depend on God alone.

"What about your Bible reading? Have you read the whole Bible?" I thought about it. Surely I had. I loved to read the Bible. Don't you eventually get to a place where you've read it all? Ron challenged me again. The Bible is the anchor for our souls. It transforms our minds and hearts and lays the foundation for our entire belief system. We must be constantly in the Word. Ron carried a Bible with him everywhere he went, and periodically through his day, he would read from it to be nourished and strengthened.

"What about evangelism, Jimmy?" I thought I had a great answer for that one because I had been on this amazing mission trip to Mexico. But Ron wasn't interested in those stories. He wanted to know if everyone in my life knew that I knew Jesus. His main question to me was, "Are you ashamed of Christ?"

Systematically, Ron went through my life and asked the hard questions. Moment by moment, I shrunk in humility. Before the end of that conversation, we were back on the floor, only this time, we were crying out to God asking Him to make me a faithful man.

It all seemed to make sense to me in this one experience with Ron: God had wonderful plans for my life, but they would never fully come to pass unless I could learn to be an obedient and faithful man.

Jeremiah 29:11-13 says it this way, "'For I know the plans that I have for you,' declares the LORD, 'plans for welfare and not for calamity to give you a future and a hope. Then you will call upon Me and come and pray to Me, and I will listen to you. You will seek Me and find Me when you search for Me with all your heart.'"

So, I began the journey of getting up every day to pray, seek God in His Word, fast, share Jesus with everyone and anyone, disciple people, and create a lifestyle of servant hood in the context of community. These simple truths have changed my life. They are still the bread and butter for all that we do at Antioch. If we can simply live out the values of the Kingdom in a very practical way, we will see the world change.

I am so thankful that God was gracious enough to bring Ron Higgins into my life right when I needed it. Not only did God reveal part of His dream to me through Ron, but He also taught me how to live a life that can see those dreams come to pass. Without this lesson, I would not have seen God's dreams fulfilled in my life.

God was shaping and forming His destiny and purpose in my life. From New Guinea to Ron Higgins, after seeing God's goodness, there was a window of time to understand deeper the truths of God's heart.

Psalm 103:7 says, "He made known His *ways* to Moses, His *acts* to the sons of Israel." It is always God's desire to show us His ways and not just simply His acts. I had seen His acts in New Guinea and was excited about what He had done. But God also made sure I knew His ways: through humility and simplicity I can stay close to Him to see His power and purposes fulfilled.

Chapter 5

Poor to Rich
1987-1989

"But we have this treasure in earthen vessels,
so that the surpassing greatness of the power
will be of God and not from ourselves."
2 Corinthians 4:7

I have found that when He calls us to obey and respond to the next step before us, He creates, leads, and guides our lives.

By the time we were married in December 1986, God was already bringing people and lessons into our lives that would teach us about His ways and how to walk with Him. After more than 20 years, we look behind us and see a tapestry of His grace. The way things have happened through the years was not always the way we would have planned, but I love how God puts all of the pieces together.

Our job is simply to trust Him, believe Him, and say "yes" to the next thing that He is telling us to do. When we do that, we will be able to look back and see His glory displayed in our lives.

Highland Baptist Church – Bigger Dreams
1987

Even before Laura and I were married, we had overseas missions in mind. We were both burdened for the nations and were convinced that God was going to send us out. Because we already had connections with Youth With a Mission (YWAM), we began looking for opportunities to serve overseas with them. However, God began to lead us in a different direction.

Within two weeks of marriage, Laura and I went to a conference in Dallas with some of the leadership from Highland Baptist Church. The speaker called for young leaders to come forward to receive prayer. Since I was not a leader, I stayed back, but Mark Buckner, the college pastor at Highland, went to the front.

As I watched Mark receive prayer, God spoke very clearly to me and said, "I am calling you to serve this man. He has carried My dreams in his heart, and I want you to serve and support him. Ask him to forgive you for the ways you've judged him over the years." Immediately, I went forward, confessed my sins, and told Mark that I was going to serve him. He then asked Laura and me to continue praying through this calling in order to learn more specifically what it meant.

For the next couple of days, Laura and I fasted and prayed for clarification about how we were to serve Mark. Two days later, we were in another meeting where a leader from Romania prayed over us with a prophetic word: "God has been preparing you. Within the next few months you will begin a process of training young men and women to send them to the four corners of the earth."

Though we really felt God's love and presence when this man prayed, I thought to myself, *Well, neat guy, but he's got to be off.* In the first place, I had just come through the most broken time in my life. Surely, I wasn't prepared; I was falling apart. Secondly, no one had asked us to train anyone. While we felt encouraged and built up that God had spoken to us, we still weren't sure what the future held.

Shortly thereafter, we talked with Mark and his wife Susan about what we thought the local church could be. They had a desire to see young men and women from the college group trained and sent out to the nations. We talked and prayed with them, and then together we came up with a proposal to submit to the Highland Baptist Church elders.

Basically, the proposal went like this: God is challenging us, the local church, to own the process of developing, training, and sending people. Usually those who want to be trained for full-time vocational ministry either go to seminary or through a para-church organization. We wanted to send out teams of people who had learned to live the

Kingdom values of loving Jesus, discipleship, and evangelism in the context of community. Out of their experiences together, they could reproduce the Church anywhere in the world.

We laid out this simple dream to be started with a training school. The elders at Highland had felt the Lord had been leading them to do something similar, and so they confirmed our calling. Graciously, they agreed to let us launch out into this ministry.

As we began preparing for the training school, we heard of a program at Phoenix First Assembly of God called "Master's Commission." We went there to check it out and discovered that it was very similar to what God was putting on our hearts. Following their example and implementing other elements from the YWAM Discipleship Training School, we started our own "Master's Commission" in the fall of 1987.

Waco, Texas – Step-by-Step into Revival
Summer of 1987

God taught Laura and me a significant lesson during the summer before the training school launched. One day when I was mowing lawns around town to take care of our needs, the reality of what we were committing to do by faith began to hit me. Financially, things were going to be tight. Though we had decided to step out by believing God to take care of us, I was struck by just how difficult things might get.

While driving down the road, I began to ask the Lord, "What are you doing with me? Am I just crazy or is this really You leading us?"

God spoke to me almost audibly: "If you will simply obey the next thing I'm telling you to do, you will be right in the middle of the greatest revival the world has ever seen." (I want to note here what He did not say to me: He did not say that I would be leading such a revival, only that I would get to take part in it.)

I was so overtaken by the voice and promise of God that I pulled over on the side of the road and cried. This wasn't just something we had come up with, but it was from God. Though I didn't know much, I knew I could do the next thing He was telling us to do. Over the years, this became our mode of leadership: we simply ask the Lord for the next step and even if we don't know what the big picture is, we choose to say "yes" today. Out of this simple obedience, God is weaving a tapestry of His grace behind us.

During the same time, Laura and I were learning how to hear God. I remember listening to a teaching on prophecy and how God still speaks to people today. As I waited on the Lord about everything that was before us, He gave me two key Scriptures. The first was Isaiah 58:11-12:

And the Lord will continually guide you, And satisfy your desire in scorched places, And give strength to your bones; And you will be like a watered garden, And like a spring of water whose waters do not fail. Those from among you will rebuild the ancient ruins; You will raise up the age-old foundations; And you will be called the repairer of the breach, The restorer of the streets in which to dwell.

While I wasn't sure what all of this meant, I began to use this verse as a guide for everything we would do. The second Scripture God gave me was Isaiah 43:18-19:

Do not call to mind the former things, Or ponder things of the past. Behold, I will do something new, Now it will spring forth; Will you not be aware of it? I will even make a roadway in the wilderness, Rivers in the desert.

Early on, God was giving us faith to believe Him for new things, for Him to make a way where there is no way.

Over and over again, I have seen these Scriptures come to pass. God speaks through His Word prophetically and then fulfills it through those who trust in Him and faithfully wait for His promises.

Eureka Springs, Arkansas – Building on Humility
Summer of 1987

Also that summer, Laura and I went on a vacation to see my brother in Indiana. On the way, we stopped in Arkansas to camp overnight. Neither of us had camped much before, but we thought it would be fun. By the time we pulled into the campsite, it was pouring rain. We slept in the back of the truck under a camper shell and woke up soaking wet.

The next morning was Sunday, and we went to a place called Thorncrown Chapel, a beautiful glass chapel in the mountains led by a man we knew. So many people were attending that day that we had to stand outside during worship.

At the end of the service, a man tapped me on the shoulder and said, "I was watching the two of you worship, and God gave me a word for you." He spoke many of the same things Ron Higgins had spoken regarding how God wanted to use our lives. Then he asked where we were staying. He invited us to go to the Passion play that evening and then stay with him and his wife at their home. Now, we had never met this man. All we knew was what he had told us: that he was a writer and had been involved in restoration ministries for both Jim Baker and the pastor at Highland Baptist who had fallen into sin.

We accepted his invitation to join him at the play and in his home. The next two days, we enjoyed hanging out with his family and learning about God's ways and their journey. One night, as I sat on the porch with him, we talked about why godly men fall into sin. He said, "You know, son, a lot of people have lived off their charisma and created big ministries but have been mediocre in their character. Others have started off humble and slow and had the opportunity to create deep character. My suggestion would be that even if your ministry is mediocre in man's eyes, deep character will allow you to have loving relationships, a strong family, and something that can last forever."

For a couple in their early twenties, at the beginning of ministry, it was significant to hear the stories of those who had gone before us, those who had made it, and others who hadn't. God had sovereignly placed this man in our path to disciple us, if even for this short time.

Master's Commission
Fall of 1987

Remembering all that God had shown us over the summer, we kicked off Master's Commission in the fall with eight students. The program was a year-long intensive discipleship course coupled with missions training: nine months in the States and three months overseas. Each morning, we memorized Scripture, studied the Bible, prayed together, and received teaching. In the afternoons, the students started different outreach ministries in our community and served the various outreaches of the church.

1st **Master's Commission Trip - 1988**

The curriculum grew out of what Ron Higgins had taught me: the simple ideas of prayer and fasting, reading the Word, evangelism, making disciples, and serving others. We believed that if we taught the students to actually live the disciplines and walk in relationship with Jesus instead of just talking about doing these things, then the transformation that took place in their lives would catapult them out to change the world.

God did so many incredible things that first year of Master's Commission. Some of my fondest memories relate to evangelism. In learning to be bold with our faith, we would preach the gospel in the university common areas and in the middle of restaurants. Some may have called us foolish, but we didn't want to let anyone pass our faces without hearing the good news of Jesus.

We were also asking God for power evangelism in which people would see the power of God and from that be saved. One Saturday morning as I prayed over one of the students, the power of God fell so heavily on him that I literally felt heat like fire in my hands. This young man then went out with his ministry partner for the day to share the gospel door-to-door. One family invited them in and gathered around to hear the good news preached. That afternoon, the whole family came to Christ.

It was also during those Saturday morning outreaches that the Lord really began to teach us how He divinely leads us if we ask Him. I remember walking through a neighborhood asking the Lord whom I should talk to. There were several people out in their yards, so my question was, "Lord, which one?" I felt the Spirit direct me very strongly to a certain lady named Sarah. As I approached her, I asked the Lord what I should say to her.

"Do you know Jesus?" I asked Sarah.

"No, I don't," she replied. "But I just got out of the hospital, and while I was there, I had a dream of falling into a black hole. I could tell that I was falling away from a light, and I was screaming out to that light. Can you tell me what that light is?"

Blown away by what I was hearing, I gladly explained to her that the light is Jesus. He had spared her life so that I could come and share His gospel with her so that she could be saved. Sarah gave her heart to the Lord that day. Her husband Michael eventually gave his life to the Lord as well, and Laura and I were able to spend time discipling them as a couple.

Highland Baptist Church
1987-1989

God's direction to start Master's Commission had been clear, and as He worked in our midst throughout the year, we felt His continual confirmation and leading. However, we did not proceed without opposition. On the first day we had class at Highland, a staff member approached me and said, "I don't think this is of God, and I'm going to do everything I can to make sure that it doesn't happen in this place." I soon discovered that he wasn't the only person who felt that way. Another man thought I was too young to be leading the school and that he should be in charge instead. He shared his opinions with different students and eventually took false accusations to the elders of the church. This went on for a couple of years, and it was a trying process.

Charles Davis was the senior pastor at Highland when we first started the training school. He is one of the most rock solid men of God that I know, a faithful husband, father, and Bible teacher. Charles had taken over for a pastor who had fallen into sin and therefore inherited many of the pains and problems of the people. During his leadership, as he was trying to repair people's broken lives, he was the target of much unjust criticism.

After receiving my first couple of challenging criticisms, I went to talk to him. "Dr. Davis," I asked, "how do you handle people's criticism even when they are not accurate?"

He pulled out a six-page letter and said, "This is a letter from a couple in the church that I am about to meet with in two hours. They are hurt and mad, and they have their own issues." He went on to explain, "I've gone through this letter and highlighted everything that I thought was accurate, accusations and observations they made about me that I think are true. I would like to see these things change in me. That is about twenty percent of the letter. I am going to lovingly listen to them, hear the pain behind their thoughts, and try to help them. Ultimately, when they leave, I will ask God to bless them and make sure to forgive them for any way that they were hurtful. But the twenty percent, I want to respond to that and learn how to change."

Dr. Davis went on, "Many times, when we hear criticism, we become defensive and we don't find the twenty percent that needs to change. I can't control whether someone becomes bitter or not, but I can learn the truth that is spoken through them. God speaks truth through all kinds of vessels, and I want to continue to grow and learn."

Charles' example, as well as the book of Proverbs, has been a mainstay for us in the challenges and accusations that have come our way. It has always been our desire to listen attentively, to ask God what is of Him, to respond wholeheartedly, to bless and forgive anyone, as well as to repent and ask forgiveness from anyone we have hurt. That means at times, we have not responded at all. Other times we have tried to clarify truth when a lie has been expelled. Ultimately, though, we have found ourselves humbled and changed by the accusations and criticism of others.

Jesus said it this way, "Blessed are you when people insult you and persecute you, and falsely say all kinds of evil against you because of Me. Rejoice and be glad, for your reward in heaven is great for in the same way they persecuted the prophets who were before you" (Matthew 5:11-12).

There are times to rejoice, and there are times to repent. Proverbs 9:9 says, "Give instruction to a wise man and he will be still wiser." Proverbs 6:23 says, "For the commandment is a lamp and the teaching is light; And reproofs for discipline are the way of life." There will always be reproof because we will always need reproof. We also believe that there are times when we just need to rejoice and not defend ourselves because God works all things together for good to those who love Him. Hopefully, we have learned lessons through others' criticisms and will continue to learn through them in the years to come.

God sustained me though these times, and I came to know that God is my Defender. Through the different challenges, He taught me to trust Him and His plan. I didn't have to worry about man's opinion or resistance as long as I knew I was submitting to the authorities around me and to God's plan that He had put before me. Again, I was led to do only the thing God put directly in front of me and not to try to create a work of God all on my own.

Waco, Texas – Living on Faith
1987-1989

When the elders of Highland gave us permission to start the training school in the fall of 1987, they told us that there were not any finances available to pay a staff or fund the needed resources. If we were going to do this thing, it would have to be by faith. Laura and I had been reading about George Mueller, a pastor in England in the 19th century who trusted God completely for finances. He took care of thousands of orphans, never asking anyone for financial assistance, but praying daily for God's provision. His journals of seeing God provide gave us faith to believe God could do the same for us.

We were both excited and sobered by the opportunity to walk with faith like Mr. Mueller. Going into the school year, we did everything we could to cut our expenses. We moved into a lower income neighborhood, sold many of our things, and then waited with faith to see God move. It was a challenging and exciting adventure for us.

I often say that the real champ in this journey is Laura. While I grew up in a middle-class family, Laura grew up upper middle class, always abundantly provided for. When we made decisions to live differently than the way we had grown up, she was amazingly sacrificial and always looked forward to see God work in response to our faith.

In the fall, Laura started working as a church secretary while I started the training school. We learned early on that the best thing for us was to minister together. However, if Laura were to quit, it would put us in an even more vulnerable position financially. Though we didn't know how it would work out, Laura quit her job in December. Mowing lawns had dried up, and we definitely needed to see God move on our behalf.

Over the next several months, we saw God provide in incredible ways. One time, we invited a man over for dinner. We didn't have any food in the cabinets, and we wondered if we should have him over at all. This man was a friend of Robert Ewing, though, and I told Laura, "Look, he knows Jesus and we will just pray and trust God. He will understand if there isn't anything to eat."

As he pulled up in the driveway, I greeted him in the front yard, and he said, "Hey, I just had to put my mother in a nursing facility, and I had bought a lot of groceries for her house. I was praying about what to do with them, and God told me to bring these groceries to you. Would you mind receiving these?"

I said, "Brother, you don't understand. You just provided your own dinner."

God provided many miracles in the area of food. We invited Sarah and Michael, the couple who came to Christ, over for dinner along with their two children. Again, we didn't have enough to feed them all. We only had a few noodles and a little spaghetti sauce. They were new believers, so we prayed about what to do.

I said to Laura, "Honey, God has multiplied food before. Let's take what we have, cook it as if it were a feast, and trust God." That night, six people ate all that they wanted with some left over. We literally saw food multiply before our eyes.

Sarah told Laura that she didn't want to come to church because she didn't have a nice dress to wear. Even though Laura reassured her that it didn't matter what she wore, Sarah still was insecure about coming. Laura asked her, "If you could have any dress, what color would you want?" Sarah said she would love to have a yellow dress, size 10.

We were on a very tight budget those days, but we really wanted to buy a dress for Sarah. As we got in the car, Laura asked, "What would Jesus do in this situation?" We thought about going to Wal-Mart to buy the dress, but decided that Jesus would go all out and get the best. So, we went to Dillard's. As we went in to look around, Laura saw a sale rack. Sure enough, there was a size 10 yellow dress, 75 percent off! We couldn't believe it. For just $10, we were able to buy a brand new, beautiful dress for Sarah. She wore it every week when she came to church.

During that season, we never missed a bill payment, though sometimes we would cut it to the last moment. Once, we owed $53.24 with no way to pay it. The day it was due, we got a refund check in the mail from the gas utility for $53.24. It was exactly what we needed.

At Christmas time, God led us in creative ways to give gifts to our friends and family and even in how to share with one another. Our second Christmas together, we bought a double cassette of Keith Green's greatest hits; I wrapped one and gave it to Laura, and she wrapped the other and gave it to me. The next year, we bought Keith Green's Gold twin cassette set and did the same thing. These were the best of times as our hearts were free and we enjoyed the simple things in life.

Though times were lean, we always had enough. Paul said in Philippians 4:11-12, "I have learned to be content in whatever circumstances I am. I know how to get along with humble means, and I also know how to live in prosperity; in any and every circumstance I have learned the secret of being filled and going hungry, both of having abundance and suffering need." God was teaching us contentment. He was extracting what I call our "suburban souls" that we might be free to live with Him in any way that He chose.

That season was not just about learning to receive His provision, but also how to give out of our need. Sometimes the Lord led us to give money that we needed for bills, gas, or food. Once, a group of missionaries from Youth With a Mission came to do a presentation at our church. At that time, we had enough food, so we volunteered to be a host home to provide a missionary with a place to stay, breakfast, and a sack lunch.

After the presentation, we were sitting around the table talking. This missionary was telling us about believing God for $4,000 to work with street kids in Brazil. Laura and I had a bill for $100 due the next day, but we only had $20 to our name. As he excused himself for a few moments, I turned to Laura and said, "Laura, we only have $20 to give. What do you think?"

She said, "Oh, I think we ought to give all that we have. We've trusted God this far, let's trust Him with everything." We gladly gave him the $20, somewhat apologetically that we didn't have more to give, but we prayed that God would multiply it for his needs.

The next morning after we sent him on his way, we went into his room to pick up towels and sheets and found a thank you note. It read something like this: "Thank you so much for having me in your home. It was a delight to be with you and talk about the Kingdom of God. As I was praying this morning, God showed me that your need was greater than mine and that I was to give you this $100. I pray that it is God's provision for whatever you need." Wow, how exciting to see God provide not simply out of receiving but out of giving.

Those first two years of leading the training school, our income never exceeded $9,000, but we were able to give half of that away. God sovereignly worked to take care of us. It was the lessons of giving, not just receiving, that set patterns for the rest of our lives. I have found if we won't give out of the little that we do have, then we won't give out of abundance either. "Give," the Scripture says, "and it will be given to you" (Luke 6:38). God takes care of those who have open hands and open hearts.

Master's Commission – Sticking it Out
Spring of 1988

The spring of 1988 brought on a whole new set of challenges for Master's Commission. A fire completely gutted the education building at Highland where we had been meeting and within the next three months, the senior pastor, one of the associate pastors, and the worship leader all resigned. These men had been very supportive of Master's Commission even when so many others were skeptical and critical. In a very short period of time, the school had lost its home and support. It was like our legs were knocked out from underneath us.

After the fire, we met in homes to conduct classes. Without the support we had the first semester and with the physical limitations and hardships we faced, I began to wonder if it was worth even planning a second year. Maybe it was time for Laura and me to move on from Highland. Perhaps God was trying to redirect us.

About the time I was struggling with these questions and concerns, I met a man from YWAM named Dean Sherman. I met with him privately and shared all of my issues. Secretly, I wanted Dean to sympathize and counsel me to move on. To my surprise though, Dean had very different words for me: "Jimmy, whose vision is this anyway? Do you expect everyone to jump up and down and get excited just because you have a vision from God? If you are not willing to put three to five years into it, your vision will never be fulfilled. So, either quit now or quit whining. If it's God's vision, He will make a way."

Those were tough words, but they were exactly what we needed to hear. At the time, only two women had signed up for the fall session of the second year, but Laura and I committed that even if it were only two students, we would still conduct the school because God had told us to do so.

Shortly after that, God gave me a word for the future of Master's Commission and the expanding work He would have us to be a part of. He told me that the first five years would lay a foundation, years six through ten would be a season of growth, and years eleven through fifteen would be a time of maturing.

Master's Commission (later known as the Antioch Training School) has been going for 20 years now. Looking back, I see how God's word came true over the first 15 years. While we have streamlined and modified the school, even changing its name a couple of times, the heart remains the same: teach people how to pursue Jesus wholeheartedly so that they can join His work in establishing His Church among the nations.

At the end of the 2006-2007 year, more than 650 students had participated in the Antioch Training School. All of them have served some length of time overseas and almost half of them have served long-term in church-planting efforts either in the U.S. or in another nation. When Mark Buckner and I, along with our wives, first talked about starting a training school in 1987, we could not have imagined all that God had planned. From humble beginnings to experiencing the awesome power and provision of God, the Antioch Training School has been an example of what it looks like for God to birth His dreams through a willing people.

Master's Commission – Foundations of Prayer
1988-1989

During the second year of Master's Commission, we were burdened to lead the church in intense prayer. We hosted several three-day, 24-hour prayer and fasting times at the church, crying out for a move of the Holy Spirit at Highland. Camping out in the sanctuary and using sleeping bags for periods of rest, we believed and asked God for a breakthrough.

After several sessions like this, I was discouraged that nothing seemed to be happening. I went to one of my mentors, Robert Ewing, and asked him what we were doing wrong. I'll never forget Robert's wise words: "Many people want to see God move, but God always raises up intercessors first. When the move of God begins, everyone will be on the bandwagon, but you and God will know that you were a part of starting it."

Those early days of learning how to pray laid the foundation for a lifestyle and culture of prayer in our community. We realized that no one has ever changed the world without becoming a person of intense, persevering prayer. The principles we learned during that year carry on even today, twenty plus years later. I believe that it is our consistency to get before God personally and corporately that has not only sustained us but transforms us day by day.

God has situated prayer in such a way that when we cry out to Him, we are able to consistently meet with Him in deep and powerful ways and are drawn into the relationship that we always longed for. Out of this intimacy, we are then able to see Him work. I love it because when He works, we can't take any credit. Prayer is geared for us to partner in relationship with God but for Him to get all of the glory.

Sometimes prayer can feel weak or unheard, but for those who persevere, there is always fruit. We are so thankful that He has consistently called us to pray because now we can honestly look back and say that He alone has done it all. After experiencing His presence and power day after day, year after year through prayer, we press on, expecting and anticipating Him to continue to move in our midst.

The training school was started as a dream to see young men and women equipped to change the world. As we look back, we have seen God's gracious hand shaping and developing all of us. The great thing about God's dreams is that He fulfills them if we just say "yes." Over and over again in the journey, we find ourselves weak and we realize that we are simply following a great God who has laid out great plans for a people who say "yes" to Him wholeheartedly.

Chapter 6

Iceland to Bulgaria
1988-1991

"But prove yourselves doers of the word, and not merely hearers..."
James 1:22

Throughout my growing up years, I loved to play sports. I was never more than an average athlete, but I loved to be in the game. One of the most frustrating things was to sit on the bench and watch others play. The same has been true in my walk with the Lord. It seems to me that Jesus has invited us all to play. Everybody has a chance to jump into this great Kingdom adventure if we simply respond to His Word.

At the very beginning of my Christian walk, I would get frustrated when people would preach messages or espouse doctrines but not teach how to walk them out. If I read or heard something, I wanted to do it. God invites us not just to read, watch, and believe, but also to experience what He is doing around us.

Reykjavik, Iceland – Experiencing Him Daily
Summer of 1988

After nine months of classroom training and service to the church and community in Waco, the Master's Commission class was ready for its first three-month overseas summer outreach. Before we left Waco for Iceland, England, and Amsterdam, we made a decision together to trust God for our finances and to mention our needs to no one. It was no longer just Laura and I but our team of six others believing God together for all of our needs.

Once in Iceland, all eight of us stayed in a small two-bedroom apartment: three single girls in one bedroom, three single guys in the living room, and Laura and me in the corner room. It was a great time together as we had opportunities to worship, pray, and learn from each other in these tight quarters.

The church that we were working with had agreed to provide the apartment and stock our refrigerator if we would just come. One Saturday night, after being there for two weeks of our one month visit, we realized that we had run out of food. As we got up that Sunday morning, everyone was asking what we were going to do. I said, "Well, one thing we are not going to do is mention our needs. We have come this far, let's just watch God provide."

So, with tentative excitement, we went to church, expecting someone to invite us to lunch. After we had ministered in the church and had a great time with the people, we returned to our apartment with no lunch and no food. While we were all tempted to grumble and complain, I got an idea. I said, "Let's figure out specifically what to ask God for. If we had lunch, what would we want?"

Someone said, "I would want a hamburger." Others said, "I would want spaghetti." But the consensus finally landed on pizza, the kind that was cut in squares, with salad and Coke to go along with it.

"Well," I said, "if that is what we want, let's ask God for it and have a time of worship." With a little bit of grumbling, we began to do just that. We had not prayed for more than five minutes when the phone rang. It was one of the elders' wives.

"A couple of families are meeting at our house for lunch," she told me. "We've got a lot of extra food, and we'd love to have you join us. Would you like to come over for lunch?"

I hung up the phone and shouted, "Guys, it is time to eat lunch!"

When we got to the house and prayed together for lunch, the hostess said, "I hope this food is okay. I made pizza, and we have salad, Coke, and other soft drinks." Not only was it pizza, but it was cut in squares, just like we had asked. We laughed and shouted and rejoiced and were able to share with them the story of God's provision.

Our cabinets were full the rest of the time, but more than anything, our hearts were full, knowing that God sees even our basic needs and is able to provide above and beyond even what we could ask or think.

In Iceland, we saw and experienced the power of God in many dynamic ways. One night, as we worshipped in someone's home, a neighbor heard us and knocked on the door. We welcomed him in and began to pray for him. As we prayed, he began to shake under the awesome presence of God falling on him. This man gave his life to Jesus. A few minutes later, there was another knock on the door and another neighbor entered. Then, the same thing: we prayed, he shook, and then he gave his life to Christ. It reminded me of Acts 2:42-47 where it describes the church meeting from house to house and living in a way that people were being added to them day by day. Literally, we were experiencing those passages right before our eyes.

Aldershot, England
Summer of 1988

From Iceland, we went to work with a church in Aldershot, England. Ministry there was difficult as many were very closed to our message. But day after day we went out to perform dramas, preach on the streets, and share the gospel from house to house.

On one occasion we shared the gospel in a neighboring city. We encountered an atheist who had a broken leg; the break was a week old. He mocked us openly, but the students just offered to pray for him. After they prayed, he left us to go to a doctor's appointment. At the doctor's office, he learned that his leg was healed! He called the church and told the elders what had happened and gave his life to Christ that day.

This man was the principal at a local school. He went to work and testified to more than 300 students that God had healed him supernaturally. Many of the students from his school came to Christ as well. The following Sunday, he came to church to testify of God's goodness, and through this miracle, the church rejoiced and grew.

On another occasion as we went door-to-door, a lady answered when we knocked. We offered to pray with her and share our testimony, but she became irate, saying, "Don't tell me that Jesus loves me or cares! God doesn't care about me!"

I asked, "Why do you think that?"

"Look at my son," she said. A little six or seven year old boy appeared. "He has mental problems and was just diagnosed with colon cancer."

Our hearts broke with her. We told her that we understood her pain and that we wanted to pray that God would heal her son. Softened by the compassion we showed for her son, she let us lay hands on him and pray. What a delightful little boy he was, smiling and hugging us while we prayed over him.

This was the next-to-last day before we left England. The boy was having surgery the next morning, and we went to visit him in the hospital to see how he was doing. When we arrived, the mother had this incredible look of excitement and shock on her face. "What happened?" we asked.

She said that when the doctors ran one last x-ray before doing the surgery, they found that the cancer was gone. She held up both of the x-rays and said, "The cancer is gone. God has healed my son." As we hugged her and cried together, we rejoiced over a God who sees the pain and need in peoples' hearts and shows up in miraculous ways.

Amsterdam, Netherlands
Summer of 1988

From England, we went to Amsterdam to work with Youth With a Mission. While with them, we would seek God in the morning and then proclaim Jesus everywhere we could in the afternoons and evenings. After one outreach, I approached a young man and asked him if he had seen our drama presentation. He hadn't, and so I told him that we were there talking about Jesus. With tears in his eyes, he said, "There is no God, and if there is, I want nothing to do with Him."

My heart broke for him, and I asked him what had happened to make him turn from God. He explained that he had survived a boating accident, but his brother and sister had died. "What kind of God would allow that to happen?" he questioned.

Desperate for God's words, I asked the Holy Spirit what I should say. I felt like God told me to tell this young man to repent. Wow, I felt so uncomfortable because normally I would empathize and grieve with him. God knew his heart, though, and I didn't. I knew I had to be bold with what God had spoken to me.

Many times in our lives, when we hear that still, small voice speak to us, we are afraid of what might happen if we step out boldly. My experience has been that if we will just obey, then God will cover us. Even if we miss it, He will teach us through the journey.

Well, I stepped out boldly that day and said, "I feel like God is saying that you need to repent, that you have misinterpreted His heart for you. It is not God who killed your family, but He is here to save you."

Suddenly, he broke down crying, saying, "I need Jesus. How do I know Him?" I shared the gospel with him, and he gave his heart to Christ. After we prayed, he anxiously looked at his watch and realized that his train for Sweden left in five minutes. One of the girls with us on the outreach was also from Sweden, and it just so happened that she was from his hometown. She got his information and was able to follow up with him.

I also was able to correspond with him over the next three years. I watched him get involved with a church and experience God's power in his life. After attending a missions' festival, he committed his life to missions. Later, I heard that he had married and was headed for the mission field. The power of the gospel is utterly amazing to take a broken atheist and turn him into a bold man of God.

Amsterdam, Netherlands – Set Free
Summer of 1988

Laura and I first met Keith while taking a day off together in Amsterdam. He was from Connecticut and approached us for money to get out of the country because he was a heroine addict and wanted to be free from it. While I don't usually give drug addicts money, I felt at this particular occasion that I should.

After I gave Keith the money, he thanked me and was about to run off when I said, "Keith, you need Jesus!"

He replied, "Oh, whatever. Thanks, man."

"No, Keith, let me pray for you." I put my hand on his shoulder and said, "Lord, get him! Reveal Your heart to him. Keith needs You, and You want to show Him that You are real."

When I finished the prayer, Keith screamed back, "What was that, man?"

I answered, "That was Jesus, and He is after you."

He said, "Whoa, dude, that's crazy. That's crazy, man," and he ran off.

I was so burdened for Keith that I prayed all day that I would encounter him again. The next day while I was heading through the red-light district to do ministry, I ran into him.

"Hey, man," he said, "that deal yesterday was a blow-away. That was amazing. What was that?"

"Man, that was Jesus," I responded.

"I thought it was just the power of the mind, you know? Like, you put your hand on somebody's shoulder and activate the power of positive thinking or something."

"No, man. It's not positive thinking. It's Jesus!"

We sat on the street and talked, and Keith told me his story. Like a

Keith Bakker – May 29, 1989 with YWAM Staff Person

prodigal son, Keith had come to Amsterdam to live a wild lifestyle of parties and pleasure. After getting hooked on heroine, losing all his money, and becoming a wanted man by the law, he was living on the streets and constantly on the run.

Before he left that day, I offered to pray for him again, but this time I told him I wouldn't use my hands. "Keith, you need to know that it is God's presence and power that is on you. It's not about me or anybody else." So I prayed again, "Lord Jesus, get him. Show him You are real and pour out Your Spirit upon him." I remember as we sat there on that curb in the red light district with the rain pouring down on us that it was like heaven on earth. God came and touched Keith again with His power and presence.

We agreed to meet that night to talk about drug rehab. As we met near Central Station in downtown Amsterdam, I challenged Keith with his need to receive Christ. He listened to the gospel and understood that he needed to respond to God. When he agreed that he wanted to pray to receive Christ, I felt I should not tell him how to pray. I said, "Keith, you know your need, and God is willing to listen. I want to encourage you to get on your knees here with me and cry out to God."

As Keith knelt beside me on the street, he cried out a prayer of desperation and need for God's forgiveness and power in his life. Once again, it seemed like heaven had come to earth as we were caught up in this incredible connection with God. When we opened our eyes at the end of our prayers, I looked up to see a circle of Japanese tourists around us clicking pictures of us. I think they thought we were part of the crazy scene in Amsterdam!

After this experience, Keith agreed to go to a drug rehab center called Victory Outreach, where they help you quit cold turkey, sitting and praying with you through those most difficult first days. After two days, though, Keith ran away.

Lars, a friend from Sweden, and I scoured the darkest reaches of the city looking for Keith. We looked under bridges, in seedy hotels, and in the drug houses of Amsterdam. My heart broke as we saw the devastation of people's lives who were addicted to heroine and the sex industry. But we did not find Keith.

A few days later when I was speaking at the YWAM base, someone came to me and said there was a man outside looking for me, saying he wanted to kill me. When I asked who this man was, they responded, "Some guy from America named Keith."

"Oh," I said. "He won't kill me," and I went outside to meet him.

"Man, you #&*!" he shouted, cussing me out and pushing me. "What did you do to me?" He explained that after he had run away from the rehab center, he had approached a lady at an ATM machine to ask for money. When he tried to talk to her though, it sounded like gibberish. He said, "My tongue was glued to the roof of my mouth, and I couldn't even speak. What did you do to me? I can't even talk. What's happening to me."

I was reminded of the passage in Psalm 137:6 where it says, "May my tongue cling to the roof of my mouth if I do not remember you."

I said, "Keith, God is after you. He's after your heart."

At that point he broke again. "What do I do?" he asked. "I don't know what to do."

I called my friend Lars over and told Keith we would pray with him until something broke. We prayed on the streets of Amsterdam until well after two in the morning. At about 1:30 a.m., as God was powerfully touching Keith's life, he looked up with tears coming down his face and grabbed me by the shirt and screamed, "He loves me! He loves me! He loves me!"

I couldn't help but shout back, "He loves me, too! He loves me, too!"

It was a great night of breakthrough for Keith, and the next evening we met again to spend time praying. We all felt that something was blocking him from total freedom. As we waited on the Lord, a picture of Keith's father came to my mind. When I mentioned his father and that he needed to forgive his father, Keith freaked out. He started pulling his hair and pacing around like a caged animal. "No, no!" he cried. "He's hurt me so bad, I can't do it."

I said, "Keith, God wants to fully deliver you, but you have to forgive."

"I don't know if I can," he responded. My heart was broken for him as he left that night.

Two days later, he came to see me before we left for the States. I remember embracing and talking about God's goodness. Again, I appealed to him to respond to the Lord. And again, he said he wanted to, but it was just so hard.

I prayed for him every day for the next four months, not knowing what had happened to him. Then, I got a letter, a picture, and a cassette tape of Keith testifying to what the Lord had done in his life. After our team had left Amsterdam, he took a severe nosedive back into drugs. He was in a car accident and had to spend a couple of days in the hospital. During that time, he realized that he had to get free somehow. Knowing that in jail he could get methadone to help him taper off of drugs, he went to the judge who works the area around the red-light district and confessed to several crimes. The judge accused him of wanting to get in jail for food and a place to stay.

"Either you put me in jail, or I will throw a brick through your car window," Keith threatened. The judge dismissed him, thinking nothing of it. So, Keith went out, found a large chunk of cement, and threw it through the judge's BMW window. He was immediately arrested and got what he wanted, thrown in jail.

During that next month in jail, Keith kicked drugs. A friend from YWAM visited every day to share with him what it means to walk with Jesus. When he got out of jail, he went to a YWAM rehabilitation facility. There, he received intensive discipleship and grew quickly in the Lord. Before long, he was back on the streets, but this time he was preaching the gospel instead of shooting up. Keith led many people to the Lord and even started traveling with Floyd McClung, a YWAM leader, to share his testimony with thousands during evangelistic outreaches.

Keith has been through his ups and downs through the years. But, God saved him, and I know I will see him in heaven one day. His journey to freedom is such a testimony of God's patient grace and power to seek out and deliver anyone who would look his way.

Reykjavik, Iceland – A Harvest Summer of 1989

The second year of Master's Commission, we took our outreach back to Iceland where the church in Reykjavik asked us to lead a youth camp. On the last night of camp, we waited on the Lord to show us what we should preach. In prayer, one of the students saw a picture of a cross. So, Brad, a Master's Commission graduate who was serving as the Reykjavik church's youth pastor, preached out of Isaiah 53 about the cross.

At the end of the message, a young man, a misfit who had been rejected by the others all week, came forward for prayer. As we lifted our hands to pray for him, the Spirit of God came on him, and he fell back. Suddenly, a spiritual barrier

Iceland Youth Revival

in the room broke, and people began calling out, "I want prayer! I want prayer!"

For the next four hours, the Lord visited us in a mighty way. Demons were manifested. People were set free. The sick were healed.

Many came to salvation, and many experienced the awesome power of God in that place.

After about three and a half hours, I broke away from the crowd and went out on the deck of the retreat center. I just began to praise and thank God for showing up, answering our prayers, and moving in power. For years I had prayed that I would see the gifts of the Holy Spirit found in the book of Acts come alive, and that night, I had seen it with my own eyes. But you know, there was something still empty inside of me. Seeing the power of God didn't satisfy me.

God spoke to me, "Remember that My gifts are sent to help and heal people's lives. *The gifts* are for them, but *I* am for you. I will always be enough for you." The gifts of the Holy Spirit are not meant to thrill us or even to prove God is who He says He is. They were sent to help hurting people get what they need. For those of us who get to be the vessels of that power, our need is only satisfied in knowing God fully.

That night, as God moved in great power among us, there was another group of college students and young professionals partying next door. As they saw what God was doing, they began to mock us in their drunken state. We talked to them and invited them to come to church that next day. Surprisingly, five of them showed up.

As we started the service, one of those guys fell to his knees crying and asking God for help. As we prayed for him, he exclaimed that he needed to be free. I told him that he needed to pour out all of his alcohol and drugs. He went with me to the bathroom and poured all the alcohol and drugs he had in the toilet and flushed them down. That night, all five of those guys came to Christ and were at the front of the church dancing and rejoicing, testifying of God's goodness.

Through the rest of our time in Reykjavik, we went downtown where young people from the ages of 15-30 hung out until the early hours of the morning. There, we did dramas, sang, and shared with people one-on-one. It was always guaranteed to be a wild and exciting time.

One young drunk guy was mocking us. As I began to talk to him, he told me, "God isn't real! This is all a big joke."

"Oh, yeah," I said, "well, then why don't you pray with me. If God's not real, then it can't matter, right?"

He said, "Ok, I'll pray with you," in his slurred drunken state.

I had him repeat after me, "Lord Jesus (Lord Jesus), I'm a sinner (I'm a sinner). Forgive me of my sins (forgive me of my sins). Come into my life (come into my life). I need You (I need You)." As he prayed with eyes closed, his body contorted. With every phrase, his words got clearer.

With this incredible thing happening, a large crowd gathered around us. After we had prayed together, I said, "God, now sober him and let him see who You are."

Suddenly, he looked me in the eye and said, "Hallelujah!"

I looked back at him and said, "Hallelujah!"

He began to proclaim, "God *is* real. He *is* real. He *is* real."

To the crowd looking on, I said, "God has sobered this man, and He wants your heart." Many people backed off, shocked and in fear. Others stayed around and gave their lives to Jesus as well. It was an incredible evening of seeing God visit a people and demonstrate His power.

We continued to see remarkable things among the youth in Reykjavik in the following days. We were in a revival. The youth would bring their friends to our meetings, and God would show up. People were saved and set free all around us.

Perhaps the most encouraging and insightful thing I learned during that revival though was that prior to our arrival, the mothers in the church had been fervently praying for the youth in that area. Their intercession had tilled the hard ground so that the gospel could be planted. As an outreach team, we had simply harvested the fruit of their prayers!

Scotland
Summer of 1989

From Iceland, the team went to the city of Banff in northern Scotland. There, we met Joe Ewen, a fisherman who had become a pastor with a passion for church planting. Joe had planted Riverside Community Church in Banff and was in the process of planting a couple of other churches in the area as well. Joe's heart and vision was not only for the city but also for the nations.

When we met Joe that first day, God answered my prayer again for spiritual fathers. Joe quickly became a dear friend of mine and has

Joe Ewen with Jimmy

proven to be a great mentor and influencer for our entire movement. Through his incredible prophetic ministry, he has consistently given me and others words from the Lord, deeply touching us with healing in our personal lives and empowerment for our futures. Today, when I ask our guys around the world about how God spoke to them about the future, many of them mention Joe Ewen.

God has literally brought people to us from all over the world to love, serve, and walk with. It is rare, however, when a dear friend like Joe comes along. We are so thankful for our friendship with Joe and Riverside Christian Church. For almost twenty years now, our hearts have been intertwined with theirs, and we are grateful for their investment in us and their example of going to the nations with the gospel and love of Christ.

One day while we were in Scotland, during one of our services, we were waiting on the Lord, asking Him where we should go that day. God gave me a picture of a horseshoe and a bar. When I asked one of the Scottish men if there was a place like that nearby, he directed me to a bar on High Street.

I followed the man's directions, found the place, and walked in. "Hey, I want to share with you guys about how much God loves you," I said to the entire crowd. No one seemed interested at first, but I went ahead and shared the gospel anyway. When I was finished, one guy waved me over. We went to a side booth, and he told me his story: The night before, he had tried to kill himself. Just as he had taken a knife to his throat, an invisible hand had stopped him and caused him to crumple to his knees. His experience made him think that God existed, but he didn't know how he could know God.

When he finished his story, I gladly shared the gospel with him and led him to Christ. His girlfriend eventually came to Christ as well, and they both got involved in the church.

That second summer outreach continued to show us that God was at work all over the world, and He wanted us to join Him. Experiencing revival in Iceland, encountering an anointed man of God in Scotland, and seeing God intervene into a man's life at his most desperate moment gave us momentum and desire to continue training and sending men and women to the ends of the earth.

Thailand – He is Worth the Cost
Summer of 1990

By May of 1990, our little family had grown from two to three with the arrival of our first-born daughter, Abby. The third summer of Master's Commission outreaches was to Thailand, and Laura and I had every intention of going with them and taking our baby girl with us. Since she was born, Abby suffered with colic. Needless to say, several people in our lives, including some family members, were not happy about our taking our frail five-month-old child to a third-world country.

In Thailand, we had to give Abby her first set of shots. She did not respond well to them and developed a high fever. With her immune system weak, she was more susceptible to illnesses.

Our team was supposed to go from Bangkok to a rural orphanage in the northern part of Thailand and out into villages to share Christ. Since Abby was so sick, Laura stayed behind and was going to fly up later with our host missionary's wife. When we reached the orphanage, we discovered there had been an outbreak of measles. I called Laura to tell her what was happening. We agreed to pray that night and then talk the next morning to decide what to do.

The next morning when I called Laura back, she told me that she had stayed up that night reading the journal of Roslyn Goforth, a lady who had risked her life for the gospel in China in the early 1900s with her husband and their loving children. Seeing the sacrifices of this lady's life, Laura said that she felt the pleasure of God in coming to join us. God was saying to her, "I will take care of you. Just go."

That evening, Laura arrived at the orphanage toting a crying baby. It was a miserable night as we swatted mosquitoes and tried to soothe Abby. We probably only slept about an hour.

Rose, the lady who ran the orphanage, had taken children in from all over northern Thailand. As they got older, she prayed with them about going back to their villages to preach the gospel. One of these young men took us to a village that as best as we knew had never heard the gospel.

It was a full day's drive to a village that was just the midway point. There, we stayed and slept on mats on the floor. The living conditions were really difficult for us since we had Abby, and we wondered what in the world we were doing out there with a baby. Had God really spoken to us?

We shared the gospel in that village the next day, and there was an encouraging response, but there were still a few more hours to our final destination. When we finally arrived at the village, the men were in the fields. In their culture, the women would not listen to us until the men came in. While we waited, we spent time among the women and children. It was crazy as they all wanted to poke, hold, and touch our plump, little white baby. Eventually it overwhelmed Laura so much that she spent most of the rest of the day in the back of the truck with Abby praying for the people and for our outreach. I am so amazed at my Laura's willingness to step out and obey God no matter the cost.

Jeff Bianchi leading children in Thailand

While the rest of us were waiting for the men, Jeff, a student in Master's Commission, began to sing the song, "Jesus Loves Me." The interesting thing about the Thai language is that because it is tonal, the people can repeat voice intonation and notes very easily. So, as Jeff began to sing, "Jesus loves me," all the children sang back in what sounded like perfect English in perfect pitch, "Jesus loves me." He went on, "...this I know..." and they sang "...this I know..." "For the Bible..." "For the Bible..." "...tells me so..." "...tells me so..." He went through the whole song, and they repeated every word and note exactly as he sang it.

Jeff got so excited that he stood up and walked through the village continuing to sing "Yes, Jesus loves me..." A crowd of children following behind and echoed, "Yes, Jesus loves me." It was awesome to realize that these children were singing the praises of God, not having heard or even knowing what they were singing. We spent the afternoon singing songs and praising God, waiting for the men to return.

When the men returned that evening, Dave Depew, our missionary host, shared the gospel. The best we know, as darkness set in, every person in that village got on their knees and gave their lives to Christ.

Wow. What an awesome experience to be a part of. The cost was great, but God honored the sacrifice.

Laura and I have seen through the years that simply listening and obeying God, no matter what the cost, always bears the greatest fruit. I am so thankful for a woman to walk with who has a heart to always say "yes" to

Dave Depew

Jesus. Oh, by the way, Abby arrived back in Bangkok healthier than when she had left.

Eastern Europe – Led by the Lord
Summer of 1991

At the end of the Cold War, Eastern Europe was an open and ripe harvest field. In the summer of 1991, our Master's Commission team headed to Eastern Europe for our summer outreach. The journey there was quite eventful. After spending a couple of weeks working in Germany with a local church, we began our trek down to Veliko Tarnovo, Bulgaria. The man that had connected us with the pastor in Veliko Tarnovo gave us a map describing how to get there. His directions went something like this: go south from Munich to Vienna. Take a right and go to Szeged, Hungary. Take the road to Belgrade, Yugoslavia, and then go straight south to Sophia, Bulgaria. Finally, go back west towards Varna on the Mediterranean Sea. Veliko Tarnovo is on that road.

Well, those directions led our Texas bunch through some interesting adventures. Outside of Belgrade, our van was broken into. Everything was strewn about, but all of our cash was in our administrator's backpack...praise the Lord. We had arrived in Yugoslavia just one week before the start of the war. After fixing our broken window, we headed out of Belgrade the next day towards Sophia, with the sound of gunshots throughout the city around us. We found ourselves in the middle of a massive traffic jam as literally thousands of people were trying to get away from the potential war.

As far as we could see on the main highway, cars were lined up trying to get out of the country. Between our two vans, we talked on our walkie-talkies about what we should do. We could see that the fence had been cut in a certain area, and we wondered if we should go off the shoulder and in through that open area. If we had though, we wouldn't know where to go from there.

Suddenly when we were almost to a stop, a van weaved through the traffic in front of us. The guy driving stuck his head out the window and waved for us to follow him. Immediately, we asked the Lord whether or not we should follow this guy. Just then, we saw a "Don't Mess with Texas" bumper sticker on the back of his van. Why in the world would a van in the middle of Yugoslavia have *that* sticker on it? Because it was too unbelievable to just be a coincidence, we took it as confirmation that God was leading us to follow him.

The van led us through the opening in the barrier toward some dirt roads. We followed him, weaving through little villages for over two hours until we found ourselves at a city near the Bulgarian border. As we came to an intersection, the van leading us turned left where we needed to turn right. The man pointed to us to turn right, waved at us, and then drove away. If we have ever seen an angel, we believe it was then.

We got into Sophia, Bulgaria at dark and began looping the city looking for the road to Varna. All we kept seeing were signs that said "Bapha." Even when we asked for directions, people would just point to the Bapha sign. Finally, after two hours of driving around, one of our guys in the back said in his thick Texas accent, "Hey, I've been looking at this map and you know what? 'Bapha' means 'Varna.'

That's that Cyrillic language." Little did we know that Bulgaria had a different alphabet, and though it looked to us like the sign said 'Bapha,' it actually read 'Varna.' We got on that road and pulled into Veliko Tarnovo, Bulgaria at 2:00 a.m. Pastor Dimitri and the people of his church met us and took us to their homes.

Veliko Tarnovo, Bulgaria – Miracles in the Streets
Summer of 1991

The next day, I met with Dimitri, and he asked us what we did. I told him, "We do worship, dramas, and dancing, and we love to preach the gospel and pray for the sick."

"Do they get healed?" he asked me.

"Well, sometimes," I responded. "We can at least give it a try."

"Ok, I will let you try tonight. We will meet at my church."

So, that night we met at his church. There were about 70 people packed in this little building. Those upstairs pressed their ears to the floor, and others were hanging in t he windows. We saw many people come to Christ that night. The crowd was so dense that we told the people to just put their hands on the place of their body that needed healing as we prayed. Three or four of them cried out saying that they had been touched by the Lord. We didn't know many details, but we thought the ministry was good.

Dimitri too thought it was good; so good that the next day he rented out the Pioneer Palace in the center of the city. This was the old communist gathering hall. That Sunday, about 400 people gathered there, and I asked the Lord what to speak on. He told me to share about

Bill Curtiss Preaching

the father heart of God. These people had been blocked from the knowledge of God for many years. Their lives were broken internally because they had no connection to the Father who loved them. As I talked about the father heart of God, people began to cry and respond.

At the end, we communicated that we would like to pray for the sick. One of the first people we prayed for was a man who had trouble seeing. After we prayed, he took off his glasses and left them because he said his eyes were better. We asked him to share with everyone how God had healed him. Then we prayed for another person whose eyes got better too. Then, a man, who was completely blind in one eye, came for prayer. As we prayed for him, he too was healed. When the blind man saw, faith rose in the room, and people clamored to be prayed for. Many, many people were touched that day, receiving salvation and healing.

That opened the door for us to share the gospel daily on the streets. Several hundred people would gather around us as we would preach of God's grace and Jesus. We would ask people to get on their knees in the streets as a sign of their commitment to Him and to give their lives to Him. And then, because the crowds were so thick, we would ask them to simply place their hands on the places that hurt so that we could pray for them.

One person had a tumor on his chest, and we saw it leave right before our eyes. Another older gentleman with a withered hand asked if I would pray for him. I immediately shared the gospel with him, and he gave his life to Christ. Then I prayed for his arm, asking God to restore the years that the enemy had stolen in his life. His hand began to crack and pop and I actually saw his withered hand become straight. He raised it in the air and shouted, "Hallelujah!"

It was as if the whole crowd knew what had happened. They began to push forward for us to pray for them. One lady tried to pay me, and I had to throw her money up in the air and tell her, "No, you cannot buy God. There is no power in man, only in Jesus Christ." To see that happen day after day was awesome.

People also wanted us to visit their friends and family. After we would spend time on the streets in the city, they would take us to other surrounding areas. One night in particular, we were asked to go out and pray for someone's uncle in a village just outside of town. When we got there, we could see red streaks starting into the man's leg as infection and gangrene were setting in. He had an open sore on the bottom of his foot that looked like it went all the way to the bone. It was green and nasty. As he unraveled the wrap on his foot, the smell alone almost knocked us over.

"Lord," we asked, "how do we pray?" Immediately I felt the Lord say that we needed to lay hands on his foot so that he could recover. *Oh my goodness,* I thought. *This is so gross.* But a long time ago I had decided that whatever God said was enough, so we laid hands on his foot and prayed. Right before our very eyes, the green began to turn pinkish and normal. We could see the wound begin to fill in. It filled half way right before our very eyes. The streaks went out of his legs, and he was being healed right there.

But the hole didn't totally fill in. We prayed again but nothing happened. I asked God, "Lord, what do we do?" I felt like the Lord said that by the morning he would be completely healed. We left the man with that word from God, and the next morning we got a call telling us that his foot was completely whole.

Things like that were astonishing to us. We would gather in the mornings and pinch ourselves to make sure this was really happening. With such revival happening, the people wanted us to pray with them and minister to them 24 hours a day. After about a week, our team was wiped out. We were tired and needed a break. I promised them that the next day, we would finish our outreach at 5:00 p.m. so that they could have the remainder of the evening to rest.

As 5:00 p.m. drew near, our team began packing up to go to the different places we were staying. The crowds of people, however, were all around; they weren't leaving. I will never forget what one of our Bulgarian college students said to us: "Why are you in such a hurry when the people are so hungry for Jesus?"

When she said that, my heart broke. I realized that God was pouring out His Spirit and showing His love to a people who were hungry. I replied, "You are exactly right. I repent. We will stay as long as the people need help."

I told the team that those who wanted to stay could and the rest could go home. About five of us stayed back and continued to minister. That night was one of the most powerful of our lives. The presence of God was so heavy that our translators kept falling down under His power. We literally would have to hold them up as they translated for us. Pockets of ten and fifteen people would come up, we would share the gospel with them, and they would be saved.

One group in particular was a group of Muslims who came to ask for prayer. As we talked about Jesus, they prayed and gave their lives to Christ. One man began to scream. Not knowing what he was screaming about, I watched him as he threw his shoe off, unwrapped something off his feet and held them in the air. There were wooden blocks under his feet to help him walk because he had bowed arches. When he prayed to receive Christ, his arches became straight, and the wood blocks were no longer needed. I can still see it in my mind, him holding up the blocks, crying, "I'm healed. I'm healed. Jesus has healed me and forgiven me, and He loves me."

Sometimes, it is when we are tired that God wants to move the most. I am so glad that we stayed around that night just a little bit longer to see God's hand at work.

Master's Commission – 20-Year Testimony
1987-2007

I look back at those first several years of Master's Commission and stand in awe of all we saw God do. We have remained committed to the practical outworking of teaching since that time because we learned that the life experiences of seeing God's provision and power at work transform more lives than just hearing or reading about His provision and power in a classroom.

The summer outreaches along with the Waco mission opportunities throughout the year have been breeding grounds for faith. I can't even keep track of all the places God has taken these students and all that He has done through them. Their lives make me stand in awe at the grace and goodness of God. Seeing Jesus glorify Himself through their sacrificed lives has been a privilege I would not trade for anything.

I started this chapter quoting James: "But prove yourselves doers of the word, and not merely hearers..." (James 1:22). He goes on to say in verse 25: "But one who looks intently at the perfect law, the law of liberty, and abides by it, not having become a forgetful hearer but an effectual doer, *this man will be blessed in what he does*".

For twenty years, Antioch Training School graduates have been proving these words faithfully by their devotion to being doers of the words of Christ. God blesses their steps as they trek the globe with the message of truth and hope.

"How beautiful are the feet of those who bring good news!" (Romans 10:15).

Chapter 7
Campus to Mexico
1989-1992

*"They were continually devoting themselves to the apostles' teaching
and to fellowship, to the breaking of bread and to prayer."*
Acts 2:42

As people developed relationships of love, community, and discipleship at Highland, our desire was to see them go to the world together in the context of those relationships. There is power in this type of community, and we believed that there were people God was calling to walk together to see His purposes fulfilled. They should grow together and then go together. Just like what we saw in Acts 2:42-47, we wanted to see communities reproducing the life of God everywhere they went.

It was that philosophy that led Laura and me to pray out of Psalm 119:63, "Lord, would you send us marvelous comrades who fear Your name." This journey that God had called us to was challenging, and it was not intended to be walked alone. God's delight is to build community so that not just one or two make it but to see His church come alive. Since then, God has sent us so many marvelous comrades, and we have been overwhelmed with this incredible tribe of people that we get to walk with. He has truly answered our prayer.

Highland Baptist Church – Called to College
1990

In the spring of 1990, Laura and I were leading the fourth year of the training school and thoroughly enjoying investing intentionally into these students' lives. At Highland, however, there had been some difficulty in the leadership. The senior pastor dismissed some elders who were dear friends of ours. It was a time of confusion and soul searching. We were asking God if we should stay there or go somewhere else. God had given us vision for the people we were leading, but we were disconnected from the bigger picture in the church and somewhat disillusioned with the problems that were going on.

During this time of prayer and deliberation, the senior pastor asked Laura and me if we would take over the college pastoring because Mark and Susan Buckner were moving on to work with Youth With a Mission. Though it was an honor to be asked, we really had no desire to lead the college group. My perception of college ministry involved mainly providing opportunities for social gatherings, pizza parties, and hanging out. We, on the other hand, had been deeply involved with Master's Commission, training soldiers for battle. So while we agreed to pray about it, we had no intention of taking the job.

That spring, while the students went off to Mexico for spring break, Laura and I stayed home to fast and pray. After seven days of fasting, I had heard nothing. Frustrated, I went for a walk and told God, "Lord, I'm hungry and You are not speaking to me. I have to hear from You. I need to make this decision. Would You please speak?"

Then a thought entered my mind: *Maybe you are asking the wrong question.* I simply responded back, "Lord, am I asking the wrong question?"

Immediately the Lord responded, "Are you in this for Me and My Kingdom or for you and yours?"

"You know I am in this for Your Kingdom, Lord," I replied. "We've sacrificed everything and sold all we had. We just want to love You."

Have you ever noticed that if God asks a question, He knows the answer? Even in the middle of my justifications, I realized I had only been thinking about what is best for me in this decision, not what was best for Him. So, I told the Lord, "Whatever is best for You and Your Kingdom, I'll do."

He spoke to me, "If you will stay, I will raise up an army of people to start churches all over the world. I've asked you to lead them and be a part of this. Stay and watch Me work."

Well, that was enough for me. I ran home and told Laura, and she was in total agreement. God was calling us to lead the college; therefore, it would be good.

Two things immediately happened that gave us great faith and encouragement for the journey ahead. The first was that when Mark and I explained to the college group about the transition, a sophomore named Jeff Abshire came up to me and said, "You know, this is hard for me because I really love Mark. I have been so thankful for his leadership, but God has put it in my heart to serve you. I am here to love, encourage, and practically serve you in every way that I can. You just let me know, and I am here for you."

Jeff Abshire, Mark Buckner

That was 17 years ago. In a lifetime, there are rarely people who come along that are the perfect balance of who you are. When I look at other movements, I see how God puts together teams of people that are the right complement of gifts and callings in order to accomplish what is in His heart. Jeff has served as my right arm over all these years (and by the way, I am left handed). What I often say is that if I implement fifty percent of the vision, Jeff implements the other fifty percent. Though God had brought many others who have sometimes done greater works in our midst, I've had no one like Jeff...faithful and consistent, loving, and a servant at all times. It was said of Jesus that He came to serve and not to be served. Jeff has done that for our movement over and over again. Antioch would not be what it is without Jeff and people like him who complement me.

What was also thrilling for us during that time was that Jeff met Dorothy Son. Dorothy had lived with us for two and a half years and was a part of our family as well as part of the leadership team for the college ministry. Eventually, Dorothy and Jeff, in their common places of serving, fell in love and married. Dorothy, the fire and zeal for revival to change the world, and Jeff, the stable and consistent one, have been markers for our movement. And, we are forever indebted to them.

The second thing that happened to encourage us in the transition to college ministry was that 12 men and women who Laura and I had invested in and spent time with over the years, came to us at different times and said, "We are in. How can we serve? How can we do this together?"

We spent time fasting and praying together with them and began to meet as a team on Sunday afternoons. The first hour, we would worship and pray. And, the second hour, we would ask, "How do we do cell groups? How do we pray? How do we connect people to the lost of the world?" Gathering with this group of people, seeking the Lord, and ministering together was really the seed bed for the beginning of a tightly knit community style of church life. It was a thrilling time, because God was truly bringing us marvelous comrades.

Not only did God raise leaders out of our past relationships and from the college group itself, but He also called out an older generation who had a heart for the students and for us as leaders. In 1984, God had told one of these couples, Darrell and Margie Atwood, that they were to serve and facilitate the coming move of God among college students. As they joined us in their 50s, they joined us wholeheartedly. Not only were they a support to Laura and me, but they were a mother and father to hundreds of students.

Danny and Kathy Mulkey, as well, stepped in to serve, love, and care for students. They eventually went to lead our second church plant in Irkutsk, Siberia. David and Becky Lockhart took one of our first Master's Commission students into their home and stepped in to serve in every way possible. Terry and Joan Hobbs came to me in 1991 and asked if they could hang out with the college students, and they have been hanging out with them ever since. Today, all these people are in their 60s and even 70s, and they continue to be the backbone and pillars, not only for our students, but for our whole movement.

While most of the marvelous comrades that God has placed in our lives are those who have grown out of the movement, people who walked with us for years from even the earliest days, God has also brought several men and women our way to join us in the midst of the journey. We discovered that there are many out there who love Jesus and carry the same values that we do, but they don't have a tribe, a place to live those values out in community. For years, we have prayed, "Lord, bring these people to us at the right time whoever they might be." God has brought men and women to us to join with our heart and vision to contribute their unique giftings and passions to see God do all He has placed in our hearts.

God has been so faithful to answer our prayers for marvelous comrades. Whether they came from among us or from outside of us, the Lord has grown them and placed them in our midst to facilitate the work He wants to do through us as a people.

Leaders' Retreat in Mid 1990s (Back Row) Jeff Bianchi, Peter Leininger, Jimmy Seibert, Jeff Abshire, Kevin Johnson, (Middle Row) Chris McBride, Danny Mulkey, Bill Adams, Ben Loring, (Front) Carl Gulley

Highland Baptist Church – Revival or Nothing 1990-1992

Agreeing to take the college position was not a decision of compromise for us. God had called us and we wanted to challenge the students to move forward. The first message I gave at the end of the spring semester in 1990 was titled *Revival or Nothing*. We had about 60 students gathered, and I explained to them that though we were going to learn how to be a community and love each other, our ultimate goal was to be a part of a move of God that we had never experienced before. Not just a few from Master's Commission, but now a whole group of college students would see the glory of God together. They received the challenge with enthusiasm and excitement as they went their separate ways for the summer, looking forward to the fall.

When we started meeting in our home on Sunday afternoons with that small group of leaders to try to figure out what the college group should look like, God showed us that it needed to be centered around prayer, cells, and missions. We believed that if we really learned how to pray and be Acts 2 type small groups that connected to God's heart for the world and reproduced ourselves through evangelism and discipleship, we would be a part of God's great work in the earth.

We began that journey with much weakness, prayer, and seeking God. Between 1990 and 1992, we grew from 60 students to about 150. We started off with six cell groups, which we call Lifegroups, in the fall of 1990. Those multiplied to nine but struggled as groups while we were learning how to facilitate and build one another up. The next semester, we multiplied to twelve and then back down to nine. By 1992, we had 24 groups but decided to cut them back to twelve.

Through the journey, we were learning how to do Acts 2 community by trial and error. Knowing this was God's heart, we pressed on. Through the willingness of young men and women to learn together, we began to see discipleship impact people's lives and evangelism take place.

Also during this time, we began "early morning prayer" which we affectionately call EMP. It began with one guys group and one girls group meeting at 6:00 a.m. to pray together. As we continued to grow, different groups started meeting two, three, four, and eventually five days a week. Over the last 15 years EMP has been a mainstay for what is happening among our students. They have consistently committed to prayer and calling out to God both personally and in communities.

As these communities grew together in prayer, we saw God move among the students' friends. Many times, groups of students would pray for the lost at their EMP. Over time, as God answered these prayers, the students' friends would come to Christ and join the college group. Seeing God move so mightily in their friends' lives really fired up our students. They were always bringing their friends to me to share their stories of how, because of the faithful prayer at EMP, they came to Christ.

One specific memory that I have of this happening was at one of our Sunday night gatherings. A student brought a friend forward who wanted to know more about Christ and how to be saved. While I was talking to this young man, there were ten people from a Lifegroup standing nearby, praying with all their hearts for him. Little did the guy know that he didn't have a chance but to give his life to Christ because the community had believed together for his salvation.

God has always given our students His heart for the lost. It has been so exciting to see thousands of students saved and transformed. Lifegroups often rally together in prayer and fasting for others until they see their friends and family come to Jesus.

One Lifegroup in particular impacted the nations by consistently sharing Jesus with a fellow student. This Lifegroup had a heart for international students, especially Muslim students. At Baylor that year, there was a freshman from Saudi Arabia named Mansour. Guys from the Lifegroup befriended Mansour, loving him and including him in their lives. He ate meals with them, played soccer with them, and eventually even came to church and Lifegroup with them. As a Muslim from a very devout family, Mansour had no intention of responding to the gospel, but he enjoyed their friendship and love. The Lifegroup prayed for him and many times even took a day to fast and pray for him as well.

After several months of hanging with our guys, Mansour realized that he had to make a decision for or against this Jesus. He began to pull back and told Josh, the leader of the Lifegroup, that though he loved them, it was getting to be awkward. Mansour was not willing to come to Christ but he saw that Jesus was a huge part of their lives. He didn't know what to do, so he backed off to reevaluate how he should relate to them.

When Mansour pulled away, our guys didn't. They didn't pressure him, but they prayed all the more asking God to break through to him. One night, Mansour knocked at Josh's door around 2:00 a.m. He told Josh, "I have had a couple of dreams this week about Jesus, but the one tonight shook me so much that I had to talk to you. In the dream, there was a holy man asking me whom I knew with names that begin with J. I told him that I know Josh and Jennifer, Jessica, Jacob and Jerry… I named ten people, but there was supposed to be eleven. The man said to me, 'There is one missing. This one is the most important one for all eternity and all the ages. This is the one you must know.' I knew it was Jesus, and I called out to Him." Mansour went on to ask Josh, "What do I do from here?"

Josh had been studying the Koran in order to relate to and understand Mansour's world. He felt that if God was speaking to Mansour, he would really let go of Islam and leave it. So, Josh put the Koran in Mansour's hand and told him to put it behind his back, pray to receive Jesus, and then drop the Koran and walk away from it. Mansour prayed a simple prayer of devotion and commitment to Christ, to have no other gods before Him. As he prayed, he dropped the Koran behind him and walked out of the room.

Mansour was established and strengthened the last couple of months before he left school to return home to Saudi Arabia. Josh and the others sent a Bible with Mansour which he hid in his room behind a dresser. One of the cleaning ladies found it a couple of months later and took it to his father. Mansour's father was outraged and threatened to disown and beat him.

Mansour found a way to get in touch with our guys and asked, "What do I do? My father will not allow me to email you any more. I cannot communicate with you. Pray for me. Please pray for me."

We didn't hear from him for about 30 days. When he was able to contact us again, we found out that his father had taken him out of Baylor and sent him to another school in the Middle East. Mansour asked us if we knew anyone in that country that knew Jesus. We were able to connect him with some people from Operation Mobilization who began to disciple him, love him, and care for him. As of our last dialogue, he was loving and serving Jesus and walking with Him.

With Lifegroups and EMP happening and growing, we also wanted to take another step in missions. We were already taking the students to Juarez, Mexico during spring break, but we wanted to give them more opportunities to go overseas.

We implemented short-term mission trips in the summers as well, beginning with trips in 1992 to our first church-plant in Siberia.

The vision God had given us for the college ministry – prayer, cell groups, and missions – was unfolding before our eyes. In two short years, we had seen growth and transformation among the students. And then something very unique happened.

During one of our meetings in the fall of 1992, God visited us. People began to stand up and confess their sins publicly. Brokenness spread throughout our community as students would spend hours on their knees pouring out their hearts to God and crying out for freedom and cleansing, confessing their sins to one another.

This went on Sunday after Sunday, in our Lifegroups and anywhere we would gather. Many of our leaders who are around the world today came out of that season of revival. We were so profoundly touched by God that there wasn't anything else we could do but simply say "yes" to Him.

In an old picture from a Juarez, Mexico trip that we took during this time with about 150 of us, we can count 120 or so that are still with us. God not only touched our hearts through revival, but He knit us together through these experiences, and we would never turn back. That visitation of the Lord set the pace for us ever since and made us hungry for nothing less than revival.

Over the next few years, the college group grew and multiplied to several hundred students meeting corporately on Sunday nights and from house to house during the week. The revival we had prayed for had come. Because we had set up structures of prayer, small groups, and missions, it continued to facilitate all that God was calling us to.

In my college years when I was involved with Campus Crusade for about a year and a half, I asked myself, *Why do I want to be involved in Campus Crusade?* I realized it was because they offered me a chance of a lifetime to change the world and be involved in a community. They were offering me everything I longed for.

As I thought about it and looked through the New Testament, I realized that the church is supposed to be offering the exact same thing: an opportunity for a lifetime. The local church should be a place to learn, grow, and develop as well as reproducing itself to reach those who have never heard. This is a lifelong calling, not just something to take part in for a season. It was really important to us that the college students understood this piece of the vision. Our desire was to set the stage for this to be a place of lifelong relationships and service and not just something to do while they were at school.

We built our ministry on discipleship and leadership development, teaching and training students to teach and train others. As a result, many of the people we had invested in began to take leadership. With the multiplication of the group, there was also multiplication in the leadership.

As we prayed and waited on the Lord during this time, God gave us Psalm 45:16: "In place of your fathers will be your sons; You shall make them princes in all the earth." Our leadership team realized that we would invest in men and women who would in turn be princes and princesses in the Kingdom. They would be used mightily by the Lord if we would just be faithful to discipleship, evangelism, and helping them to be all that God has called them to be.

Those early days of learning about prayer, cell groups, and missions laid the foundations for everything we do. Today, they have become commonplace. I am so thankful for a group of young people and leaders who were willing to learn the journey together. Ultimately, we are all thankful to God for pouring out His Spirit on us and putting fire on simple offerings of faithfulness.

Juarez, Mexico
1989-2007

Since 1987, we have used spring break as an opportunity to take students on a mission trip. It began in Guatemala in 1987. In 1988, we went to Guadalajara, Mexico with a Mexican pastor named Daniel Valles. On our third year, Daniel moved to Juarez, Mexico and invited

us to come down and do an outreach there. Every year since 1989, we have taken a group of students to Juarez and seen God move in amazing ways.

What we found early on was that this spring break mission trip was as much about us as it was about the Mexican people. It was an opportunity for us to live out the values of the Kingdom

Morning Worship Time - 2007

together in an intense environment, to deal with issues that we may have been distracted by at home, and to see the power of God like we had never seen it before. You have to be there to understand it. But, every year, God visits us, and all the community gets ignited with fire from heaven and our lives are changed.

Over the 18 years we have been going to Juarez, we have taken thousands of students. In the early years, we took about 30. This year (in 2007), we took more than 500. Obviously logistics have changed over time to accommodate the larger groups, but the heart and method of the trip have remained the same since the beginning.

Every morning, we gather to worship and pray together. These are some of the most powerful sessions we have all week. People share their hearts and stories with their friends. The community weeps together, prays for one another, and ministers to each other. In the afternoons, groups go into the barrios to serve and share the gospel. Every day, people get saved and healed. For many of the students, this is the first time they see God move in such power. They experience His presence in their midst, and they taste His goodness. In the

On the Streets of Juarez

evenings, we go out to share through drama, music, and speaking. And again, we see God move in power.

What is so amazing to me today is that when I talk to those serving on church-planting teams around the world, about eighty percent of them point to either Juarez or World Mandate (our annual missions conference) as the time when God spoke to them about serving on a church-planting team.

In Acts 13, we see the church come together to fast and pray, and from that time God called out Paul and Barnabas to take the gospel to other nations. There is something about the corporate gathering of God's people that God gravitates toward. As people lay their hearts out before Him, He speaks. In Juarez, an environment free from daily distractions, in a context of running hard after God, in an expectation of encountering Him, He regularly calls out laborers for the harvest field.

I can think of no better way to communicate the awesome experience of Juarez than to let you hear testimonies from a few of those who were changed by it. The following are stories from former students who went on a Juarez trip and are now serving God faithfully.

Holden, 2001

I ended up going to Juarez on a whim. I was planning to go to the beach with a few college friends, but several people at Antioch had put me on their "VIP" list and had started praying for me. They were always talking to me about going to Juarez. I did not go to Antioch at the time and was very skeptical of the church and the whole Juarez trip.

The night before we left, I was at a party drinking with my friends. The next morning, I woke up and really felt like I needed to clean my life up. I decided to go to Juarez.

I started off the trip extremely reserved and would not sing during worship, and I stood towards the back during the sermons. However, after the second night, I was sitting at a meeting when a guy leaned over and said he felt like God had spoken something to him about me. He proceeded to sum up exactly what I had been going through the last few years and how I was feeling in my heart. I was really disturbed as he spoke because I had never shared these things with anyone. It caught me off guard to listen to someone with that much insight into my heart.

The next morning, Jimmy spoke on loving God with all we are, and I was convicted that I had not been living that way. Jesus was not Lord of my life. I pulled a guy from our team aside and started confessing all my sin to him. Then, I started sharing with another guy who looked really spiritual to me. He started praying for me to receive the gift of tongues and be baptized in the Holy Spirit. Theologically, I did not believe in the baptism of the Holy Spirit or in tongues. But, at that point all I wanted was God, and I was willing to try anything.

After a few minutes of lying on my face before God, I felt a new language bubbling up, and I started speaking in tongues. At that moment, I felt joy and peace like I had never experienced before. From that moment on, all I wanted to do was to live for Jesus and glorify Him in my life.

After my week in Juarez, I came back and stopped living a life of rebellion toward God. God led me to reach out to everyone I knew with the power and truth of the gospel. Over the next five years, I traveled to Morocco, Tunisia, Lebanon, Jordan, Iraq, Pakistan, China, and Macedonia. I completed the training school and am now leading a section of young adult Life Groups. I live in Waco and continue to lead short-term trips overseas, but one day I plan on going out with a church-planting team long-term.

Marci, 1999

My freshman year of college, I knew nothing about the power of the Holy Spirit or sharing boldly with the lost. I went on the Juarez trip ripe for change.

Every morning, we would spend one hour with God alone and then would gather together for corporate worship. These times were powerful as I learned to hear the voice of God speak to me and prepare me for the events each day. We would wait on God to reveal words or pictures of people He wanted us to share with or minister to that day. I was so surprised to hear God so clearly in the morning about things that would happen in the afternoon.

Once, we got a picture of a woman needing healing. We prayed for her healing before we went out. Later, as we were doing an outreach, we saw a woman and shared with her. She wanted to accept the truth of Jesus, and we then prayed for her to be healed. God healed her of stomach problems.

Other times God told us that we would see many salvations that night. After we would share, we realized that 100 people gave their lives to Jesus.

These experiences of seeing people so hungry to know Jesus and immediately accepting Him broke my heart for people who have never heard about Him. As I watched masses gather around us to hear the gospel, many of them deciding to follow God, my heart stirred and came alive. I knew this was what God wants us to do all the time, wherever we are.

Juarez taught me what God expects from our daily life with Him: to spend time with Him and to minister all day out of a place of intimacy with Him. We should listen to His voice and get prophetic words for people so that they can see how much God cares about them personally.

Jeannie, 1994

Two years after my conversion to Christianity, I went to Juarez, Mexico. Having recently begun the practice of hearing God, the mission trip challenged and stretched me. One particular afternoon, half of our team went out to work (paint) and the rest of us stayed back to pray for that night's outreach. During the prayer time, I sensed that God wanted to free someone from bitterness and to heal someone's back. I submitted this to the leadership and continued to pray for the evening.

That night, I was sitting on a low wall in the barrio where we were doing the outreach, praying over the crowd. I spotted a woman with a severe hunched back and immediately sensed that the Holy Spirit wanted to move in her life. With the help of a translator, we discerned that the woman was a Christian who had severe scoliosis. With her son standing nearby, we began to pray for her physical healing.

Nothing happened as we prayed, and then I felt the prompting of the Holy Spirit to ask her if she had unforgiveness in her life towards her parents. My hands gently touched her spine as she tearfully confessed rebellion in her teenage years. As she confessed, I was shocked as I felt individual parts of her spine popping and moving.

At this point, a crowd began to gather because it was obvious that she was being touched by the Holy Spirit. A few minutes later, the activity stopped and I again felt prompted to ask her if she had any more unforgiveness. She began to repent of multiple things, and again I felt and heard her spinal cord moving. Her blouse was thin, making it possible for me and others to see her back moving in my hands. It felt like an electric current ran through me, and I just responded in awe.

After an hour, the team was packing up to leave, and the woman stood straight up. No one could believe what they were seeing as the woman cried out, "Gloria a Dios!" over and over. On the bus ride home, we sat silent. The wonder of witnessing the supernatural overwhelmed us to speechlessness.

I am forever marked by that experience. God is a healer of the body, soul, and spirit. Today, my husband and I live in England, a land *mostly unfamiliar with dramatic healings. I love to share this story with my English friends because it reminds me to believe God for the impossible.*

Robert, 1997

Juarez was my first mission trip experience. The entire week had been amazing with extended times of worship and prayer where God touched all of us in deeply powerful ways. It was like a curtain being pulled back to let light into dark places.

In the middle of the week, several of us were asked to stay back from the day's normal routine of manual labor to pray for the evening's outreach. I gathered in a room with a dozen others and sat down on the floor. Our leader encouraged us to wait on God for a moment to see if He would show us anything about that night. This was totally foreign to me, and I felt awkward and nervous thinking I would be the only one without a "word" from God. Nevertheless, I closed my eyes, quieted my mind, and wondered if the Lord would speak to me at all.

He did.

Instantly, I saw a clear picture of an old woman in a red dress. Something was wrong with her leg. A minute or two later, everyone began sharing what they had heard from God. When my turn came, I spoke with a mixture of awe and doubt, amazed at the clarity of the image, but wondering if it had been imagined rather than received. Right when I finished sharing, another guy spoke up excitedly and said that he had seen a picture of a woman healed of a leg problem and dancing. We would no doubt keep our eyes open for an old woman in a red dress!

That night, I was leading worship in a poor neighborhood church. People were singing and dancing before the Lord throughout the room. About midway through the service, someone came up to me and pointed to an old woman sitting on the front row that I had failed to notice. She was wearing a red dress and was one of the only ones not standing up. I immediately grabbed a translator and knelt before the woman to talk with her.

I discovered that she wasn't dancing because she had a great pain in her calf muscle that kept her from standing for long periods of time. Several of us laid hands on her leg and prayed. Suddenly, she smiled from ear to ear and stood up. She began to jump up and down, raising her hands in the air. Everyone nearby was elated. The worship team played another song, and within a moment, the entire congregation was doing a worship train around the room. The old woman danced like mad for a good ten minutes, tears streaming down her face.

During that week, God did something else amazing. In my times with Him in the mornings, before the Mexican sunrise, He would bring the nation of Turkey to my mind, as well as the city of Istanbul. At the time, I had no idea they were even related. With each passing day, I wondered if God might be calling me to these places, but I mentioned it to no one.

A few days later, a good friend of mine was praying for me during church. I'll never forget his words: "I pray for Robert, God, that you will give him the strength and courage to go wherever you want him to go, even if it is Istanbul. Bless him, Lord!"

I looked up at my friend dumbfounded. "What made you say Istanbul?"

"I don't know," he said. "It's just the city that came to mind." I went home that night simultaneously overwhelmed and elated, wondering what road lay before me.

Three years later, I moved to Istanbul with a church-planting team. I felt like I was coming home.

Juarez, Mexico – A People Passionate about Jesus
1989-2007

The stories from Juarez could fill up an entire book on their own. God has chosen to use that place in Mexico to open the eyes of thousands of college students to His power. Over the years, we have seen salvations, healings, and miracles. Without fail, every time we take a group to Juarez, the lives of the students are just as changed as the lives of the Mexicans we minister to.

One of my favorite parts of the Juarez trip is coming home. Watching these young people come back changed is exciting. They are bold. They are passionate. They are sincere. They have become world changers. Many get more involved in their Lifegroups and the church. Many enroll in the training school. And many go on to take part in church-planting teams around the world.

The faith-building power of God that the students encounter in Juarez stays with them through the years. One of the main reasons we continue to go to Juarez every spring break is because an overwhelming majority of those who go come back to us years later and tell us how that one week set them on a path of pursuing Jesus with everything they have and expecting Him to show up in their lives and ministries.

Mindy put into words the impact of Juarez in her current ministry in a Muslim country:

I wish everywhere I went I had a Juarez experience. I mean, who wouldn't love to live on the mountaintop their whole life. I guess deep in my heart I live believing God wants to touch and move in people like this all over the world. Memories of my times in Juarez have carried me in seasons of sowing and seeing less fruit. It fuels my prayer life and keeps me believing that God's power really can overcome all things. It has given me real life experience that I can't deny. God exists and He is eager to move on behalf of weak people who love and call on His name.

When God called Laura and me to lead the college ministry at Highland, we were afraid that it would not be as fulfilling or exciting as leading Master's Commission, but we were so wrong. Inviting hundreds of students over the next few years to join the adventure of knowing and loving Jesus was more thrilling than we ever imagined. Watching Lifegroups grow and multiply…praying with broken young adults ready to submit their whole futures to God…training the next generation to pursue a passionate relationship with Jesus in their prayer closets as well as in their daily lives…this is what we were created for: A *passion for Jesus and His purposes on the earth.*

Chapter 8

Tents to Desolate Cities
1991-1994

*"Now to Him who is able to do far more abundantly
beyond all that we ask or think...be the glory in the church
and in Christ Jesus forever and ever."*
Ephesians 3:20-21

In 1991, I visited Fuller Seminary School of Missions in California. While I was there, a man I didn't know came up to me and said he had felt impressed by God to give me this passage. He handed me a scrap of paper with Isaiah 54:2-3 written on it. I tucked it away in my pocket and went on my way.

A couple of days later, I was back in Waco when Kurt, a dear friend who now serves with us overseas, came up to me and said he had been praying for me all week. God had led him to give me the Scripture Isaiah 54:2-3. *Wow*, I thought, *that is amazing.* I was looking forward to going home and meditating on these thoughts.

When I got home late that evening, I received a phone call from Joe Ewen, our dear friend from Scotland. He said he had been praying for me all week and God had told him to give me this Scripture: Isaiah 54:2-3.

Now, I may not always hear the Lord well, but I knew this time that God was speaking. As I opened up this passage and read, I was astounded by the words and promise of God:

Enlarge the place of your tent;
Stretch out the curtains of your dwellings, spare not;
Lengthen your cords
And strengthen your pegs.
For you will spread abroad to the right and to the left.
And your descendants will possess nations
And will resettle the desolate cities.

God was calling us as a people to believe Him for even greater things, to continue to branch out by faith and trust Him to do above and beyond what we could ask or think. He wanted us to reach desolate cities, places where people have never heard the gospel before.

This passage continues to be a centerpiece for all that God has called us to be. We go back to it when we are seeking Him for the future. It has been a rally cry for us through the years to continue to stretch out and believe that we can see the world impacted and changed even from our little town of Waco, Texas.

Praise the Lord. I didn't have to wait long to see the prophecy begin to unfold, nor was it a short-lived promise. The first fruits came only months later, and we continue to reap the harvest even today.

Amsterdam, Netherlands – First Fruits
Summer of 1991

In the spring of 1991, we felt that we were to begin phase two of our vision to send out long-term church planters. Even though we didn't know where we would send them or how it would happen, we offered an opportunity to Master's Commission graduates to take four months of training in the fall and then be sent out to plant a church somewhere in the world. Four people responded to this challenge, and we all took a blind step of faith, believing that God would show us the way.

That summer, we had friends exploring possibilities from Asia to Europe. Our eventual team leader, Ben Cox, felt like God had told him that it would be right where Europe and Asia meet, that we would minister to both Asians and Europeans.

The Master's Commission trip that summer was to Eastern Europe, and we saw crowds come to Christ, miraculous healings, and great revival. At the end of the trip, Laura and I split from the team. She went to be with some friends in Germany, and I traveled to Amsterdam. As I rode all night on a train, I reflected on all that God had done in Bulgaria, Romania, and Hungary. Then, I began to think about Russia, wondering how the end of the Cold War had affected it. So I prayed this simple prayer: "God, if all of this is happening in Eastern Europe, would you show me what is happening in Russia?" I found myself praying like this several times throughout the night.

When I arrived in Amsterdam the next morning, I had a breakfast appointment to meet my friend Derryck McLuhan, one of the leaders at the YWAM base in Amsterdam. We barely said "Hi" when Derryck spoke up, "Hey, let me tell you what God is doing in Russia." It looked like God was going to answer my prayer immediately. This was not a coincidence but God's divine appointment.

Derek told me incredible stories of revival across Russia. They had seen hundreds of people saved through outreaches in many of the larger cities west of the Ural Mountains. At one outreach in Moscow, a concert promoter from Siberia was saved. Afterward, he told the mission team that he wanted to help them tell people who had never heard about Jesus. He offered to set up an eight-city tour throughout Siberia, Mongolia, China, and Uzbekistan for other teams to come and sing and share this message of Jesus.

As the leaders of YWAM sought the Lord on this, they felt like God gave them a specific plan to partner with churches in North America and Western Europe in this venture. YWAM would put on the initial concerts in these cities, and the partner churches would provide laborers to stay behind to plant churches. Derryck explained this vision and offered us an opportunity to partner with them. After a month of prayer and consulting with our leaders, we agreed that God was leading us to be a part of this new adventure.

God's leadership is so amazing. The city YWAM asked us to help plant a church in was Ulan-Ude, Siberia, a place where the Buryat Asian people live in full unity with European Russians. The first fruits of the Isaiah 54:2-3 promise were about to come to pass.

Ulan-Ude, Siberia
Fall of 1991

Three months after meeting with Derryck, I went to southern Siberia with Ben Cox and Terry Hobbs to meet this Christian rock band from Amsterdam. After a crazy trip, we went to the hotel where

**Terry Hobbs, Jimmy,
Ben Cox in Red Square**

we were supposed to meet the YWAM team. When we arrived, we found out that we were not welcome. Ulan-Ude had a military city attached to it that was not on the map. It was an arms inspection point for NATO, making the city closed to foreigners. Though the lady behind the counter at the hotel did not speak English, she clearly communicated that we would not be staying there. Screaming at us in Russian, she let us know that there was "no room at the inn."

When the band arrived with their Russian translator and helper, they showed that they did have reservations for us for one night, and she was forced to let us stay. Not knowing what we would do after the one day at the hotel, we went to the concert that night. There was a major blizzard, so only 120 people came; 30 of them made decisions for Christ. When the new Christians came up on stage, the translator looked at me and said, "Well, they are all yours. What would you like to do?"

Realizing that the band was leaving the next day, leaving us without a translator, my first question to the new believers was, "Do you know anybody that speaks English?" When we polled the crowd, one person said he could ask his teacher at the college who spoke English to help. We made an appointment the next day at noon with the English speaker, and the translator told the group of 30 when and where we would meet with them the following evening.

Back at the hotel, I asked the Russian translator what we were supposed to do about staying in the city. His response was, "As you say in America: 'Every man for himself.'"

We went to bed that night, not knowing what the next day held. After we ate breakfast, we spent some time in prayer, asking God for a translator and a way to stay in the city. We met the English teacher, Julia, at noon. Her English was very good, and she said that she would love to help us but that she was a Buddhist.

"It won't bother us if it won't bother you," we said.

"Great," she said. "Just tell me what to say and I'll say it." Wow, what a start to a church-plant, with an English-speaking, Buddhist translator.

Well, there was more fun to be had that day as Julia explained from the lady behind the counter that we had until 3:00 p.m. to be out of the room before they would throw our stuff into the snow. We knew God had led us there, so we were going to have to trust Him to take care of us. In prayer, we sought God and asked Him to intervene.

When we had checked in at the embassy in Moscow on the way to Ulan-Ude, they had given us the name of the only other American who would be in Ulan-Ude the same time we were there: Captain Scott Cerone, U.S. Army arms inspector. Ulan-Ude is a city of about 350,000 people, and we had no idea where this man was or how to find him. Since our only option was to find Captain Cerone, though, we knew we had to trust God to lead us to him.

Walking out the front door, we prayed, "All right, Holy Spirit, which way do we go?" We all felt like He was leading us to go left, so we did. About 100 yards away, at the next intersection, we asked again, "OK, Lord, which way do we turn?" We felt like we were to turn left again, so we did. After walking about 300 yards, we saw a lady with a big video camera on her shoulder. When we got close enough, we heard the man she was filming say, "This is Captain Scott Cerone of the U.S. Army, signing off."

Overjoyed, we screamed, "Scott Cerone, it's you!" We all but hugged him to death. Overwhelmed, he questioned who we were and how we got there since we were not supposed to be in that city. We explained what we were doing and how we needed help to stay in the city. His suspicions only grew with our explanations.

Praise God that his wife was there with him, as women tend to be more compassionate than men. She looked at her husband and said, "Honey, we need to help them in some way."

Scott had a scheduled meeting that afternoon with the Defense Minister of the Soviet Union. He told us he would see what he could do and then call around 2:00 p.m. to let us know what happened.

We went back to the hotel, prayed, and felt it was in God's hands. Having stayed up most of the night before, we decided to take a nap. The phone rang around 2:00 p.m.. Scott was downstairs with the Defense Minister. After greeting them in the lobby, the Defense Minister asked in a deep Russian accent, "Vhat do you need?"

I told him that we needed to stay for three weeks because we were telling people about God's love and wanted to finish what we had started. After he heard my request, he spoke with the woman who had been screaming at us for the last 24 hours. Suddenly, a big smile came over her face. She waved us over, welcomed us, and checked us in for three weeks.

For the rest of the time that we were there, we met nightly with the new believers, building them up in the Lord and encouraging them in God's ways. We did all we could to prepare for our long-term team to move there three months later. When the long-term team did arrive, they found the original 30 believers; 10-12 of the group were still meeting faithfully from house to house, continuing in the things we had taught them. It was a great beginning to this opportunity of a lifetime: to see a desolate city, once without the gospel, become a beacon of light to that whole province.

Ulan-Ude, Siberia
1992

As I think back to those early days in Ulan-Ude, there were so many wonderful stories of God's faithfulness. Two, however, stand out.

The first summer we were there, in 1992, we were having our first baptisms. The only place we could find to baptize was at an old pioneer communist camp that had a cement swimming pool with green algae growing in the water. People began to show up on buses from the city to be baptized.

Tanya was a new believer in the church, glowing with the life of Jesus. She loved the Lord and was so thankful to know Christ. When she stepped out of one of the taxi vans, I saw her beautiful white chiffon dress. *Wow,* I thought. *That dress must have cost her everything she had.* Knowing how expensive it must have been, I also knew we could not risk ruining it in the nasty water.

"Tanya," I said, "you look beautiful. Surely you don't want to be baptized in this dress."

Her response was, "Well, of course. Only the best for today because it is the day that I marry Jesus."

What could I say to that? Here was a woman who understood the love of God, who wanted to present herself to Him and consecrate all that she was to Him. We still have the picture

Tanya, "Married to Jesus"

of her coming out of the water in her beautiful white chiffon dress, draped with a blue jacket; the glow, joy, and life of God on her face is so evident. Yes, she had come to marry Jesus, and she would continue to walk with Him the rest of her days.

God continued to move powerfully in Ulan-Ude as believers met from house to house and in regular Sunday gatherings as well. During a visit to Russia in the fall of 1992, a group of us stood in a crowded train station waiting for our train. It was ten degrees below zero, and the people were packed in trying to stay out of the cold.

One of our guys came up and asked me, "Have you ever seen a dead guy?"

"I don't think so," I responded. "Why?"

He walked me over, pointed to a man, and said, "That guy is dead."

"Are you sure?" I questioned. He looked pale and gray, and about that time he slid out of his chair and bounced on the floor. Some people looked at him but kept on walking as he lay there stiff.

Immediately, I thought, *Lord, what do we do?* I went over and leaned against the wall, asking God whether we should pray for him to be raised up, send for help, or what. For a moment, I thought, *I've read about things like this. This might be the big moment where we see someone raised from the dead. Surely we should go over and pray for him.*

While one of our teammates made sure that an ambulance was on the way, Fred and I, along with one of our Russian translators, went over and knelt down next to the man. As I put my hand on his arm, he was cold and clammy. What do you pray when you are laying hands on a dead man? Different phrases began to come to mind from the words of Jesus: "Come forth...Rise up...Be healed." But none of those phrases seemed to work for me.

As I opened my eyes after voicing different hopeless prayers, I realized that people were pressing in all around us. Suddenly, it hit me. Spontaneously, I turned to our Russian translator and said, "Whatever I do, you do."

Then, I jumped up and began to cry out, "This man is dead, and someday you will be too! The question is: Do you know Jesus? Have your sins been forgiven? Do you know He has a place for you in heaven? Everyone will die, and everyone needs to know that Christ is in their lives."

When I finished sharing the gospel, I asked if anyone needed Jesus. They all raised their hands saying, "I need Jesus!" I led them in prayer to receive Christ. Then, I told them to place their hands on a part of their body that needed healing. We prayed and believed God to touch their bodies and make them whole. People began to scream and testify that God was healing them. The commotion drew an even larger crowd, so I went through the whole thing again: "This man is dead..."

An Outreach in Ulan-Ude

Even after the man was taken to the hospital, we continued to preach to the crowd. Hundreds came to faith that day in the train station. People tried to offer us money and gifts if we would pray for their children, but we declared to them that no man can heal, only Jesus has that power. Our train arrived to take us to a gathering of believers several hours away, but I told the members of our team who were not going with us to stay at the train station and pray for people. They stayed for another two hours as God moved and saw many more saved and healed. And the church continued to grow in Ulan-Ude.

While some of us were away from Ulan-Ude for a few days, Kevin Johnson, who eventually became the team leader and pastor of the church in Ulan-Ude, stayed behind. He met with one of the cell groups and taught them how to hear the Lord. He told them to wait and ask God if there was anything He had to speak to them. If God gave them a picture, a word or a Scripture, they should speak it out.

One of the precious young girls in the group had a picture of a map. Crosses were going out from Ulan-Ude down to Ulan Bataar, Mongolia and into China; they also went to the right and the left, to places around the globe as far as she could see. She felt like the Holy Spirit spoke to her: What has started in Ulan-Ude will go into Asia and around the whole world. Little did she know that she was seeing the same thing God had been showing us. Isaiah 54:2-3 was not just for Waco but for the whole world around us.

Ulan-Ude, Siberia to Tashkent, Uzbekistan –
Passing on the Dream
1993-1994

Ultimately, everything that has life reproduces itself. When an individual gets on fire for God, they can't help but invest in other people. This produces a small group. When a small group grows together in the life of God, it can't help but bring more people in. Those small groups reproduce into churches. When those churches are obedient to the call Jesus gave His followers, they can't help but go to the nations with the gospel. Those churches reproduce and become more churches. When new churches catch the vision of their parent church, they too can't help but continue the work and plant even more churches. Church-plants reproduce even more churches and become movements.

One desire God planted in our heart for the church in Ulan-Ude was to train and send them out to the nations just like we did in Waco. Kevin and a great staff of people established a training school there and led it for the year. There were 17 students, approximately half

Russian and half American, and the classes were taught in both English and Russian. It was a trying and stretching year for the whole leadership team as they were running both a church and a training school.

The prophecy from Isaiah 54:2-3 had said, "…your descendants… will resettle the desolate cities." At one time we believed that scripture had been fulfilled, as the church-planters among us went out to Ulan-Ude. But, now we believed that as this church had become an extension of our body, they too should go forth to inhabit desolate cities.

Through a series of divinely orchestrated interactions, we all agreed that God was leading us to Tashkent, Uzbekistan. Kevin, Jeff Abshire, and I went there on an exploratory trip in the beginning of 1994. It was obvious to us that the doors were open, and God was leading us to walk right through. So, in May of that year, an outreach team from the Waco training school met an outreach team from the Ulan-Ude training school to plant a church in Tashkent.

Altogether, 22 leaders and students from two countries converged to pray, minister, and work together. Having just emerged from communism, the city was still very closed to the gospel, not governmentally, but spiritually. The team was believing for 20 new Christians to start a church, but as the first few weeks went by, that seemed unlikely.

The team was sharing the gospel with anyone and everyone that spoke either English or Russian. While many friendships formed between Uzbeks and Russians and between Uzbeks and Americans, still none of the Uzbeks were interested in accepting Christ. Dayna, one of the American students, suggested they fast and pray for breakthrough. No one was really excited about that idea because most of the team had contracted dysentery from the poor sanitary conditions in the city. Many had already lost a lot of weight and were struggling physically.

Despite the health concerns, though, the team knew they needed God to show up in power. So, they fasted for two and a half days. The plan was to seek God during this time and to end the fast with a big American meal and invite all of the new Uzbek friends. The party was a hit, full of fun, laughter, and games.

At the end of the party, the entire crowd went outside where the team performed a drama entitled *Life or Death*. Kevin then shared the gospel with the crowd and encouraged all of the Uzbeks to find the friend who had invited them to the party and ask them about Jesus. That night, 14 people came to Christ! The team also prayed for healing and many experienced miracles. One man had come to the party limping, but before the night was over, he was dancing and praising God. God had honored the fast with 14 eternally changed lives.

The Russian team had to go home shortly after that night, but the American team stayed behind and saw six more people saved. God gave the team the 20 new believers they had trusted Him for that summer in Tashkent, and as a result, a church was planted. Before leaving, the team baptized the new believers, discipled them as much as the short time would allow and left them with Bibles and other resources for growth. Four months later, a long-term church-planting team returned to invest in this group of new believers.

Of the original group that came to Christ that summer, several influential church leaders emerged. Four or five went on to serve in other nations. A young church in Ulan-Ude had risen to the call of the Great Commission and helped plant a church in another nation. As the two teams of students caught the vision and made it their own, God showed up and glorified Himself in their midst. What is beautiful about the whole adventure is that not just 20 people were saved, but a church was planted in a place where there was not one before. And that church has grown and matured and has sent out missionaries to other parts of the world. Even today, the fruit of that dream continues to bud and bloom in Tashkent and beyond.

As we obeyed, God did as He always does. He blessed. I believe today we continue to see Him come through with His end of the bargain. Ulan-Ude was just the beginning. Over the next five years, we watched Isaiah 54:2-3 unfold before our eyes. We sought to be obedient and faithful to its commands: enlarging our tent, stretching out our curtains, sparing not, lengthening our cords, and strengthening our pegs. Just as He had promised in Isaiah, we have "spread abroad to the right and to the left." Our spiritual descendants in the churches planted are possessing nations. Desolate cities are being resettled.

Chapter 9

Dreams to Reality
1992-1999

"Delight yourself in the Lord
And He will give you the desires of your heart."
Psalm 37:4

Throughout the first five years of ministry, 1987-1992, I often heard from speakers and authors about what God was doing around the world. When I would learn about the unreached in the earth, I would dream and think of different ways we could be a part of taking the gospel to them. I would always ask the Lord, "What are we supposed to do about this? How do we respond?"

Every time I asked, He would simply say, "I have called you to fast, pray, disciple people, and share the gospel. Invest in those around you." It seemed that God was asking me to use my desire for missions to facilitate others, as the foundations of our ministry were being laid.

Around 1992, I was talking to Sean Richmond, a former Master's Commission student who had become the youth pastor at Highland. We were talking about how to determine which dreams are from God and which ones are not. Sean asked me, "Jimmy, what are your dreams?"

Before I knew it, I found this coming out of my mouth: "You know, Sean, I don't have any dreams any more. I have found God to be so good that all I want is His dreams."

It was like God was speaking to me in the midst of the conversation. I went home that night and said to God, *"All I want are Your dreams. If You have a dream on Your heart, give it to me. If there is something that You are thinking about that no one else wants, Lord, I'll take it. I don't mind if I'm the second or third choice or even the tenth choice. I just want a dream that started in Your heart. I want to change the world. Dream Your dreams through me."*

Suddenly, it was as if a light bulb went off. God spoke clearer than ever. He had called us to plant churches around the world out of a community that was living out the values of the Kingdom. He desired not just individuals to plant churches but a people to plant churches. If we would let Him shape and change us into that people, then we would be able to reproduce the life of Jesus anywhere He sent us.

Laura and I have prayed this way through the years, and hundreds, if not thousands, of people have joined us in saying: *"Lord, dream Your dreams through me."* We have seen God do above and beyond what we could ask or think. I want to share several stories as examples of God living out His purpose through humble, willing vessels.

Bret and Jackie – Impossible Dreams
1986-1993

Jackie came to Baylor as a freshman in love with Jesus. She was tender and compassionate and shared Christ boldly. Though her love for Jesus was genuine, she struggled with an eating disorder. This bondage led to her dropping out of school after her third year. After counsel and help, she returned to Baylor, still loving Jesus. She and Laura became close friends towards the end of their college years.

When I was a senior, in 1986, I met a young man named Bret. Bret had suffered a sports injury in high school that caused him migraine headaches almost daily and severe pain 24 hours a day. The pain was so intense that he could hardly focus to study. Doctors had tried everything, but the ligaments had been so damaged that there was nothing they could do to help him cope. Bret met Jesus in that journey in such a powerful way that he found focus and peace only in abiding in Jesus. The rest he found in abiding allowed him to study, learn, and function socially.

Bret was a broken man, hungry for Jesus. He was intent on knowing all there was to know about God. When he and I talked for the first time outside of his apartment, the presence of the Lord filled the car. Throughout Bret's college years, we met regularly to jog together, to talk about God and the Spirit, and to worship and pray together in the mornings. More and more, Bret entered into the power and joy that God had for him.

These two humble people, Jackie and Bret, met the weekend of Laura's and my wedding. They soon discovered that they had kindred hearts and minds about living wholeheartedly for Jesus. Eventually, they married, having a common heart for the nations, willing to do whatever God had for them. On their honeymoon, they took one day to visit the Epcot Center at Disney World. They wanted to visit the Asia section because they knew God had called them to Asia. As they watched and heard about a nation in the Himalayas and about Mongolia, the presence of the Lord surrounded them. With tears flowing, they stayed in the movie theater for three showings as people filed in and out.

Jackie and Bret were a part of the original team that led college Lifegroups in 1990, learning how to disciple, evangelize, and reproduce the life of Christ. They multiplied their group four different times and were diligent to serve wherever possible in our growing movement.

Mongolian Believers

As we labored together, we continued to ask the Lord, "Is it now? Is now the time for you all to be sent out?" One day, as Bret walked out of work, a lady who had been praying for him approached him and asked about Mongolia. When she did, the presence of the Lord touched him in such a strong way he had to lean against the wall for support in order to not fall over. He went home and shared the experience with Jackie, and the presence of the Lord touched her as well. They realized that it was time to go.

Mongolia
1993-2006

After finishing the training school in 1993, Bret and Jackie, a single guy named Greg, a single girl named Sharon (who were later married and are now church-plant leaders in another Muslim city), and another single girl named Lynn (who has since married and is now serving in another Muslim nation with another organization) launched out to Mongolia to see a church established. During the early days, they saw a good number of college students come to Christ, and they began to meet from house to house. Though they saw fruit, they found it difficult to develop leaders and see people stick in their newly found faith.

Bret and Jackie began to pray and ask God for a man of peace, someone who would rise up to take leadership among the people to move them forward. Around that time, Jackie developed a relationship with her neighbor Chuka. She was a broken and desperate lady, having lived with the difficulties of an alcoholic husband. Through her relationship with Jackie, she heard the gospel and came to Christ. Jackie began teaching Chuka to pray for her husband, Tsolgi. Bret began to engage Tsolgi in conversations about God's wisdom for the family in Scripture and about Jesus. After many times of worship together, prayer for Tsolgi, and one key time of spiritual warfare, Tsolgi eventually gave his heart to Jesus.

As Bret discipled Tsolgi, he told him that he needed to share Christ

Tsolgi, Chuka, Their Children, and Tsolgi's Mother

with his family. The first person he shared with was his mother. This 70-year-old woman was a devout Marxist, teaching Marxism at the only medical school in the nation. Every medical student in Mongolia had to take her class. When she heard the message of Jesus and saw the changed lives of Tsolgi and Chuka, she also gave her life to Christ. As passionate as she had been about Marxism, she became about Jesus. She led 17 adult members of her family to the Lord. This family became the core of multiple cell groups all over the city. God did signs and wonders in their midst and many were saved.

While God was doing great things among them, this new church knew there was more. They began to pray for the villages and towns that had never heard the gospel. Then they took a short-term trip to another city in Mongolia. After sharing with 200 people, 50 gave their hearts to the Lord and began meeting from house to house.

Over the ensuing years, Bret and Jackie handed the work over to Tsolgi, Chuka, and the team of national leaders. Today, the church has spread to 15 different locations with multiple house churches in those locations. A church-planting movement is spreading in Mongolia.

The Joy of New Life!

Mongolia – Raised from the Dead 2006

In 2006, we received testimony about a village of 12,000 that the Mongolian church was trying to reach. The Mongolian believers were going into the town regularly to evangelize and reach out to the neighbors and friends of the ones who had become Christians.

During their visits, they had heard of a man who was very sick and dying of liver cancer.

On one visit to the village, they found that this man (not a Christian yet) had died. For 38 hours he had no signs of life, so the doctors said to take him home for burial. All the man's family had gathered and were preparing for the funeral.

One of the Mongolian believers thought God wanted her to go and pray for the dead man. However, the family was Buddhist and did not allow it. They actually felt at first she was making fun of them. But, the man's mother finally relented and allowed the believer to pray for her dead son.

The Mongolian believer placed her hand on the dead man and prayed for him to live. His eyelids moved some but nothing else happened. Then, she and the other believers left the village and went back to the capital city.

The following week she returned to the small village, and the "dead" man was there waiting for them...ALIVE. He said that he was dead, "there was nothing at all," but when she prayed for him, he suddenly heard her praying in Jesus' name and saw a brilliant, bright light. Then, his consciousness returned, but he could not move. He tried to speak to her as she prayed but couldn't move at all. After she left the house, his strength slowly returned.

He asked for something to drink about four hours after the prayer, and his family was so shocked because a DEAD MAN was talking to them.

Then he got out of bed and started walking around the town looking for "the Jesus people." His family was astonished that the man they thought was dead was up and speaking, asking them where "the Jesus people" were.

When the newly living man found "the Jesus people," he prayed to Jesus and was baptized. His family, all of whom where Buddhist and previously had no interest in Jesus, also prayed and were baptized. A total of 14 people were baptized together with him including his wife, the doctor who pronounced him dead, family members, and villagers!!

This man is a 47-year-old taxi driver, well known by the people in the village. It appears that all 12,000 people in the village have heard about it. Glory to God!

A freshman with an eating disorder and a young man with a physical disability said, "Jesus is enough. He is my portion and my cup. I will not let go of the hem of His garment. I will find my inheritance in Christ alone and give myself to the nations of the earth." They went from wounded freshmen at Baylor to seeing a church-planting movement established and the dead raised. Today, Bret, Jackie, and their children live in the Himalayas reaching two other unreached people groups, believing for another church-planting movement to be established.

Dayna (Curry) Masterson – Dreamed through a Servant
1989-2001

Dayna came to Baylor because her mother wanted her to attend a school that didn't allow smoking in the dorms. In her testimony, Dayna openly shares about her struggles in high school with alcohol, drugs, and eventually having an abortion. When she came to Baylor, she joined a college Lifegroup at Highland and the people in the group began to love and care for her.

At a Friday night gathering, Mark Buckner had a word of knowledge: someone there was like a puppy in a corner whom God was calling out to be healed and restored. Dayna had literally been sitting under a table, feeling exactly that way. Mark eventually saw her and prayed for her. She began to come alive and to discover worship and the love of God to be the centerpiece of her heart and life.

Dayna began to serve in Lifegroups, learning how to disciple, evangelize, and find Jesus as her sufficiency. After finishing college and being involved in leadership at Highland, she went through the training school. When we asked Dayna where she wanted to go in the future, her basic response was, "Wherever I am needed."

At the time, we were sending a long-term team to Tashkent, Uzbekistan after the outreach from the training schools from Waco and Ulan-Ude. We already had a family and another single lined up to help establish this church, and we asked Dayna to join them.

Right before Christmas in 1994, Dayna (Curry) Masterson and Erica (Greenwald) Denney arrived in Uzbekistan. The plan was for these two ladies to remain together until the team leaders showed up a couple of months later at which time Erica would return home. Dayna's time in Tashkent was fruitful as she worked under her team leaders and alongside many short-term workers. However, due to a number of difficult circumstances, the team leaders had to return home.

I met with Dayna and discussed what should happen next. Again, Dayna's heart was, "Just tell me what is needed." There was still a need for these new believers to be established. Since there were other believers and friends already living in Tashkent that Dayna could live with, we decided that she should stay. Dayna became the leader of the Tashkent church-plant.

Simply wanting to serve, Dayna found herself leading out. Over time, we transitioned from her leadership into an emerging leadership team in the Tashkent church. As Dayna sought God about the future, Kurt and Karen, another missionary family, invited her to be a part of their team in Afghanistan. Dayna accepted their invitation and later moved to Afghanistan.

Dayna is an awesome evangelist, one who serves the poor and cares for the needy. She found herself living out the purposes of God, not by a force of her own will, but by simply wanting to be a servant. Little did she know that she and Heather Mercer would have the opportunity to share the testimony of Jesus with millions of people through the media and print after she was imprisoned for three months for sharing the gospel in Afghanistan.

Dayna's dream has never been to be somebody in the world's eyes but to be somebody in God's eyes. She wants to love Him with all her heart and her neighbor as herself. Today, she and her husband serve in North Africa as team leaders of a church-plant. They are reproducing the life of Jesus, the very life that had captured her heart as a freshman and continues to lead her to touching the nations of the world.

Irkutsk, Russia – Inheriting the Dream
1993-2007

We sent a second church-planting team to Russia in 1993, this time to the city of Irkutsk. A training-school team from Waco had gone there and shared the gospel with students, many of whom were either interested in Jesus or were new believers. When the long-term team led by Danny and Kathy Mulkey arrived in 1993, the group was already meeting regularly on Friday nights.

Over the next couple of years, the church in Irkutsk multiplied their small groups until about 100 were gathering on Sunday mornings. They devoted themselves to relationship, discipleship, and community. Modeling what they had learned in Waco, the team saw the church in Irkutsk established. After Danny and Kathy returned to America in 1995, Lyle and Melissa Smith emerged as the team leaders, and the church continued to grow and mature in discipleship.

Alexey Kuschenko was only 16 when he joined the church in Irkutsk, but he quickly matured in the Lord. He had been saved as a high school student during one of our first summer outreaches in Ulan-Ude in 1992 and had later come to Irkutsk for college. Alexey eventually married a young woman named Margarita. She was saved through one of the Irkutsk church outreaches and was already active when Alexey moved from Ulan-Ude. Both became leaders, disciplers, and evangelists, giving their hearts wholeheartedly to the work in Irkutsk.

When it was time for the church-planting team to return to Waco in 1999, it was obvious that Alexey should take over leadership in the church. Though he was only 21 at the time, God had blessed him with wisdom and steadfastness.

God continued to grow and develop the church in Irkutsk through the years as He gave them a heart for drug addicts and people with AIDS. Working with some of the most extreme needs in their city, they saw many come to Christ and be set free from drug addiction. They also saw so many people healed of AIDS that the local newspaper printed their stories.

Irkutsk Pastors: Alexey & Margarita

Many family members of those miraculously healed were saved as well. At one time, Alexey communicated to us that eighty-five percent of the church had been saved out of drug addiction, healed in some way, or was a family member of someone who had been saved or healed. God has done a great work in Irkutsk and continues to multiply that work for His glory.

China – Multiplying the Church
1998

Even as Alexey and the leaders in Irkutsk were experiencing the purposes of God in their midst, it was spreading to others as well. A young Chinese man, whom we call Larry, came to Irkutsk to do a language program. He met Christ through some of our team and got involved in a Lifegroup where he was discipled. Larry eventually became a Lifegroup leader and learned how to invest in others and to reproduce the life of Jesus. After being with the church in Irkutsk for about a year and a half, his visa expired, and he had to return to China. Our team prayed for Larry and sent him out, hoping to keep in touch.

Two years passed without any contact from Larry. Michael, one of the leaders in Irkutsk, and his wife Linda, an American team member, had a heart for China. God had given them a desire to go to Larry's city to see a church established there.

When they visited, they found Larry and asked him, "Are you still following Jesus?"

Larry looked at them strangely as if to say, *Well, of course I'm still following Jesus.*

They went on to ask him, "Have you found the underground church or other people to worship with?"

Larry responded, "All I did when I got here was what you told me to do. I gathered my friends and told them about my faith and what God was doing. Many of them came to Christ, and we began to meet in my home to talk about growing together in Jesus. They began reaching out and starting their own groups. Now we have about 120 people meeting in different homes in the city."

Michael and Linda spent the next two years with Larry and saw the group grow to 300. God's plan is always to capture peoples' hearts, allowing them to invest in community and to learn to reproduce that community wherever they go. I believe we have stepped into what Jesus proclaimed when He said, "I will build My church; and the gates of Hades will not overpower it" (Matthew 16:18). God is looking for anybody to join His purposes of reproducing His life through the church for His glory.

World Mandate – Birthplace for Dreams
1989-2007

Over the years, one of the main places we have talked about the nations and encouraged students to dream God's dreams has been at our annual mission conference, World Mandate. When we started World Mandate in 1989, our vision was to encourage and inspire students to go to the nations. Attendance grew incrementally through the early 1990s and then began to grow exponentially. The first year, about 60 students came. For the last three years, we have sold out the Waco Convention Center with more than 2,700 in attendance.

World Mandate was, and is, one of those dynamic times when God shows up in a powerful way. Much like the Juarez, Mexico trip, World Mandate is a time when God speaks to students about how and where they can be involved in His plan for the nations. Every year, we bring in speakers from around the world, missions' leaders who share their lives and hearts. Through these messages, along with the dynamic worship, lives and futures are changed for the glory of God's Kingdom.

To give you a taste of what God does through World Mandate, here are some quotes from students who have attended. These prayers were laid before the alter as a sign of their commitment to follow what they heard God saying. Many were written by people now serving all around the world.

God – I, Christi...will go to the nations to proclaim your glory at any cost, as scary as this pledge is. Make me worldless! Fearless! I will carry your burden for the cross. Dream your dreams through me...not my own American dream! Teach me how! You want me to do this. I will go unless you change this by your will.

By the grace of God, I will go wherever and whenever God leads me to people who have not heard -- no matter what it costs me: friends, husband, children, health, life...I just want to live for the cross of Christ -- no matter how it looks. First, the Palestinians: that they would be church planters to the Arab world. Second -- the next place in my heart: Iran and Tajikistan ...Rebekah

World Mandate: A Call to the Nations

Dear God, I make it my ambition to take myself and my family to Central Asian Islamic nations within the next 2 years -- eventually to end up in Tajikistan. Praise you most High God! Jeff

141

Dear Jesus, I want to go. I don't want it to be a thing that I promise to do and every time I think about going my heart races and tears flow and chill bumps spread all over me. I want it to be more than emotion. When I think of China, my heart breaks. I break. I think of the women who are so trod upon and abused and all I want to do is hold them. I want to be a lover of that people. All I can see myself doing is just that. How can you let me love them and grieve for them even though I've never seen them? There would be no other way I would want to die than loving one of them the way you have loved me. Yes, Lord, I will go. I will even go if it's just you and me. I had put that stipulation on you, but I'll lift it. I will go. I love you, your daughter.

Father God, Give me your passion for the people of this world. I will go out and serve in a foreign place unless you want me to stay here. But Father, until I leave I want to share your word with my friends here. Kill the fear of man in me, Father. I will serve you wherever you lead me. Tell me what to do, God. May my every whisper, my every breath be an outpouring of love for you, a libation that others would come to know you and that I would be stronger in you.

God's presence is near when you are dealing with matters that are close to His heart. At World Mandate, we talk about the lost; we pray for them and commit our lives to God's ultimate call to go to those who don't know Him. When we gather each year to do this, He can't help but visit us with His presence and power because His heart is for the lost. Over and over again, He has shown up in powerful ways.

There are hundreds of stories of how God birthed His desires for nations and people in the hearts of those in our midst. Some stories I can't tell to protect those who are serving in closed countries in the world. But wherever they serve, we know that God's desires are becoming reality: the values of simply loving God, each other, and the lost in the context of community are being reproduced all over the world.

In the 1980s, God put a love for Him and for His church in my heart. I believed then as I do now, that He wants passionate worshippers to emerge who love His church in such a way that they can reproduce an Acts 2:42-47 community around the world.

I am convinced that today we are in the middle of God's plan. We are a simple people living out the gospel in our own location. By being the church in Waco, Texas, we can reproduce church anywhere with a few cultural and language adaptations. Because of this, we can then be sent anywhere in the world to reproduce the life of God.

Chapter 10

Foundation to Growth I
1992-1997

*"But by the grace of God I am what I am, and His grace toward me
did not prove vain; but I labored even more than all of them, yet not I,
but the grace of God with me."*
1 Corinthians 15:10

In the early part of 1992, we were about to launch our first long-term church-plant team to Ulan-Ude when I received a letter from someone who had worked with us before but had moved on to another mission agency. The letter was well meaning, but very challenging, basically outlining twelve reasons why we had no business planting churches.

Immediately, I was defensive in my heart and began to pray, "God, how do I respond to this?" I felt like the Lord said, "I want you to reread each one of the reasons listed and see if they are true."

As I reread all twelve reasons I realized ten of them were true. The Lord went on to tell me, "Call him and tell him that he is right, but that I have called you to do it, so you have to do it anyway."

Criticism like that sometimes made our work difficult. Though we didn't know what we were doing, we trusted that God would be bigger than our weaknesses. So, we launched out with all of our hearts and learned lessons along the way; some lessons were challenging but others were glorious as we watched God work.

As I mentioned earlier, God spoke to me very clearly that years one to five in our ministry would be foundational and years six to ten would be growth. 1992 to 1997 were these years of growth. Some of the greatest highlights of our lives happened during this time, along with some of our most painful experiences. Growing pains were real as all of the changes and struggles made growth awkward, and we were not sure where it was all going. We knew, however, that if we survived the growth stage, we would learn things that would propel us into the future.

Training School Growth
1992-2007

One of the most apparent areas of growth in 1992-1997 was in our training school. We went from roughly 10 students in 1991 to 30 plus in 1992.

At each phase of growth for the training school, God brought men and women to the team to help with the transition and changes. A mentor once taught me that I should try to work myself out of every job. So, from the very beginning of the ministry, my goal has been to turn it over to others who are capable of taking it even farther. About half way through 1991, I handed over the leadership of the school to Jeff Bianchi. Jeff had been transformed by the grace of God and helped shape our training school over the next five years.

After Jeff moved to Berlin in 1996, Kely Braswell stepped in to help us navigate some changes in the training school as we refined it more towards church planting. Kely and the team were there for the transition years until God led him, his wife Jennifer and their children, and a team to plant a church in Turkey. At that time, God brought back our dear friends Ty and Erica Denney, who had grown up in our college ministry, to lead the next five years of our training school.

In 1998 we also began our night training school, pioneered and developed by Kevin Johnson. This was an exciting development because it allowed us to also invest in people who were working full-time and wanting to be discipled and trained as church planters. Tad Smith began leading the night school in 2001 and when he became our church-plant leader in Belton, Texas, Danny Mulkey stepped in.

As we continued to look ahead to the future, God brought Nate Bobbett to lead the training school during yet another transition. Instead of one school that focused both on discipleship and church planting, we split it into two: Elevate and 24:14. Elevate is now our discipleship training school that is offered as both a 9-month day school and a 12-month night school. 24:14 (from Matthew 24:14) is an intensive 6-month church-planting school.

At every step along the way, God has brought in the right leadership and team members to help grow and shape our training process. I also want to point out here that while we often mention team leaders in the training school, we all agree that it takes a whole team to run the school. We have always had an incredible staff of men and women who have sacrificially given themselves to equip and strengthen students in the training process. Many times, the staff has a higher impact on the students than even the leader does because they spend consistent one-on-one time with the students. Only eternity will tell the power that these individuals and teams have had on our training school students and their work around the world.

When enrollment at the training school more than tripled in the fall of 1992, we found that the students had really caught the vision and were ready to go. We did, however, run into some problems. A few of the students had needs that we were not aware of and this caused some issues going into the year. Some were minor and even a bit funny, but others turned out to be hurtful.

One family, who had taken a student in, asked me about the student's home life. When I told them that I thought it had been pretty normal, they told me that no one had ever taught him about basic electricity. To heat the room in the morning, this student would turn the shower on full blast and open up the doors to let the steam heat the room. When confronted by the couple, the student said that was how he always did it growing up. We found out that many of our students needed basic life skills. While learning how to change the world, some of them needed to learn how to better take care of themselves.

Another of the more interesting challenges came up early one morning when one of our students asked to meet with us and relayed this story: Ann and Jane (their names have been changed) were roommates living with one of our families in the church. Jane was sharing her frustrations with Ann about life and the training school. As they began to talk and pray, Jane's face became contorted, and she began to speak in a deep, guttural voice saying that she had been sent to destroy Master's Commission.

Ann was completely overwhelmed and called on the name of Jesus and prayed for the peace of God. After things had settled down and Jane had gotten back to her normal state, she communicated that she was frustrated and tired, and she was going to go to bed. To say the least, Ann was a little overwhelmed that morning, wondering what to do. I have to be honest; we were a little overwhelmed too. Eventually Jane was asked to leave the school for a number of reasons, but it once again shows that our battles are not against flesh and blood. There are things that happen and go on in people's lives that can help us all to learn how to respond to the love of God and deal with the challenges of moving ministry forward.

Also during these years of growth and transition for the training school, we had different people challenge the leadership. One person on staff thought they should be leading the school instead of Jeff. This person did not choose to walk it through with us but instead talked to other students and staff. Eventually, this person left with another staff person and embittered many of the students as well.

These situations are not abnormal in church life, but for us, they were new places of growth, learning how to bless and forgive, how to release, and how to take correction even when correction was done wrongly. Though these challenges seemed devastating at the time, each was a part of God's process to strengthen us through the journey.

God continued to visit us with great power in our morning sessions in the training school, so much so that many times everyone in the room was on their face meeting with the Lord. There were times of deep intercession for the nations and seasons of brokenness as God shaped and changed us. The growing pains were part of the process, but they did not stop God from moving in peoples' lives. Eventually, the problems ironed themselves out, and we were a better training school because God had changed us and continued to work in our midst.

With the launch of the Ulan-Ude church plant, we knew we needed to gear the training school more towards preparing people to reproduce the church in other parts of the world. What started off as a discipleship school transitioned as we began to focus more specifically on church planting. We developed several new training procedures to equip and train the students to do what God was putting on their hearts.

People need to have a basis for what they are learning both within the Word and in practical application. As we discovered that leadership is not only caught but taught, we started a Lifegroup Leader training weekend as well as ongoing meetings for development, support, and encouragement.

The more church plants we sent out, the more we realized that our people needed more training than what we offered in our training school classes. So, those who wanted to be involved with us long term attended a seven-week staff training course to better prepare them for the mission field. And as we saw specific training needs on the field for individual teams, such as ministry in the Muslim world, we started providing these opportunities before church-planting teams departed. The more we learned about what our people needed, the more we grew in the areas of training and development.

During this time, we were introduced to a model of learning that has stuck with us ever since. Steve Nicholson, the head of U.S. church planting for the Vineyard, once explained to me: if you keep people's ministry experience one step ahead of their knowledge, it will always make them hungry for more. Ongoing training seemed to be more effective than frontloading all the information. Initially, we trained ongoing out of sheer practicality. But we have found over time that when we take the attitude of being lifelong learners, ongoing training is what keeps us growing and learning on the job.

Church-Planting Growth
1992-1998

Russia, Mongolia, Uzbekistan, Afghanistan – within a few years, we were in all of these locations and more. To keep up with this rapid growth, we had to send people out quickly. We soon found out that it is better to send out the right laborers than just to send out an abundance of laborers.

Not everyone we sent out was prepared and mature enough to handle the challenges and complexities of cross-cultural missions. Basically, if someone had faith, wanted to go, and was not in major sin, we sent them. Later on though, we realized that it is not just faith in someone's heart that makes them able to be involved in a cross-cultural church plant. Several other things in their lives have to line up as well.

Because of the multitude of laborers we sent out and the pace at which we sent them, we experienced some backlash. A couple of people fell into immorality. There were team conflicts that sometimes hindered what we were trying to do. We had to adapt and respond quickly to these new experiences and emergencies on the field. To say the least, it was a crazy time as we visited teams and spent eighty percent of our time resolving difficult issues.

As we struggled through team issues and conflicts, we learned better how to function as a team. Even as the disciples went out two by two, God added to them along the way, making teams of people who would reproduce the life of God to plant churches around the world. God has called us to minister as teams, and it is never just about one person or leader. He calls together groups of people to influence and disciple others. In Acts 2:42-47, we see a people gathered together, living out Kingdom values. That is the type of community we have tried to reproduce.

In response to all of these challenges, we changed some of our training and leader evaluation processes. One of our favorite sayings is, "I'd rather deal with it on this side of the water than the other side." Eventually, all these things worked together for good as we learned the balance between releasing people quickly and making sure they have everything they need to do what God had called them to do.

With our people spread all over the globe, it was obvious to us that God was moving in and through us, and we were very aware that it was Him and not us doing it all. The pains and striving through this season were places where we found His grace and strength to be more than enough in the journey.

In 1997, after five years of doing a few things right and a lot of things wrong, but staying consistent in loving and developing leaders in Ulan-Ude, we were ready to turn the church there over completely to Russian leadership. We had been the first foreigners to work in Ulan-Ude, but after 1992, other mission agencies, some of the largest in the world, had come. They had better strategies and ideas than us and had often been critical of our methods.

On the day that we turned the church over to the national leaders, several guys from the other organizations came and sat in the back. Joe

Ewen, one of our close friends and mentors, was also there. The men asked Joe, "How did these guys do this? We see so many holes in their strategy and missiology."

Joe simply said, "You know, sometimes I've wondered the same thing. One thing I know is that they love Jesus with all their hearts. They fast. They pray. They give their lives sacrificially for the people. I

Ulan-Ude Pastors Zhenya & Lena Levandovsky

guess God just honors that and overlooks their weaknesses."

I love the passage that says, "…we have this treasure in earthen vessels, so that the surpassing greatness of the power will be of God and not from ourselves…" (2 Corinthians 4:7).

Berlin, Germany
1997

After our first year in Ulan-Ude, I realized that even when God speaks incredible dreams, dreams that are possible only with Him, few people actually implement His vision. There are a lot of opinions and ideas about how to plant churches, about how to do missions right, but the pain and the process of what it takes to see it all the way through is many times left undone.

We are committed to not just dreaming, but to letting God change us, rearrange us, and reshape us so that the dream can be fulfilled. Implementation is as important as vision. Dreams just don't happen. They require hard work and a willingness to continually be changed along the way.

Sometimes though, things don't turn out the way we intend. In 1997, after four years of leading the training school, Jeff Bianchi, along with Jennifer Smyer and Lisa Miller, left to plant a church in Berlin, Germany. Our desire was to reach people for Jesus in that nation but also to set up a European hub to launch into the Middle East and beyond.

Jeff has always been a catalyst for renewal and revival as his passions for worship and prayer have impacted us greatly. But as Jeff, Jennifer, and Lisa headed out, something none of us expected happened: Jeff began to experience clinical depression. The issues and challenges of life, ministry, and what God was doing in him, seemed to be crashing all around him. After the team had been in Berlin for three months, I went to Europe and brought the team home.

This was a very difficult time for all of us. As a church, we loved Jeff dearly. We didn't understand how this could happen after all of our fasting, praying, and seeking God. However, we did learn a lot through the process, specifically, that we are all just weak vessels in the hands of a mighty God, and He is doing different things in different peoples' lives at different times. No matter who we are, where we have come from, or how much training we have received, we are all still being made and fashioned into His image. For those of

Marathoners (L-R) Kevin Johnson, Jimmy Seibert, Sean Richmond, Jeff Bianchi, Ty Denney

us who walked with Jeff, we learned that it is just as important for us to love and to restore as it is to empower and equip.

I must say on Jeff's behalf, he had a sweet spirit through the whole time. Even when life was confusing, challenging, and darker than he ever imagined, he kept a tender heart towards God and people. One year later, after Jeff was well on the road to recovery and experiencing the grace of God in a new way, he sent me a coffee mug that read: "Never, never quit." I still have that mug on my desk as a reminder that we don't always understand why our challenges happen, but if we will never quit growing from our mistakes and understanding more of the character of God, we will see the goodness of the Lord and the glory of God in the nations.

Today, Jeff serves as an associate pastor and training school leader with his wife Sarah at our church in Boston. He has been a Barnabas to me, Laura, and our whole movement. Also today, we have a new church-planting team in Berlin, Germany, flourishing in the grace of God.

Opening Nations
1992-1998

God has always called us to believe Him for the impossible, to see Him as bigger than ourselves. For years, I have meditated on Isaiah 40:12-17:

Who has measured the waters in the hollow of His hand,
And marked off the heavens by the span,
And calculated the dust of the earth by the measure,
And weighed the mountains in a balance And the hills in a pair of scales?
Who has directed the Spirit of the LORD,
Or as His counselor has informed Him?
With whom did He consult and who gave Him understanding?
And who taught Him in the path of justice and taught Him knowledge
And informed Him of the way of understanding?
Behold, the nations are like a drop from a bucket,
And are regarded as a speck of dust on the scales;
Behold, He lifts up the islands like fine dust.
Even Lebanon is not enough to burn,
Nor its beasts enough for a burnt offering.
All the nations are as nothing before Him,
They are regarded by Him as less than nothing and meaningless.

Isn't it awesome to know that God measures the waters in His hands, weighs the mountains in a balance, and sees the nations as a drop in a bucket. It has caused us to believe that God can do the impossible and will always make a way for us, whether through new strategies or divine appointments.

Many times, people talk about closed nations, ones not open to God's people coming in to share the gospel. Our belief is that every nation is open all the time. There is no closed nation.

As a part of the holistic message of the gospel, God has called us to find practical ways to serve as well as proclaim the clear message of His love and salvation. As Chris and Rebekah and their team looked for ways to serve the Palestinian people, they saw that one of the biggest needs around the world was for job training and skills development. In light of that, Chris established a non-profit organization in the States that allowed us to set up non-governmental organizations (NGOs) in different parts of the world. These NGOs have allowed us to facilitate the two hands of the gospel: caring for people's practical needs as well as clearly proclaiming Christ. We are so grateful to Chris and his team for their service to us in setting up this organization. It has become vital to how we fulfill Christ's commission to the uttermost parts of the earth.

One closed nation that we were knocking on the door of was Afghanistan. In 1995, Kurt and Karen, Allison, and I were trying to find a way to get into Afghanistan as Kurt and Karen felt led by God to serve that nation. We arrived in Tashkent, Uzbekistan not knowing how we would get into Afghanistan since visas were difficult to obtain and the borders seemed to be closed.

Our second day there, I spoke at the international church in Tashkent and shared out of the Isaiah 40 passage. I told them that the nations are as a drop in a bucket to God and that we were trying to get into Afghanistan. Even though everyone had told us that we could not get in, we believed that God would make a way where there was no way.

At the end of the service, a young man named Aiyup introduced himself to me. He had come to the Lord through some aid workers in Afghanistan and had since moved to Uzbekistan to work with that organization. He told me that his father was a cabinet member under General Dulstom, the leader of the Northern Alliance in Afghanistan. Aiyup went on to explain that if we wanted, he could arrange for us to meet Dulstom and possibly get into the country.

Immediately we said yes, not knowing what the next few days held. The first day, armed guards with machine guns picked us up and took us to a holding spot. After a few hours, they told us that General

Dulstom could not meet with us. The next morning, they picked us up again, and within 30 minutes, we were pulling down a side road in a neighborhood in Uzbekistan. They told us to get out of the car very slowly and not to make any sudden moves.

Out from behind a high wall walked a large dark-skinned man with two large bodyguards armed with AK47s. Aiyup told us that this man was General Dulstom. As we slowly walked up and greeted him, he invited us into his palace beyond the wall. Walking down the red carpet, we were all constantly praying, *"Lord, what do we say? What do we do? Help, help."*

Once we sat down together, he simply asked the question, "What is it that you guys want?"

I told him that we were followers of Jesus and that we had a small NGO that offered medical and educational assistance around the world. But specifically, I told him that we wanted to know how we could help him. We asked, "Is there something on your heart that we can help with and pray for you about?"

He looked at us somewhat teary eyed and said, "If I shared with you everything that is in my heart, there would not be time. Come to my guest house in Afghanistan. We will meet again."

His aids immediately made sure that we had visas, and the next day we were flying down to Termez, the border city of Afghanistan and Uzbekistan. Some missionary friends picked us up at the border and drove us to Mazar-e Sharif, the capital city in the north. As we got into the city, we went to check in with the town council. When we pulled up, our doors were opened for us, and we were ushered into a big room to meet dignitaries, generals, colonels, and the U.N. negotiator. We were treated to a feast and then invited to spend the night at General Dulstom's guesthouse.

The rest of the day we spent time in the city looking for opportunities where we could serve. We met the president of all of the hospitals in the Mazar-e Sharif area and then met the president of the university. With each of these men, we spoke of our faith in Jesus. We were also invited into classrooms and medical facilities. Then, we were brought to General Dulstom's guesthouse with the expectation to meet with him the next morning.

A servant literally stood outside our door all night, waiting on us hand and foot as we stayed in this 18th century fort. I stayed up late that night praying and seeking God, asking Him what I was to say to General Dulstom. At the same time, the training school students back in Waco were fasting and praying on our behalf, asking God for a breakthrough. I felt that I had a clear message for General Dulstom and resolved to be bold.

The students' prayer and fasting ended at 2:00 a.m. Afghan time. At 3:00 a.m., I woke up violently ill. This went on all morning, and even as I was trying to hold it together, General Dulstom had to fly off to the military front, and we were not able to meet again. I often wonder what would have happened if the fasting would have continued and the opportunity would have come. God had other great plans though. We had opportunities to meet with other leaders in the country, sharing our love for Jesus, praying for them, and eventually leaving with a letter inviting us to return to the country.

Since that time, as we have listened to and obeyed the Lord, we have been brought before kings and have slept on the streets. We have had opportunities to minister and live in countries that people thought would forever be closed. God has called us to be pioneers, to walk by faith and not by sight, to not worry about what everybody says you can't do, but to believe that God can make a way for anyone who believes that nations are a drop in the bucket.

As we started to go into these more difficult places, we found out that many of them were not in revival and were very resistant to the work that we were doing. Other mission agencies in these countries did not appreciate our youthful zeal and passion to believe for the impossible. God had been so gracious to allow us to experience revivals in Russia, Mongolia, and Uzbekistan, but as we moved into Afghanistan, Pakistan, and other nations, we realized that it wasn't always going to be that easy. There was a reason a church hadn't been planted for hundreds of years in some of these cities. The soil was hard, and we would have to learn new ways to share the love of Christ.

A key element in seeing church-planting movements happen in these more difficult areas is the willingness to suffer and sacrifice. This is a hard fact, because I am more willing to die than I am to suffer. But if Acts is the normative for how New Testament believers lived to see a church- planting movement started, then we have to expect suffering. Instead of being surprised by it, we must rejoice, knowing that it will change us and bring God glory.

We have found that what makes suffering significant is not that it is a catalyst in and of itself but that it is simply one cost in following Jesus. Jesus and the apostles were dangerous to be with, not because they were foolish, but because they were lovers of God and had to proclaim what He had done for them. Suffering is the path of Jesus, and it is in following Jesus that we will see Him establish His church in the nations. When hard times come along, we never question our calling. We do not consider it foolish to have shared the gospel even when there are difficult consequences.

Fear and intimidation are destroying the work of God in and through the North American and western church. There are also biblical indications that tell us that it is never foolish to count the cost of suffering and then to go and share Jesus in spite of it.

There are 2.1 billion people on earth today who have never heard the gospel in a clear way. Reaching these unreached has always been the heartbeat of what we are all about. We have always prayed, "God, if there are people who have never heard or places where no one will go, send us." In Acts 1:8, Jesus told us to go to the uttermost parts of the earth. We like to say that we will go to the "st" of the uttermost.

From the beginning, God has given us that pioneering spirit. Sometimes, we are the only westerners in places; where others have said you could never get in, our people go and live. Though I cannot communicate all of these places and people openly, I am so proud of them and rejoice that they have really taken on the "st" of the uttermost. God is using them for His glory.

U.S. Church Planting
1997-2007

As God led us to the uttermost parts of the earth, He also reminded us that we are called to Jerusalem, Judea, and Samaria (Acts 1:8). Sean Richmond, who was the youth pastor at Highland Baptist Church at the time, carried the nations in his heart. But he also knew that God had called him to reach the United States. As we began to dialogue about it with Sean and his wife Laura, we realized that God was calling them and us to plant churches in the U.S. as well as facilitate more laborers for the harvest around the world. Sean and Laura moved to Boston in 1997 to get more education and learn the "lay of the land." In 1999, we began our first U.S. church plant there.

Many people went with Sean and his family to invest in Boston. Two of the hardest to let go of were Jeff and Dorothy Abshire, who had walked with us from the beginning. It was difficult to release them after they had been such strong foundational pillars among us. Jeff was the backbone of administration, and Dorothy had been the initiator of our creative arts and was a stirrer and lightening rod for revival. However, we knew that God was leading them during that season in the process of teaching and empowering them for future ministry, as well as healing their hearts after the devastating loss of a child at birth. Part of growing up is learning to let your best go so that the Kingdom of God can be furthered. After helping the Boston church get off the ground, the Abshires returned to Waco in 2000 to work with Antioch Community Church.

Boston Team: First US Church Plant

Today, Sean and Laura and their team lead a flourishing church in Boston. After they left, others began to sense God's leadership for U.S. church planting as well. Our commitment has always been to get behind people's dreams and visions from God. Robert Herber, our college pastor, also began to get a heart for U.S. church planting. As we dialogued together, we came up with a vision statement: *We want to see a church planted in all 50 states of the U.S.*

That spurred a fresh wave of church plants. In 2001, Ben and Ruth Loring headed out for the inner city of Dallas with a vision to reach the homeless as well as to empower men and women from all economic strata of that community. Our dear friends, Amy and Jonathan Gulley, led a team to Chicago in 2004, followed by other great leaders and teams to Belton, Knoxville, Portland, Seattle, Los Angeles, Durham/Chapel Hill, and San Diego. This is just the beginning of a future wave of church plants.

God spoke to us that we were to create more hubs in the U.S. for reaching people and for touching the nations. As they have gone out and established churches in cities around the country, each of our U.S. church-planting teams has taken with them a heart for reaching the nations. Even in their early years of development, all of our church plants have made it a priority to go to the nations, either by starting their own training schools, sending short-term mission teams, or gearing toward sending long-term workers around the world.

Antioch Ministries International
1992-1998

By 1993, we were out of control administratively. Jeff Abshire, Ruth Reese, and I, along with a host of volunteers, worked as hard as we could, but it just wasn't enough. We needed an army of administrators and a complete mission arm to facilitate training, care on the field, developing local ministries, and fund-raising.

Originally, we incorporated under the name Training and Sending Centers (TASC) in 1992. The more we sought the Lord though during the following years, He asked us what we wanted to be. Looking through the Scriptures, we saw the church at Antioch in Acts 11 and 13, and realized that was who we wanted to be: a people trained and developed by the local church who are sent out in power by the Holy Spirit to do His bidding. So, we changed our incorporation papers to Antioch Ministries International and renamed the training school Antioch Training School.

We also raised up a local staff to service our growing missions arm, which proved to be a challenging experience. At our first staff training, with about ten people preparing to join us either administratively or elsewhere, I talked about our commitment to live a disciplined devotional life. We emphasized at least an hour of prayer a day, a consistent lifestyle of fasting, rigorous Bible study, in-depth Scripture memory, sharing Christ on a daily basis, investing in and discipling people, and sacrificial giving. All of these were Biblical norms and admonitions that were given as ways to help us draw nearer to the heart of the Lord.

Later, when I wasn't around, one young lady voiced that she was overwhelmed by the expectations that had been shared. She felt she wasn't good enough to get it all done. A few others voiced similar concerns. The leader of the training session tried to explain that we were not trying to pressure them into works, but after several days of talking things through, some of them left us having decided that they were not ready to do what we were asking.

I didn't understand why they were feeling overburdened by the standards and commands of the Lord. You see, I had grown up with a father who was a peacemaker, always affirming and resolving conflict when things were difficult in the home. Therefore, I didn't struggle with the Father heart or love of God. God had so devastated my heart in the early 1980s that I had fallen in love with Him. For me, the only thing I wanted to know was how to get closer to Him and how to change the world. But we realized that for people to live out the standards of the New Testament there had to be a deeper and wider understanding of God's love, faithfulness, and character in order to tap into His grace to do all that is in His heart. Without an understanding of the grace of God, each of these disciplines become dead-end streets, works of the flesh instead of works of grace.

We like to say it this way, "We need to know how loved we are so that we can live out of acceptance and not for acceptance." Many people in our midst were running for acceptance, acceptance from God and acceptance from others. It was obvious that we needed to change. I began to make it a habit every time I spoke to talk about the character of God for at least one-third of every message. I share about His character, His love, His affirmation apart from our works, and His grace that enables us to do the will of God and overcome sin so that people can be grounded in their acceptance to do what the Bible commands out of love and not for performance.

Ultimately, it had to be God that transformed and led us. We are committed to disciplining our lives before Him because we want to see Him work, but that discipline is not the ultimate answer. God Himself must be enthroned in our hearts 24/7. This truth is something that we continue to grow in today.

My heart still hurts for the people who were wounded during those early days. Our immaturity and lack of discernment about what people really needed in order to run this race caused most of the pain. We began to realize how overwhelming it can be to walk this journey without being fully established in God's grace. We needed to change, adapt, and adjust so that all of this would be moved and empowered by grace alone.

God provided all the right people to help us through our administrative crisis, and He also provided a place for us to work. Highland graciously gave our staff a house to be our office, and we sectioned off old bedrooms into cubicles. With a staff and an office, we began to take on challenges of communicating with people all over the world. There was so much to learn and do, organize and plan. It was a real challenge!

For example, in 1992 we sent out our first church-planting team of two single guys and two single girls to Ulan-Ude. A YWAM chartered flight dropped them off with all their luggage and only a phone number of a contact we had met. Over the next two weeks, they moved nine times to different apartments around the city, trying to find two places to rent, one for the guys and one for the girls.

Toward the end of those two weeks, I got a phone call from the team leader, Ben Cox. We were literally screaming at each other on the phone because the connection was so bad.

I heard him scream, "Jimmy, you're not going to like this!"

"Not like what, Ben?!" I screamed back.

"They put us in one apartment. We are all living in only one apartment." (Again, this was two single girls and two single guys).

I wasn't worried about any of them morally; I was worried about how it appeared. My mind began to race quickly about what to say. Ben was not only apologetic but was trying to find a solution. So, I screamed back, "Ben, whatever you do while you are working this out, don't tell anybody back home!"

As I screamed this over the phone in our small office, the whole church staff heard me. When I walked out a few minutes later, everyone walked out of their offices grinning and asked me, "Don't tell any of us what, Jimmy?" Those were funny times of learning the rhythms of trying to administrate a church plant thousands of miles away during a Siberian winter.

Jon Petersen, a leader at YWAM, came in during this season and observed what we were doing. He pulled me aside and said, "This is the make or break of the organization. Either you learn to administrate what God has given or this thing will implode."

As a staff, we read the book <u>Seven Habits of Highly Effective People</u> to try to get our own lives in order administratively. We looked at procedures and researched other mission organizations like Campus Crusade, YWAM, and the Southern Baptists to see what worked and what didn't. Like a junior high boy, we were growing quickly but were all over the place trying to catch up with our body.

God was moving, and we needed to put procedures and training in place to follow what He was doing and take care of our family that was spreading around the world. Our goal was never to become so bureaucratic and centralized that we stifled the life of God. Instead, we looked at it like this: to run a family, there are certain disciplines and processes in place to raise and develop the children into all that they are called to be, eventually becoming parents themselves. We can't be totally non-administrative and undisciplined if we want to see our people grow and have all that they need.

Growing in every area, both internally and externally, we were learning lessons on how to walk in the grace and love of God. In the midst of this intense zeal to pioneer new areas and develop an organization, we experienced God in very practical ways as He walked us through every challenge so that we could do all that He was calling us to do.

Chapter 11

Foundation to Growth II
1992-1997

"If we are faithless, He remains faithful, for He cannot deny Himself."
2 Timothy 2:13

Several years ago, I had a conversation with a man who was a part of leading a movement in England. When I asked him some of the lessons he had learned, one thing he told me was that the health of the local church body directly affected the health of the church plants and what was happening around the world.

"When we were doing well," he explained, "they were doing well. When we were waning, they were waning."

Because God had called us to do local church-based missions, the local will always be tied to those we have been sent out. Because we are family, it is so important that we remain healthy, life giving, innovative, changing and growing all the time. Looking back to the Isaiah 54:2-3 passage, we wanted to make sure that as we lengthened our cords, we also strengthened our pegs. As we expanded our reach around the world in the 1990s, our home needed to be strong and secure enough to withstand all the growing and changing that was stretching us to our limits.

Growth in Discipleship
1992-1997

In the mid-1980s, I spent a year as a college student involved in Campus Crusade for Christ. I remember hearing Bill Bright talk about the exponential power of discipleship: if three will invest in three who will invest in three, then it would only take 20 years for the whole world to hear the gospel and have the opportunity to be discipled. Challenged by the truth of his statement, I started the process of meeting with three guys. Even though none of us knew what God wanted from our time together, at least we were meeting. By the mid-1990s, this simple step of obedience had led to a lifestyle of meeting with 10-15 guys a week, believing that those investments were the best way for me to be a part of impacting the world.

Discipleship was the foundation for everything we had started in 1987 and continues to be a major part of everything we do today. But as things got bigger through our years of growth, we discovered that our discipleship process needed some refinement. People were still doing Lifegroups and discipling the best they knew how, but we needed a fresh infusion.

At that time, we were blessed to have our friend Mark Masterson join us. Before Mark came to us, he already had a passion for evangelism and discipleship. With us, he continued to work out that which God was already doing so wonderfully in his life. In one meeting, we were talking about our need for new Lifegroup leaders, and Mark said something that really convinced me that something

Mark Masterson Sharing the Gospel in the Philippines

needed to change. "I don't think we have a leadership problem. We have a discipleship problem. Whenever we don't have enough leaders, it means we are not discipling thoroughly and well enough."

Mark introduced us to two books: The Master Plan of Evangelism and The Master Plan of Discipleship, both by Robert Coleman. While we had always focused on discipleship, these resources helped us reshape and clarify some of our thoughts. When God reveals a truth, there are always multi-levels to that truth, and so there is always a need to grow and develop even in the things God has already revealed so that they do not grow stagnant and begin to lose ground.

Mark not only encouraged us and helped us get clarity, but he also led by example. He and Amy (Hamilton) Tarter, along with Noel Tarter and Pete and Jennifer Leininger, began focusing their Lifegroups specifically on discipling young men and women. Out of their initial investment and their commitment to teaching discipleship, as well as modeling it, we saw a whole new wave of leaders emerge, many who are planting churches and leading our local ministries today. These young leaders, along with so many others, partnered with us during those days to lead, disciple, and reproduce their lives. I could list names for days of people all around the world whose lives have been influenced and impacted as a direct result of this season of discipleship.

In 2 Timothy 2:2, Paul admonishes Timothy, "The things which you have heard from me in the presence of many witnesses, entrust these to faithful men who will be able to teach others also." This is the way God's Kingdom has always worked: life on life, people investing in people for the glory of God. Antioch is a collection of strong discipleship relationships, not just one or two people, but hundreds who have invested in each other purposefully and intentionally. Over the years, this type of community has created a sense of family and maturity even among the young college students.

Early on, I knew that it would take all the giftings that the Scripture spoke about if we were to become the people that God called us to be. But one thing we have taught our people is that no matter what your gifting is, God has called us all to be abandoned to Him. Everybody should be earnestly seeking Jesus every day. No matter what our

Early College Leaders: Brian Bundy, Robert Fuller, Robert Herber

calling, all of us should be involved in discipleship. No matter how we serve, all of us should be involved in evangelism. All of us should be leading holy and sacrificial lives.

As we saw leaders emerge from our accounting department, administrative positions, pastoral roles, children's ministry, and worship ministry, we kept the same standards for everyone. All of us would live out the basic values of the Kingdom: loving God, discipleship, evangelism, being men and women of prayer, and living intentionally in the context of community. We didn't want anyone, from a secretary to a bass player on stage, not being a fully devoted follower of Christ who was involved in our community. Keeping these standards has allowed us all to be of one heart and mind together. These truths mark us and drive us, and it is through discipleship relationships that we will see these truths reproduced and lived out in generation after generation of new disciples.

Growth in Pursuing God
1992-1997

From the very beginning, prayer has been the centerpiece of everything that we do. Throughout our times with the training schools and the college, we would call everyone to three and five day fasts. Sometimes, we would spend 24 hours a day, seven days a week taking shifts praying and crying out to God. Often, a cluster of Lifegroups hosts half nights or whole nights of prayer. Every year in January, we challenge the training school students to fast longer than they ever have before. This has led many of us into doing 40-day fasts where we find that God is able to do more than we ever thought or imagined in the area of finding grace to fast and pray.

In the early days, Kurt Mahler led us in establishing *Prayer for the Nations,* a place where individuals and groups pray for different nations around the earth. Eventually, as we sent out more church plants, we developed what are called Prayer Shields. These start out with individuals or couples who have a heart for a nation. They gather others to pray with them, and when a team goes to that nation to plant a church, they leave a Prayer Shield in place to cover them. Many of these Prayer Shields are still around today, where people are covered in prayer by home base and are also learning how to pray on the field.

Jesus says we should always pray and not lose heart (Luke 18:1), that if we will ask, we will receive (John 16:24). He has called us to be a house of prayer for all nations. In Isaiah 56:7, God says, "....My house will be called a house of prayer for all the peoples." Our delight and desire is to continue to have a 24-hour prayer room that fuels what is happening around the earth. Some of our most dynamic gatherings are not just preaching and teaching times but corporate gatherings at the end of prayer and fasts.

Before the days of growth during the 1990s, we were already established in prayer, but we found that becoming even more established would give us endurance through the challenges to continue to propel the movement forward. Even today, prayer is the centerpiece for everything that we do because we know that none of this is possible without the power of the Lord.

Also, out of our desire to love God, extravagant worship has always been a part of who we are. Worship had to become practical so that it could flow through the whole fellowship. To help people lead worship in their Lifegroups, we offered classes and resources such as teaching basic guitar. We like to look back and joke about the time when we counted around 300 people in our midst who could play G, C and D on a guitar to lead their Lifegroups in worship.

William Whittenberg on Outreach in Amsterdam

Marcus Mohon and William Whittenberg were instrumental in this process by helping us go from one acoustic guitar to several bands serving at different gatherings. William and others also began to write songs that captured the heart of what God was doing among us. As more worship leaders began to emerge, William invested in them. He spent time with James Mark Gulley, a young man who carried our heart and values. Even as a 17-year-old, James Mark led some of our Sunday night gatherings. When God led William and his wife Sheila to be a part of the church-planting team in

Germany, James Mark became our worship leader. Today, he continues to lead us into new places of intimacy with God.

Beyond expressing our worship through singing and instruments, Dorothy Abshire had a gifting and passion to see the arts emerge.

James Mark Gulley at an Early World Mandate

Under her leadership and encouragement, people started to write dramas and dances. As expressions of worship, the creative arts began to impact what we were doing around the world. This initial stirring in Dorothy's heart became the catalyst for raising up hundreds of creative people in our midst who tapped into their gifts for God's glory in the nations.

These elements of prayer, worship, and expression can never be underestimated. Our people are intercessors and worshippers who seek God wholeheartedly, and they multiply that passion all over the world. Whenever I travel to visit our church plants, I find nationals who passionately worship God and lead lives of intercession, all because of passionate men and women who have led us and taught us how to pursue God better through the years.

Growth in Ministry
1992-1997

In 1995, Highland asked me to be the Pastor of Ministries. What was happening among our students and single adults, the church wanted to see happen throughout the entire body. So, as Antioch Ministries International, Antioch Training School, and the college group grew, I began to serve the families of the church. We organized and guided the adults into doing Lifegroups that could multiply.

The first year that Lifegroups were up and running in the whole church, we saw incredible numbers of people saved and baptized. It was awesome. But this new growth also challenged the structures and relationships in our staff. It seemed that at every turn where we saw new developments and growth happening, new challenges inevitably came too.

Also, setting up Antioch Ministries International helped us invest more in the inner city. People stepped up to raise support and help develop our Backyard Bible Clubs, tutoring programs, and ministry to hurting kids in the inner city. In the early days, Kim Cutler, Angela Adams, and Robin Fink led us in these ministries by sacrificing their time, energy, and lives. Through the years, many people came to the Lord and were transformed.

A while back, I was in a local convenience store when a girl smiled at me and said, "Mr. Jimmy, is that you?"

"Yes, that's my name," I replied to her. "I'm sorry, I don't know you."

"My name is Shaunte. Don't you remember me? You used to come pick me up when I was about 5 years old until I was about 9 or 10. I'll never forget those days of you and Laura loving me and sharing Jesus with me. We moved away and then came back. I had a challenging high school time, but today I am serving Jesus and involved in a church here in town. I'm so excited for what God is doing in my life, and I just wanted to say thank you for investing in me. I'll never forget those early days. It helped me so much in my walk with Jesus later, during difficult times, to remember that He is always near."

There are so many stories like Shaunte's of investing in people and watching God carry them through even the most difficult circumstances, bearing amazing fruit in their lives years later. In the end, if we are not faithful in the things that God puts before us – loving people, sharing Christ, and investing in the neighborhood He has placed us in – then I don't think we will be effective in the other places God sends us. That is why we have always emphasized that local ministry is as important as anything we do around the world.

At Highland, our journey of sharing Jesus with our city started out by identifying 350 homes nearby. We would go door-to-door sharing the gospel, praying for the sick, encouraging people, and starting Backyard Bible clubs with kids. When word got out that we were a church who loved our neighbors, people started seeking our help. We eventually saw so many benevolent needs coming through our door that we started the Care Center, an outreach that allowed us to provide food, clothing, and counseling for those in need. While many times we were able to give financial assistance, our goal was always to help people find long-term solutions through counseling and personal care.

Our heart is not to be a church with missionaries but to be a church with a mission. Still today, at our core, we want to be driven by the purposes of Jesus, whether we are at home or in a foreign culture. Focusing energy, love, and attention on our neighbors here in Waco is our heart's investment in what God has placed before us. Even as we aggressively send people around the world, we desire first to go to our neighbors.

Growth Through the Gospel
1992-1997

Getting more involved in the city also gave us more of a heart for the lost. Many times, after our Sunday night service, students would go out spontaneously in evangelistic teams and hit parties around town. They would stand up in the middle of the crowd, get everyone's attention, and preach the gospel. After they shared, they would make themselves available to anyone who wanted to talk.

At one of these parties, a guy named Kyle was listening. In his younger years, he had been in church. But as a teenager and college student, Kyle had fallen away from his faith. When our guys showed up at the party, Kyle was amazed that they were actually sharing the gospel and that they actually believed what they were saying. His heart was drawn. Our guys stayed late into the night talking to Kyle. Before the night was over, he gave his life to Christ and poured his drugs down the toilet, choosing absolute surrender and freedom with the Lord.

The next Sunday, Kyle came to be baptized. He shared his testimony before the congregation, and then I baptized him. Just as I was bringing him up out of the water, a man on the back row stood up and shouted over hundreds of people, "My son was dead, but now he is alive!" Kyle's father, who had also not been to church in a long while, had slipped into the back of the church. Seeing the power and grace of God, he couldn't help but stand up and shout. The place erupted with rejoicing as we celebrated the power of new life.

In those days, we were seeing people saved daily. We actually went for months where someone was saved every day. Acts 2 talks about people being added to the church daily, and this Acts 2 experience was dynamic and powerful. It was the outflow of the revival we had seen in the years prior. God doesn't want us simply to enjoy the blessings He gives, but He wants us to pour those blessings out to people who desperately need Him.

Growth in the Seibert Family
1992-2007

Even as we were growing as a movement, the Seiberts were growing as a family. Laura and I had our second daughter, Lauren, in 1992, and Caleb came along in 1994. In 1997, we had a miscarriage before our final blessing, Daniel, came in 1998.

There are so many lessons that we learn from being a family that carry over into being part of our extended spiritual family. One of the biggest lessons we have taught our kids along the way is how to obey. From the youngest days, when Abby was only two and a half, we have had

The Seiberts in 2006

daily family devotions in the morning. A common question we would ask them when they were young was, "How do we obey?" Abby, and every child since has responded, "Cheerfully, quickly, and completely." Then we ask them, "Why?" And they respond, "Because when we learn how to obey Mommy and Daddy, then we will learn to obey Jesus, and life will go well."

Laura and I have always told our kids, "The reason you want to obey cheerfully, quickly, and completely is so that you don't turn out like Mommy and Daddy." Laura and I have realized that many of the hang-ups and issues that we continue to work through are related to the areas that we didn't allow Jesus and His Word to rule and reign completely in our lives. We want our children to learn how to follow Him wholeheartedly as early in life as possible. It has been a delight to see our children grow, develop, and learn, not only in response to us, but ultimately to their heavenly Father.

Through the years, our kids have been involved in everything that we have done, from believing God for finances to sharing the gospel to going on mission trips around the world. They have been able to live in the Kingdom and therefore have not been caught up in the normal world of American expectations and life. Laura was diligent to home-school them in their early years, and we put them in private school later on. These years of establishing our own family gave us the impetus to focus and strengthen marriages and families in our church community.

We, as parents, have purposed to do our best to include them on this journey we have taken, with the hope that they would see opportunities to believe for more than we ever imagined. As we are now looking to send our first daughter away to college, I can honestly say that Laura and I have many wonderful memories and blessings and few regrets.

It has been a great blessing to raise our children among people who radically pursue Jesus. A particular blessing was having people live with us. For 17 of our 20 years of marriage, almost all of our kids' growing up years, the men and women living in our home became part of our family as they invested love and care into our children and had a high impact on their lives.

With the challenges of a growing movement, travel, and the expectations of the ministry, there were many times of stress and strain on our family along the way. Laura and I, over and over, had to evaluate how we should partner together so that our family would be first in the long line of needs around us. I am so thankful for Laura, who has always chosen the kids and family first. Her tireless commitment to disciple, encourage, and strengthen our children in the midst of the journey has already been, and will continue to be, rewarded as we see our children walking with Jesus and loving Him with all their hearts.

Through the child raising process, we learned how to prioritize our schedules. The key was to live out of a sense of these simple priorities: the first face we see every day is Jesus; then next would be each other, to talk and pray about the day; finally, we would be committed to family devotions. Also, one night a week is family night, and one night a week is date night for Laura and me. These rhythms and patterns have served us well.

We had great counsel along with way from some dear friends that were a part of a similar ministry. They told us that the greatest memories for their family came from vacations together. As the years went on, we too made room for family vacations. These have been places of recommitment to one another and God's purposes in our lives. We have also taken these times together as opportunities to learn how to minister together and to share Christ. One of the fun things that we have done on our long drives together has been to break up into teams of two to hand out tracts and share the gospel along the way. We have been with all of our kids when they led their first person to the Lord.

Through the years, standing side-by-side with our kids, seeing them share their testimony, preaching the gospel, doing dances and dramas, and being able to teach the Word of God have been the most rewarding experiences of Laura's and my life. We often say, when we think about the years of our kids growing up, we are thankful for every decision that we made, but we will always want more time with them.

I am so thankful that Laura and the kids know that they are my greatest joy. I would rather be at home strengthening and nurturing them than anywhere else. Even as God has given our family this great joy of serving our spiritual family, we still strive to make our family a priority because we believe that this is our first place of service.

Growth Through Families
1992-2007

As the student ministry grew during this season and so many lives were transformed in our midst, we began to see how the students' families were affected as well. Over and over again, parents and siblings have been impacted by what happens in their child's or sibling's life. When the students go back home and share what God is doing, He begins to restore and heal their families. Sometimes family members even move to Waco to join us or to find a place of service in missions.

Pat Murphy, one father who ended up partnering with us because of what he saw God do in his daughter's life, shares his story here:

My wife Tanya and I both graduated from Baylor and all three of our kids went there too. Our daughter Brooke came to school unsaved. She didn't know Jesus and was walking far from the Lord. In high school, she had rejected God and the church because she said it had no relevance in her life, and she didn't see anything very real there. The sad part is that she was pretty accurate, though we thought we had a great church at the time.

So, she came to Baylor as a rebellious pothead. Early in her freshmen year, she just started crying out to God because she was so miserable. God met her one night when she cried out to Him, 'If You are real, You have to show me.' Well, He did show her, and she broke down and surrendered her life, 'God You are real. I'm not making things work by myself, I'll let You do it.' She went from darkness to light. It was the kind of powerful, radical transformation that only God can do.

As Brooke told my wife and me about it, we were in Kansas City praying that this was real and would last, because 18- year-old kids can run very hot and cold, going through phases and swings of emotions that are extreme. Two months later, she came home from college, and she knew God better than we did! We had been "walking with God" for 40 years, and in just two months, she had passed us up. It was one of those shocking, sobering wake up calls, and very confusing because we didn't know how it could be possible. The personal, intimate relationship she had with God was something I had talked about my whole adult life but never really had.

We started looking into Antioch and heard that it was a crazy church. The next time we were in Waco to see our kids, we went to visit. What we saw was not a crazy church but a whole lot of people who unashamedly loved God and had a real and dynamic relationship with God that we didn't have. We just fell in love with them.

Brooke was discipled in the college ministry, and people really walked with her through her junk and did all of the things that very seldom happen in community. It is talked about a lot and is needed like crazy, but it is hard to do. The kids and leaders here are willing to do it. It dramatically transformed her through the power of the Holy Spirit.

The more Tanya and I got to know the people, we felt drawn to what God was doing here. I had worked in business for 25 years, but God allowed me to have enough dissatisfaction for what I was doing that I would leave where I was. I took a position at Baylor thinking that just living and working in Waco was the next step God had planned for us.

Then, Jimmy talked to us about coming to work for Antioch to do development. It was kind of a shock, and initially we said we didn't feel it was the right time. When we were in business, we were the typical affluent family. We had a couple of houses, kids in private school, good income... The thought of leaving that nice life, well, we had never even thought about it. I wanted to leave the pressure and misery of business behind but keep my nice life too.

A few months later, we went on the Juarez college trip because our younger daughter really wanted us to go. What we saw was astounding; not just the power of God, but the support structure in the college ministry was powerful as well. The leadership model was incredible. Our team leader was 24, and we had a team of 70 people. I had just come from 26 years in business and professional life, and I was wondering what this kid was going to try to do. A couple of days later, though, I was thinking, 'I could really learn from this kid, and I would follow him against the gates of hell.' I was very taken by it all.

A few weeks later, we decided to leave Baylor for another business opportunity. I called Jimmy and asked if we could do the development work part time. He said no. I had heard that Antioch paid in a unique way, and I asked him how that worked. He said, 'Well, it's not a lot, but we have great benefits. The god of money is the most worshipped god in this country, and we just don't want to be anywhere near that. We have people all over the world living on very little. We don't want to be living fat and happy when they are living very meager, simple lives and are really laying their lives down.'

When he told me how much they pay, I thought, 'Yeah, that's not very much.' Jimmy said, 'We want to meet your needs, but we want you to trust God for your wants.'

'OK, then, tell me about retirement?' I asked.

'That's kind of a want,' Jimmy responded.

Having just come from a professional career where people's entire focus is to be financially independent, free to travel, and do whatever, I suddenly realized all of that is a want and not a need.

Early that next morning at about 2:00 a.m., Tanya was tossing and turning, and I finally woke up and asked her what was going on. She told me that she was really drawn to come to work at Antioch like I was, but she too was feeling the death of a dream to be able to keep our house in Colorado, travel to Europe, take our grandkids wherever they wanted to go ... At about 6:30 that morning, she said, 'If we do anything else, then we are going to miss what God has for us.'

We didn't know how it would work, but I called Jimmy and told him that we were in. It has been awesome. God has provided in wonderful ways. We don't have our house in Colorado, but we have access to one and don't have to pay for it. We went through the training school with Brooke, and she went to Morocco for a year. Her life and our whole family have been incredibly shaped and marked by the people here.

If God is moving in people's lives, it will affect their families. Many of the parents near retirement age have moved to Waco to live and work with us and are major contributors to our movement. This really is a family thing, not just in the Spirit, but in our daily lives.

1992-1997 were definitely years of growth as we trusted God through the challenges and rejoiced in His faithfulness to us. In those five years, we grew from one church plant to eight. We started with no official staff and ended up overseeing about 35 people. We started a mission agency. The influence of the movement began to spread through families and around the world. Laura and I turned over responsibility of the training school, led a college ministry of several hundred people, and became the pastor of ministries at the church. At the same time, we had two more children and even brought a dog into our home. It was, in the words of Charles Dickens, "the best of times and the worst of times."

Hopefully these stories of struggles and victories will encourage you as you grow. There are great seasons of glory, but there are also great places of pain. During both of these, we have found God faithful.

We continued to persevere with the vision even when we thought it was all going to fall apart. When staff would turn and leave, when people would falsely accuse us, when challenging situations that we didn't know how to cope with came up, we found God to be faithful over and over again.

I'm so glad He had already given us the promises of Isaiah 54. From the beginning, it was His promise and initiative and not our own. He was moving us, growing us, and leading us into His great desires and adventures for our lives.

Chapter 12

Growth towards Maturity 1997-2002

*"Then the cloud covered the tent of meeting,
and the glory of the LORD filled the tabernacle."
Exodus 40:34*

God's wisdom is amazing; He sovereignly places each of us into particular families, and He uses our experiences to shape and form who we are.

God wisely placed Laura and me under the care of Highland Baptist Church to grow and mature. Being young, zealous and energetic, we needed older, wiser men and women to counsel and shape us into who we needed to become. Our mothers and fathers at Highland encouraged us to live out our dreams and provided a haven of protection to help us to mature.

Highland Baptist Church – Sent Out
1997-1999

As in most family situations, children grow up, reach adulthood, and become mothers and fathers themselves. Laura and I were not only growing naturally, having our third and fourth children, but the training school was growing, and we were sending out more church plants around the world.

Highland was supportive, encouraging, and empowering in a thousand different ways during these growing years, but by 1997 we came to a time when particular nuances of our philosophy and vision differed from the leadership at Highland. Highland comes from a wonderfully rich history of supporting missions of all types, not just church planting, and they had a variety of equipping opportunities. Though they had given us complete liberty to develop Lifegroups within the whole church, as well as champion mission causes around the world, their focus remained much broader.

The elders at Highland, under the leadership of Barry Camp, were both patient and kind with Laura, me, and our leadership team as we began to work through our differences. We were all committed to do everything we could to work things out together. Many hours of discussion and communication about what would be best eventually led to a decision in the spring of 1999: Highland would send us out to plant our own fellowship, a community that is now called Antioch Community Church.

This was a hard decision for all of us. Through Barry Camp's humble leadership and the willingness of the elders at Highland to support the vision God had given us, we were blessed by a peaceful and joyful release. Barry and I both shared our hearts about the different visions God had for the two churches, and when we announced to the congregation in April of 1999 that Highland was sending us out, they communicated their heart to release us with tremendous blessing. In fact, Barry told the entire staff and congregation that they were welcome to go with the new church plant if they wanted.

Highland not only released us, but they also continued to support Antioch Ministries International missionaries and encouraged the staff and others who felt led to go with us. Though it was not perfect, we were all committed to moving forward with what we knew was God's leadership.

About 400 people came to our first Sunday meeting as Antioch Community Church on June 6, 1999. Before we left Highland, they were averaging about 1,300 on Sunday mornings. Over the next few years, not only did Highland recoup that 1,300 but it continued to grow. Today, both churches average between 1,800 and 2,000 members. The Kingdom literally multiplied in Waco, and I believe it was because of the commitment to communication, blessing, and encouraging one another. We are forever grateful for our mothers and fathers at Highland for the way they raised us and released us. We are who we are because of Highland, its leaders, and its people. This was a big win for the Kingdom of God.

Antioch Community Church – Pilgrims
1999-2000

For the first several months as a new church plant, we met all around the city of Waco. We were sojourners, pilgrims in our own city, wandering and looking for a place to land. During the week, Lifegroups gathered in homes. Then on Sundays we met in all kinds of places from the convention center to a local theater to the fairgrounds.

Our first meeting place was in the exhibit hall in the Heart of Texas Fairgrounds (H.O.T.). On Saturday nights, there were usually parties at the H.O.T., so on Sunday mornings we would come into the wonderful aroma of beer and cigarettes lingering from the night before. Sometimes there would be a funky backdrop left over from a wedding reception or other party, but we would just clean up and then set up.

Traveling around so much made us a volunteer-driven church. It took more than thirty volunteers each week to load the trailer, unpack it, set up the venue, take care of the kids, and tear everything down in the end. Those volunteers not only made church happen on Sundays but really carried the values of who we were around in their hearts and practically lived them out. Though sometimes this process felt unstable, having to rely so heavily on God and one another really forced us to be a people who lived out the things we said we believed.

One particular Sunday, after we had outgrown the H.O.T., we met at a place called Melody Ranch, a local country and western bar. It was a lot of fun, and we felt right at home walking into the smells that came with meeting in a bar. In weeks past, we had used a six-foot horse trough for baptism. We just took it with us wherever we met, filled it with water, and baptized people in it. The guy at Melody Ranch told me that instead of bringing our own, we could use the horse trough they used for beer. What he failed to tell us was that it was only a four-foot trough and not a six-foot one like ours.

Several people wanted to be baptized that morning at Melody Ranch, including a local anesthesiologist. When he had invited his family to witness him testify of the goodness of the Lord, he did not know that we would be meeting at Melody Ranch. His family had not come from an Antioch-style background; they were more of a formal bunch. There, on the back row, in coat and tie, they watched as I literally stuffed this grown man into a four-foot trough. He was a great sport, testifying of what the Lord had done for him. It was hilarious and joy-filled, and I think even the doctor enjoyed it.

Somehow, the local newspaper heard about our crazy church and sent a reporter to do a story about us. She was at Melody Ranch the morning of the four-foot horse trough baptisms. It just so happened that we were sharing our vision that morning: we want to be everyday, normal people who live out the simple things of the Kingdom with all of our hearts. We explained that if we will just do that, we could change the world.

Her article, "Everyday Walk with God," landed on the front page of the paper. She did a great job capturing our heart. For us, it seemed like a prophetic message to our city that expressed our desire to be a simple community that walks every day with Jesus, serving a big God. The irony was that the reporter was not a believer at the time. God used her to get our message out to our city even though she didn't agree with us. Eventually, she joined our church and began loving Jesus with all of her heart.

'Everyday walk with God'

Fast-growing Waco congregation on the move — literally

By MARLA PIERSON
Tribune-Herald staff writer

The Rev. Jimmy Seibert of Antioch Community Church stood before the stage at Melody Ranch looking over the nearly 1,000 people who came to worship last Sunday morning in a cowboy hat.

In front of him, a Melody Ranch horse trough that holds beer for the club was instead filled with water for a baptism.

"This is what it's all about," Seibert said before baptizing in the name of the "father, son and holy ghost."

Indeed Antioch Community Church — a non-denominational congregation that grew out of Highland Baptist Church last summer — holds missions and evangelism high.

Seibert, 35, joked Sunday that the booming congregation was trying to be traditional — "We started a tradition of baptizing in horse troughs."

The contemporary music seems to belie that statement. And the movable congregation meets for worship not in a sanctuary, but in spots ranging from the Waco Hippodrome Theatre and the Waco Convention Center to Melody Ranch.

Yet the core of the church is

Staff photo — Kelly Lemons

Baylor student Elizabeth Horton (left) and McLennan Community College student Christina Fyke raise their hands while singing praise songs at Melody Ranch during a Sunday service for Antioch Community Church.

SANCTUARIES FOR THE SPIRIT

In a series of occasional stories, Tribune-Herald reporter Marla Pierson will profile the churches, fellowships and temples where Central Texans explore the spirit and define their values.

cell or life groups that meet weekly in homes — a model members say harkens back to small gatherings of the New Testament church.

"Our Sundays are just times of celebration or vision but not really the make or break of everything," Seibert said. "We really emphasize what's happening in the small groups as the core of our church.

So while there were 973 in worship last Sunday, in the preceding week 950 participated.

See CHURCH, Section Back

Since we floated from place to place each week, Lifegroups became even more vital to our church's communication and structure. The Sunday morning gathering place was announced each week through our Lifegroup leaders, so people had to be connected to a small group to find our Sunday morning services. In those first two or three years, more people met in Lifegroups than on Sunday mornings. It was a God-ordained time. We had long desired to see people established in house-to-house ministry. It motivated us to learn how to do an even better job of facilitating these cell groups. As these groups matured, we saw the church multiply and reproduce in our city, not through a corporate gathering, but through individuals reproducing the life of Jesus.

Antioch Community Church – Building 1999-2000

Even before we started roaming the city, we knew that we had a long-term commitment to Waco and began to seek God about whether we should own a building or just rent one. During that time, I met with a man who had helped start one of the most significant movements in Great Britain. As his church had grown and developed, they found that they needed a "mother ship," a place for people to come home to, a place that didn't change. When their lease had come up in their rented facilities, they were scattered, and it affected their people who were coming and going around the world. His encouragement to me was to put down permanent roots to commit to our city, much like someone buys a house or a cemetery plot.

After considering this advice and praying through the decision, we decided to purchase property that would both establish us in Waco and be a home base for people to come and go from.

As we began to look around, our heart was drawn to the inner city. We work with the poor around the world, and because we want to do church in such a way that it can be reproduced in the nations, we wanted to put ourselves in a multi-cultural situation at home. We found a building, an old grocery store and cafeteria connected together – 36,000 square feet of dirty, rodent infested warehouse with a collapsing ceiling. When we inquired about the place, we learned that though it had not been officially inhabited in ten years, prostitutes and drug addicts were living in it at the time. What a great place to start.

We needed $150,000 to purchase the building. Two or three times a week, 120 of us gathered to pray and seek the Lord about how to see this come to pass. We were committed to not going into debt. If we were going to buy anything, we would pay cash. As different groups gathered, we asked everyone to pray and give towards that end.

By midnight of the day that the money was needed, we had $152,000 to begin this great journey.

Across the street from our newly owned building, a couple of our friends employed in real estate bought an old house for us to use as office space. It was a real beauty. The years of chipped paint made the walls multi-colored. The cracked windows made for nice air-conditioning in the winter, and the rats running through provided ample distraction as we tried to work. It was a great place to start the process of seeing God's work established in and through us.

Buying the building was just the first step in establishing ourselves in Waco. The huge task of renovating lay ahead of us. It wasn't much to look at, dilapidated inside and out, but the structure was strong. To start work on this old building, we knew that it would really help to have the architectural drawings so that we could see the structural layout. The last company to own the property was the HEB Corporation, a grocery store chain in Texas. When we called the records department to get the drawings, they told us that they had shredded everything pre-1990. They asked us which particular building we were looking for, and we told them that it was a structure built in Waco in 1960.

The man on the phone said, "Oh, you won't believe it, but I am from Waco. I thought this particular building was so interesting that I took the drawings and threw them up on the top rack. I think I still have them right here." Isn't it sovereign that when other things were being shredded, God knew we would need those drawings, and He had them set aside just for us? He is so good.

The church family stepped up with volunteers doing a lot of the work on the building. People sacrificed a tremendous amount of time and energy to clear it out and get it ready for the renovation. Every once in a while, we conducted a service in the parking lot to encourage everyone through the process. We based our initial fund raising service on the Exodus 35 concept. When it was time to build the tabernacle, God told the children of Israel to give whatever they had to the cause: jewelry, wood, fabric, anything. We asked our people to do the same; give what you have.

The day of the parking lot service, we set out tables for people to place their gifts on. It was amazing to watch. People brought TVs, fur coats, diamond rings, computers, furniture…you name it, they brought it. Even those who didn't have financial resources brought what they had. That morning, we took up $294,000 in cash and miscellaneous items that we either used or sold to begin our journey of restoring the building debt-free.

With the building cleared out and a financial foundation laid, we were ready to get going on the actual work of rebuilding. I approached a contractor who had been coming to our church and wanted to give back in some way. I said, "Jerry, what I need is somebody to take the bull by the horns to move this thing forward." Wow, he was just the man to do it. Jerry Dyer jumped in with both feet along with our foreman, Don Birchum, and things started moving quickly. I told Jerry, "You just keep pushing forward, and I will take care of believing God for the money with our people."

What a journey that was. We felt like we were putting a 747 together in flight. There were many challenging days because we had committed to staying debt-free and paying every vendor when the bills were due. To make that happen, we decided to abandon our church operations budget and just use the money in our account each day to pay whatever needed to be paid, whether salaries or contractors.

There were several times when we called the staff together and asked who needed their paycheck that day and who could live without it for a while. We would ask them to write their answers on a piece of paper, and all around the room, people would respond with a silent "yes" or "no." The only people who saw those responses were our administrators who had to get the checks out. I am blown away at the kind of people we had; they were willing to sacrifice what they were rightfully owed for this journey.

In July of 2000, we realized that we were spending about $1,500-$2,000 a week renting space to meet on Sundays. We had already met in the parking lot for motivational services, so we thought it was a good idea to just meet there every week. It would save money that could go towards our goal of restoring the property debt-free.

Sunday morning services in the parking lot were awesome. Because we didn't have money for chairs, we asked people to bring their own. People carried lawn chairs in the back of their cars, and our college students showed up each week with couches, recliners, and even park benches. We used to call it the "Lawn Chair Convention." On a trailer in the back of the crowd, we provided water and sunscreen in the summer and hot chocolate and coffee in the winter. On the mornings that it rained, we would pray and ask Jesus to stop the rain for us. I can't tell you how many times it would stop just in time to start the service and then start up again as soon as we were done packing up after the service.

One day, though, it started to pour right in the middle of my sermon. I wondered what would happen to the crowd. Some people just popped up their umbrellas and stayed where they were while others ran under the awning at the front of the building. Everyone stayed through the end of the service. I stood in the rain getting poured on, but the crowd stayed with me all the way. It was awesome! That morning, we prayed for people and some even got saved. It was amazing to see a people who were so abandoned to Jesus that they would do anything to be in the presence of the Lord and with the people of God.

The "Lawn Chair Convention"

When I look at Acts 2:42-47, I see a church that met daily in the temple and from house to house, breaking their bread together and sharing their lives. This journey for Antioch Community Church was about all of us together, sharing our lives, sacrificing for one another, and working together to see God's divine purpose realized. We look back on those days with incredible joy and fondness for how God laid the foundation of our church in the midst of facilitating the great purposes that He had for us.

Antioch Community Church – Abundant Provision 2001

By December 15, 2000, we were in the building. Not everything was completely finished, but it was at a point that we could meet inside. Things had been moving along, and God had provided so much for us to get to that point. We had honored all of our commitments to all of our builders and did it all debt free. I remember one Sunday, though, in January 2001, when we realized that we needed $150,000 by Monday to pay the next round of bills that were due.

Now, it wasn't like our people hadn't already sacrificed abundantly; they had given so much over the past year. The staff purposed never to pressure them into giving but simply to create an opportunity for people to give and be a part of what was going on. From day one, we knew God would be our provision. If He were leading us to do something, He would bring the money in.

When Sunday came around, I communicated to the church that it was time for a family meeting. I read 2 Corinthians 9:6-8:

Now this I say, he who sows sparingly will also reap sparingly, and he who sows bountifully will also reap bountifully. Each one must do just as he has purposed in his heart, not grudgingly or under compulsion, for God loves a cheerful giver. And God is able to make all grace abound to you, so that always having all sufficiency in everything, you may have an abundance for every good deed...

I told them, "This building will be built out of cheerful giving, not out of coercion...we just want to tell you where we are. We need $150,000 by noon tomorrow. We don't know what to do except to lay on our faces before God between now and Monday morning."

Immediately, people began to give, and that morning we saw $70,000 come in. A businessman ran up to me and said, "Hey, we've got $70,000, and I know where we can get a loan for $80,000. Let me go get it."

"No," I replied. "We have all said, 'God, You are our provision. We will live and die off of what You have spoken to us.' Let's hang in there."

The elders were slated to meet at noon on Monday to assess the situation. All morning, people called and came up to us giving what they had. One guy told me that he had just started a savings account with $1,000 and that he would give it all. Kids brought in piggy banks and emptied them. One family was saving up for a much-needed second vehicle, and they gave their entire savings. Young and old alike brought in change and possessions, everything they had.

When we met at noon, our accountant tallied up all that had been brought in and reported that we had made it. We had $153,000.

We were so excited! We whooped and hollered, celebrating over God's amazing provision. Just as we were about to go tell everybody the good news, I got a phone call. The caller was contacting us on behalf of a foundation in another large city in Texas. A donor had told them to call us at noon to tell us that someone was anonymously donating $100,000! Now, no one knew this at the time, but I had been secretly praying, asking God to provide a $100,000 gift for us. I had heard of such things happening for other organizations, and so I asked God to bring such a miracle to us as well. And He did. After our people had given everything to get us to the amount we needed, God gave us $100,000 more.

I got so excited that I ran over to the building where people were working, many of them unbelievers from other companies, and I told them to stop their work and gather together. "I just wanted to tell you all what God has done for us!" I exclaimed. I told them the story of the miraculous provision of God and then I shouted, "And you're gonna get paid!" We prayed and worshipped together, and I think the workers were a bit overwhelmed. It was a great testimony to them of God's abundant faithfulness to His children.

With the extra $100,000 that had come in, we were able to shoot for the finish line. As in every war, sometimes the last battle is as challenging as the earlier ones. One particular day, we realized we needed $8,000 by the end of the day to pay a vendor. This wasn't just any vendor; it was one of our dear friends who had given us hundreds of volunteer hours. His company needed the money that we owed him by the end of the day.

I got together with the elders and said, "If this doesn't come in by 5:00 p.m., I am going to go sell my truck at the local dealership." The others there were also seeking their hearts to see what they could do to help. We were willing to do anything. After praying together, we felt like we were just supposed to wait and watch God work. At about noon, I locked my office door and got on my face before God, determined to stay there until He provided. The phone in my office rang at about 2:00 p.m. It was the front desk telling me that someone had dropped a check by and that I might want to come see it.

As I walked out and looked at the check, I saw it was for $13,000. A young man had brought his tithe from his signing bonus with a major league baseball team. He had been a student at Baylor, and since we were his church, he felt compelled that particular day not to wait but to go ahead and bring his tithe in. Little did he know that he would be part of an amazing testimony of the Lord's goodness to us. I love how God works, causing us to depend on Him wholeheartedly so that He can glorify Himself by providing for us in the end.

The building was complete in April 2001. Finally, after a year of giving, sacrificing, working, praying, and trusting God for every penny, the Antioch community was able to rejoice together in the building God had provided.

When we moved in that first Sunday, I asked God to give me His word. We had been talking about the glory of God coming upon the temple, and God gave me a picture of the belly of our building bowing out, bursting with a hundred different rivers flowing over the horizon. It seemed to me that God was saying that if we will simply love, honor, and obey Him in this place, then, the people will burst forth and be poured out over this nation and the nations of the earth. In those early years, we began to see this happen as one church plant after another was sent out and our people began to affect our city with the love of Jesus.

To this day, people look back on our first two years as the pilgrim church with extreme fondness. We bonded as a family during that season as God stretched our faith to the limits. I am extremely privileged to have walked with that group during those days.

Antioch Community Church – Establishing Foundations 1999-2002

As with every new venture, there is an opportunity to establish foundations and impart values. At Highland, we had already been a team that carried the same values in our hearts. But when we stepped out in faith into the adventure God had called us to as a church, things began to expand, and there was a need to rally everyone around the vision and purpose that God was laying before us.

Our desire was to help people go from unbeliever to church planter. We would provide equipping, encouragement, and nurturing care along the way so that the lost could be saved, and our people could share the gospel consistently. For the first year of gathering as Antioch Community Church, we taught and reiterated our values so that they would be clear. We asked the questions: *Who is God? What do discipleship and community look like? How do we live out evangelism?* And as we answered them, we began to develop these values in every area of our community.

Ken Lorenz, Becky & David Lockhart - A Few of Our Early Pioneers

In our children's ministry, we asked the workers to pray for God's purposes and plans over even the littlest child. They developed mission trips for kids and got them involved in engaging the community through evangelism and discipleship. Our youth group really embraced our multi-cultural call by beginning to both love and care for both inner city and suburban youth. Our college students became fully integrated into all that we were doing and were not just a separate ministry of the church. Our adults took seriously the call to discipleship and commitment. Together, we began to become a people of common values.

On a leadership level, we structured ourselves with multi-level leadership teams: a senior leadership team (which eventually became our elders), a pastoral leadership team, and an administrative team. Every one of these teams has been consistently filled with people who are willing to do anything for the gospel.

The initial elders in 1999 were Ben Loring, Darrell Atwood, Kevin Johnson, Danny Mulkey, Kely Braswell, and me. Each of these people has been committed to doing whatever was best for the Kingdom.

For example, when ACC started, Danny Mulkey was the International Director for Church Planting. When it became obvious that it was time for change and growth, Danny was the first to suggest that Kevin should take over his position and that he would become our Family Pastor. Every time we gathered, we would ask, "Jesus, would you speak to us about what is best for Your glory and Your people?" God always answered those simple prayers. In 2001, God put it in

Ben's heart to plant a church in Dallas, and we released and blessed him and his wife Ruth to reach out to inner city Dallas. Many times we have had to rearrange our staffing and teams to better facilitate the grace of God. Walking with a people who are not about protecting their position or prominence has made these times joyful.

As we looked at the structure for staffing the church, our desire was to create an environment of equality. No matter what someone's gifting, we wanted to communicate that we were all in this together as a team. So, we adopted a pattern of paying the same base income to everyone on our full-time staff. This is supplemented based on marriage and dependant children. We used the median income of our city as our base income, designed to provide everyone's needs. Our staff would have to pray for their wants.

This element of faith has kept people from wanting to be on our staff simply for a position or salary. It has also kept us out of the hireling system so that we can focus on those people who are truly called to serve with us. This simple structure has kept our hearts honest in believing that everyone on our staff is called to wholehearted service. Whether it is an administrative assistant or one of our pastors, because the base pay is the same, everyone is called to the same sacrifice, even when there is a need to spend extra time or energy. In systems like this, it never works perfectly, but God has blessed and honored the intention of our hearts.

We have always committed to being debt free, not just in our building projects, but in our personal lives as well. Living simply is a value we all share in common. I like what one man said, "However you run your personal checkbook is how you will run the church if given the opportunity."

Also, from the very beginning, we have set aside ten percent of the money raised for our building projects to be used to bless the poor. I've seen God abundantly bless us as we have given away literally thousands of dollars to other ministries, both in our city and around the world. In our missions giving, ninety percent goes towards our own people, and the other ten percent goes to other ministries. We have done this through the years to make sure that we know that God is blessing different people and different types of ministries and to keep our hearts focused on giving and not just on taking care of our own.

One unique opportunity came up a few years ago when a cell phone provider came to us and asked to use part of our parking lot to build a cell tower. As we prayed about it, we felt like God gave us the passage in the Old Testament where it says to leave the corners of the field for the poor (Leviticus 23:22). So, a cell tower sits on the corner of our parking lot. The monthly income that comes from the lease goes toward feeding the homeless at a regular activity we call the Feast.

As we laid out all of these new structures, procedures, and visions before our people in the early days of Antioch, we also carried over other values from our time at Highland. We continued to establish five-day-a-week prayer on the campus and multiple other prayer meetings through the week because we knew that prayer had to be the foundation. Just as we had done before, we hosted neighborhood parties to love the people in the inner city around us. Antioch Training School continued to raise up church-planters, and Antioch Ministries International continued to send them out. In many ways, we just kept walking out the same purposes and plans God had placed in us for the past 15 years.

Those early days were times of putting down roots and foundations. The wisdom of God is always greater than the wisdom of man. We would have rather had a secure place to walk into with all the problems worked out. But God knows that there is something about the journey that allows us all to become more like Him and closer to one another. It takes God and the church to see miracles like these happen. We look back on those days as some of our sweetest times of meeting with God and of needing one another desperately to see the purposes of God fulfilled.

Chapter 13

Prison to Praise
2001

"But in all these things we overwhelmingly
conquer through Him who loved us."
Romans 8:37

God often is preparing us for the future when we don't even realize it. Trials and triumphs are not always ends in themselves, but God's way of getting us ready for bigger things that are coming in the future.

That was exactly what Antioch's journey of coming together in 1999-2001 was. As we laid foundations by sacrificing to complete the building and giving ourselves to become the people of God, He was teaching us how to face trials together. Learning how to pray together, trust together, give together, sacrifice together and hope together, we had no idea that we were about to encounter what would be the greatest challenge and trial we have ever had to confront as a church body. It was in the fires of faith that God equipped us with the tools we would need to believe Him for a miracle.

Afghanistan – Never a Dull Moment
Summer of 2001

After Antioch had officially paid our last bill for the completion of our building in July of 2001, Laura and I went on a little vacation with the kids. As we were heading back to Waco on August 2nd, about twelve hours away from home, we got a phone call from Dawn Manoleas, the administrator for our international work. She told us that

193

the Vice and Virtue Police, a Gestapo-type group that worked for the Taliban in Afghanistan, had imprisoned Heather Mercer and Dayna Curry, two of our missionaries, with eight other international aid workers and 24 Afghanis.

Our mission teams had been working in countries like Afghanistan for several years, so this news wasn't particularly alarming when I first heard it. We were aware that Christians in certain parts of the world who told others about Jesus risked their own safety, but usually with a bit of negotiation, the prisoners can be released. The uniqueness of this particular situation, though, was that the Taliban had been threatening aid workers in Afghanistan for months. They had gone so far as to pass a law stating that if foreigners were caught proselytizing, they would be imprisoned and possibly even executed.

I had just been to Afghanistan a few months prior to visit the team there. For four years they had lived under the Taliban regime. The team leader and his family lived between a Taliban commander and a mullah (an Islamic priest), and over time had developed a good relationship with both of these men. Until that time, the team had successfully navigated difficult circumstances as they ministered to the nationals and shared truth with those who were hungry and open to the gospel. Their hearts were to serve the Afghanis as long as there were people to love and minister to.

When I was with them that summer, we worshipped and prayed together and sensed the presence of the Lord. We discussed the intensity of the concerns among the foreign community, especially for the believers sharing their lives and the gospel. We talked about how we should respond to the Taliban's restrictions and what their daily ministries should look like. In agreement, we decided that no one should try to be a hero, but at the same time, no one should pull back from sharing truth. Because we knew we could trust God to lead us, everyone promised to only share the gospel with nationals when they felt led by the Lord to do so.

I remember hugging Heather, Dayna, and the rest of the team before I left, as we all realized that we might never see one another again. Everyone in the room agreed, though, "Jesus is worthy."

Antioch Community Church – Coming Together
August-November 2001

When I received that initial phone call from Dawn so many things raced through my mind. The first was to call our people to prayer. I didn't want to cause a huge alarm, so I asked Dawn to gather the Lifegroup leaders to intercede for Heather and Dayna. I got back into town late that evening and went straight to the church with my sleeping bag in hand, thinking we might be there two or three days praying for the girls' release. When I arrived at about midnight, the prayer room was already full. After two years of trusting together, our people already knew how to rally around the cause of God. All of the prayer that had gone into the very building they were praying in had prepared them for this challenge. Juleigh (Beckham) Smith, a prophetic singer and intercessor, led us in prayer during this season. She carried Heather and Dayna in her heart and motivated the church to get involved.

Juleigh (Beckham) Smith

During the first few days of Dayna and Heather's imprisonment, we tried to keep the situation out of the press. The State Department was working with the Taliban to negotiate their freedom, and we didn't want to complicate matters by connecting them with our church. As the details began to unfold, though, we realized that this had not just been a random arrest. Mohammed Omar, the leader of the Taliban, had ordered it with at least Osama bin Laden's support, if not his encouragement. The situation was far more serious than we first thought, and we realized that simple negotiation would not be enough to see them released.

There are so many stories I could tell about the miraculous escape of the rest of our team in Afghanistan as well as Heather and Dayna's incredible journey in prison. Perhaps you have read *Prisoners of Hope* by Random House, which chronicles their imprisonment and escape. (We purposely left out their connection with Antioch in that book because of our other workers around the world.) However, I am not going to focus on these stories because I want to take the opportunity here to share Antioch's journey as a people through this challenge.

On the very night Heather and Dayna were arrested, the people at Antioch began to pray around the clock. This prayer continued throughout the entire 104 days they were in prison. From the very beginning, we sought God on how we were to pray for our friends. He gave us hope in a passage from Acts 12:5-17:

So Peter was kept in the prison, but prayer for him was being made fervently by the church to God. On the very night when Herod was about to bring him forward, Peter was sleeping between two soldiers, bound with two chains, and guards in front of the door were watching over the prison. And behold, an angel of the Lord suddenly appeared...saying, 'Get up quickly.' And his chains fell off his hands. And the angel said to him, ...'Wrap your cloak around you and follow me.' ...When they had passed the first and second guard, they came to the iron gate that leads into the city, which opened for them by itself; and they went out and went along one street, and immediately the angel departed from him. ...he went to the house of Mary...where many were gathered together and were praying... Peter continued knocking; and when they had opened the door, they saw him and were amazed. But motioning to them with his hand to be silent, he described to them how the Lord had led him out of the prison.

We clung to this passage over those three and a half months. When doubt crept in, we prayed fervently as the church did for Peter and believed that God could and would deliver Heather and Dayna along with the others in prison.

I and other staff members from our church went to Pakistan to meet with the U.S. Ambassador and State Department as well as care for the team who had escaped the Taliban's raid. Danny Mulkey, our international director at that time, spent ten weeks in Pakistan gathering information and working with whomever necessary to see the girls released.

When the 9/11 tragedy of 2001 occurred, just a few weeks after Heather and Dayna's capture, we realized that there would be immediate ramifications for the eight foreign workers and 24 Afghans being imprisoned for their faith. This was now an international incident with grave consequences. As we grieved with the rest of the country over the loss of 9/11, we also poised ourselves for what lay ahead.

Until that point, press coverage on the situation had been limited. However, after 9/11, we recognized an incredible opportunity to get the story out so that other believers could stand with us in prayer. Soon after, we held our first press conference with reporters from several national papers and the Associated Press to answer questions the media had been asking about the ladies' imprisonment. Our prayer was that they would pick up the story in its purest form so that we could effectively call people to pray for Heather, Dayna, and the nation of Afghanistan. Miraculously, that is exactly what happened.

One key writer worked for the *Austin American-Statesmen*. He was particularly drawn to the story, though he was not a believer, and the paper he wrote for was not particularly conservative. However, he considered himself to be a spiritual man and was struck by the girls' plight. After sitting down with me to get all of the details straight, he wrote an article that clearly represented our hearts in the matter. His full-page story was picked up by the *Drudge Report*, a news website, which communicated the story to millions of readers. Suddenly, we were not the only ones called to prayer, but people all over the country heard the story and began to intercede with us.

Over the entire three and a half months, 104 days, the people who interceded in our prayer room so faithfully were deeply affected. Whenever we pray and give our lives to someone else's cause, God can't help but give back to us. Life and renewal happened in our midst, even as we were going through the greatest challenge of our lives.

This life and renewal didn't just happen in the Antioch community but all over Waco. Greater New Light Baptist Church, an African-American church nearby, felt led by the Lord to pray for Heather and Dayna one Sunday evening. They stayed up all night praying for the girls' release. A group of our businessmen were in the prayer room that Monday morning for their weekly 5:00 a.m. prayer time when the Greater New Light group knocked at the door. When the businessmen answered, the two groups joined together seeking God's deliverance for Heather and Dayna.

The body of Christ in Waco and around the world was unified, rallying behind the cause of two young women being held in jail for sharing the gospel. We received letters from all around the country. People were stirred by the Lord to pray. We believe that millions were interceding for these prisoners in Kabul.

Our perspective, and I think the perspective of those imprisoned, was that God allowed them to be captured in order to awaken the world to His heart for Afghanistan. The Taliban, a regime that did not believe in liberty and freedom for men, women or children, were oppressing the widow and the orphan. The widows were not allowed to work and had no way to feed their families. God wasn't just interested in our two ladies being released from prison. He was interested in an entire nation being changed.

God allowed some of His kids to be put in prison so that the cry of the orphan and widow could go up to the nations of the earth and the prayers of God's people could break the back of that oppressive regime. Three and a half months of 24/7 prayer...missing our friends and deeply concerned for their lives...all of this was a part of a plan so much bigger than we could have imagined at the time. A burden on God's heart brought the world together and then moved God in a mighty way through the prayers of His people. Out of this crisis, God brought justice and mercy to a land that had only known cruelty for many years.

Worldwide Media
August – November 2001

Perhaps one of the most unique opportunities that surfaced during this season came through our daily interaction with the U.S. and world press. Overnight, we went from an unknown church to a sought after interview. As requests poured in to meet with us, we asked God for wisdom on which ones to take and which ones to turn down. We knew that the press could either be a blessing or a curse, so our desire was never to become celebrities but simply to be obedient people. So, wanting to be solely led by the Holy Spirit in our decisions, sometimes we said no to the famous news agencies and talk shows while other times we said yes.

As we met with so many people in the press during those few months, we took the opportunity to minister to them. We wanted to love and encourage them, while not being intimidated or impressed by them. Their words could either crucify us or make us heroes, and we had no control over which they chose. We just trusted God for protection and chose to love them and share the gospel with them.

I remember one particular group from one of the largest news agency in the world. They visited our service as part of their interview process. After filming that Sunday, tears filled the main reporter's eyes as he asked me, "What was that presence? I've seen a lot of religious services, but there was something different here. What was it?"

"That's Jesus, the real Jesus, the One who loves you and cares for you and died for you," I responded.

Then, another man began to ask questions about the reality of Jesus. Before it all ended, these three men, who are well known in media circles, were asking for prayer and more insight into the life of Christ. Time after time this happened. People were deeply touched by our journey, and God moved in them with love, mercy, and grace.

During this season, several questions came up both in conversations and interviews about our beliefs and values. One common one was, "Do you believe that Christians are the only ones going to heaven and that Muslims are going to hell?"

I would always pray and ask the Lord to help me answer this question. My response was, "Jesus said, 'I am the way, and the truth, and the life; no one comes to the Father but through Me' (John 14:6). Whether someone calls himself or herself Christian, Muslim, Hindu, Buddhist or atheist, these words are still true. It is not the label that we call ourselves, but the god that we choose that determines our eternal destiny. If it were my opinion, that would be one thing, but this is how Jesus said it, and I have chosen to live my life through Him and His word."

Another question that came up was, "Is it right to offer aid and also share Christ? Doesn't that confuse or deceive those you are evangelizing?"

My answer to this was to explain that when I look at the life of Jesus and His followers, they were always doing both - boldly proclaiming Christ as the way to eternal life *and* sacrificially giving everything they had to serve the poor and needy. I would often describe to the press, "We want to be like both Mother Theresa and Billy Graham. We want to be clear with our message of salvation as Billy Graham has been through the years, and we want to serve the poor as Mother Theresa did. No matter what the response of the poor, we want to give ourselves to them." These two hands of the gospel communicate the heart of God at every turn.

Perhaps the question I got most often revolved around Heather and Dayna's fate: "What will you do if the girls are not released but instead die for their faith?" My response was to explain the three scenarios in Scripture related to the imprisonment of believers. The first was that people were imprisoned for long periods of time and from their jail cells they wrote great letters that have helped people for hundreds of years. The second scenario was that people were imprisoned and eventually died for their faith. The most honorable deaths in Scripture are those by people who gave their lives for what they believed in just as their Lord did. And thirdly, there were those imprisoned who, through the miraculous intervention of God, were released and able to testify of the goodness of God in the midst of their imprisonment. All three of these scenarios brought glory to God and served as testimonies to the world.

To those questioning me, I told them that we always believed that God had chosen scenario number three for Heather and Dayna. This is what we prayed and had faith for. But if one of the others happened, we would still trust and love God. No matter what, we know He is enough for us, and His ways are perfect.

During a radio program interview with Heather, Dayna, and me after their release, a well-known pastor asked me if I felt responsible or guilty for the ladies being put in that position in Afghanistan. He asked me, "How did you deal with the question of what might happen to their lives?"

I remember thinking the question somewhat odd considering the Biblical implications. I told him, "When I was with them in Afghanistan in June, we knew the consequences of living out our faith wholeheartedly in an oppressive Muslim regime. We knew that people had gone before us and sacrificed their very lives for what they believed in. I cried many tears on behalf of Heather and Dayna because they are like daughters to Laura and me. Our love for them is deep. It would have broken my heart if they had lost their lives because I believe they have so much to live for. But, we all realize that this mission we are a part of is worth our lives. Jesus is worthy of our very lives. Whatever the outcome of our journey of faith, we will come out fine if we are loving and serving Him by sharing the good news and laying down our lives for the people He has called us to."

Antioch Community Church – To God be the Glory
November 14, 2001

On November 14, 2001, the worldwide press descended on Waco. Russian President Vladimir Putin was meeting with President Bush at his ranch in Crawford, which is only 30 minutes from our church. Media from Russia, Europe, as well as the U.S. were in town to cover this story. That morning, since the press was in town, we held a press conference to give an update on the situation in Afghanistan.

Throughout the entire time Heather and Dayna had been in prison, we received many false rumors about their release. We had learned not to get too excited until we could verify whatever news we heard. During the press conference that morning, one reporter told us that the Taliban had fled Kabul with the ladies. We had heard that rumor before but could not validate it, so we dismissed it and went on with the press conference.

That day went on as most days: we prayed and continued taking care of the basic needs of the church. Then, at 5:30 p.m., a man from CBS busted through the front door of our offices with a big camera screaming, "What's your response? What's your response?"

I asked, "My response to what?"

"All the foreigners have been found and are being flown to Pakistan right now!" he told me. "Lock the doors down! I get the exclusive!"

"Who did you get that information from?" I questioned.

We ran to a TV and turned on the CBS evening news with Dan Rather. There we heard them reporting just what the man had said and showing a Pakistani helicopter landing in Islamabad. Spontaneous joy broke out in the office, and I immediately got on the phone to Pakistan to get clear information about what was happening.

In the midst of the chaotic rejoicing, I told the news crews that were streaming in the front door that we would do a statement at 6:15 p.m. in our auditorium. One of our pastors called the Lifegroup leaders with the news and invited everyone up to the church to celebrate. People began showing up until hundreds were gathered in the auditorium. Everyone was giving high-fives, celebrating, and rejoicing. Our people had owned this in their hearts and were seeing with their own eyes the very things they had prayed for.

LOS ANGELES TIMES

RESPONSE TO TERROR

Texans' 104-Day Vigil for 2 Held by Taliban Ends in Joyous Fest

By DAVID LAMB
TIMES STAFF WRITER

WACO, Texas—The converted grocery store on North 20th Street roared with clapping and joyous tumult until the early hours Thursday. "Praise the Lord!" worshipers shouted. "Jesus has heard the prayers."

Heather and Dayna were coming home from their Afghanistan nightmare.

For 104 days, the congregation of the evangelical Antioch Community Church had held a round-the-clock prayer vigil for two members whom the Taliban regime had jailed for allegedly trying to spread Christianity in the Muslim country. Now the news had come that they were free.

And the party rolled on and on until pastor Jimmy Seibert realized that it was 4 a.m. and time for bed.

Robert Herber and wife Stefanie, left, join in celebration at Antioch Community Church in Waco, Texas, of the release from Afghanistan of church members Heather Mercer and Dayna Curry.

Our worship leader, James Mark, was there, and I asked him to set up the sound and lead a time of worship and thanksgiving after the statement. As he warmed up, it sounded so good that I told him to just go for it right then and there. The press was setting up a multitude of microphones for my statement when James Mark started leading a song that he wrote about the nations. Our people joined in with tears, raised hands, and much joy. As we all began to dance and sing, the press went crazy. They were running around with cameras, taking pictures, watching us shout and jump, amazed at what was happening.

Then I started thinking to myself, *You know, for the last three months, the press has never really let me share my whole heart. When I talked about Jesus, they edited it out. Now, I am about to go live across the world with an unedited version of our testimony. This is an incredible opportunity! I just have to preach the gospel.*

When we finished the song, I got on the microphones and said, "First of all, we want to thank our Lord Jesus Christ because He has delivered our friends, not just from this one situation though. When Dayna was 17 years old, she gave her life to Christ, repenting of her sins and turning to Him with all of her heart. When Heather was 15, she turned to Jesus and found Him as a faithful friend, and she has walked with Him all of these days..." I shared Heather's testimony, Dayna's testimony, and my testimony and proclaimed the gospel right there on live TV for the world to see.

"We love the Lord Jesus. We are so thankful for His faithfulness. We are thankful that He offers that love to all men. Whoever calls upon His name can be saved from all of the junk that goes on inside of us. We can be free because of what He has done... we see people like Heather and Dayna who are willing to lay their whole lives down for that precious good news that Jesus is Lord. We are so proud of these ladies, who they are, and what they stand for; and we are thankful most of all to the God who makes a way where there is no way..."

I still remember one news agency in Dallas that had shown the live feed from our auditorium. When the camera went back to the anchors, they looked frozen for a couple of seconds before they finally said in an awkward tone, "Oh, well, they are really excited in Waco, Texas." It was awesome!

That night we worshipped and prayed for two hours, doing interviews with the press, sharing the gospel, and proclaiming the goodness of God. For the next 24 hours, the lead for the BBC radio news brief went something like this: in the background a song that James Mark had written called *Jesus Loves Afghanistan* played and the BBC reporter came on with his British accent saying, "*Jesus Loves Afghanistan* was the chant from a church in Waco, Texas last night..." and then he would proceed to describe what had happened. On the front page of many newspapers across America the next day were pictures of our people dancing and rejoicing.

It was an incredible night of celebration for all of us. For Heather, Dayna, and six other aid workers, it was a victory. For the body of Christ, it was a victory. Eventually, for the orphan and widow of Afghanistan, it would be a victory.

Ultimately, though, it was a victory for living out Kingdom values. Our ability to respond in prayer, to navigate the pressures of the media, and to steer through the complexities of working with parents and governments all came from God's simple love and wisdom that He poured out on us as we walked in close relationship with Him every step of the way. Heather and Dayna were able to endure prison and go on to serve Jesus in other nations because they lived out those simple values too. When you have an every day walk with God, whether the whole world knows about it or nobody knows about it, it will impact the world around you.

Dayna and Heather's lifestyles represent hundreds of others in our midst that live the same way. As they were in prison, getting up daily to pray, read, share, and live out the Kingdom values, there were hundreds here in Waco at the same time, getting up to pray, read, share, and live out the same values. We were all in this together, on different sides of the world.

Heather and Dayna – An Enduring Testimony
November 2001

When I met Heather and Dayna in Pakistan before they came home, I told them that they were about to enter an incredible new world of people wanting to hear and exploit their story. I told them they had to decide, "Do you want to be like Mother Teresa or like a Christian rock star?"

They both immediately responded, "We got in this for the poor and the lost. How do we stay true to that?"

"First of all," I advised, "you have got to decide what to do with the money."

They decided to set up a charity to give all of the money to help people in Afghanistan, pouring back into the lives of those they went to see set free. No matter where the journey took Heather and Dayna, from their book to national TV shows, they were never motivated by money but simply to testify of the goodness of the Lord.

That conversation took place only a couple of days after their rescue, on November 16th. In the sovereignty of God our annual retreat for Antioch missionaries from around the world was slated to start in Germany on November 17th. I flew from Pakistan with Heather and Dayna, and we were able to be at the opening session together with our people. As these young ladies shared their story with their friends and co-laborers from around the world, it stirred all of our workers' faith that God could meet us in the challenges of working in some of the most difficult countries in the world; He could meet us in the challenges of being imprisoned for our faith. Their testimony wasn't something that caused us to pull back but to rise up and believe God for even greater things.

The first Sunday I was back in Waco after the overseas retreat, I asked the Lord what I should speak on. I felt strongly that He led me to Revelation 2, where it talks about returning to our first love. Our first love was not in being known in the press or having two famous people in our family. Our hope and strength are in Jesus alone.

We do not want to be known as the "Heather and Dayna church" or "the church that prays" but as the church that loves Jesus with all of our heart, soul, mind, and strength. Through the years, God has brought of us back to this message over and over – loving Him, honoring Him, and keeping Him first. For you see, when He is first, we get to see His heart and then all of the great things that He does happen right before our eyes. But when we only focus on the things that He does, we miss His heart. We never want to miss His heart.

Behind the story of two aid workers who were imprisoned in Afghanistan for their faith, there are a thousand other stories. There was the story of the body of Christ rising up to pray so that Afghan widows and orphans would be freed. There was the story of other team members miraculously escaping the country with the help of Taliban leaders who cared for them. There was the story of the people in the press hearing the gospel. But whether the whole world knows all of the stories or not, we know that when we simply love Jesus, live in community, and reproduce the life of God everywhere we go, there will always be fruit, and God will always be glorified.

Chapter 14

Crisis to Catalyst
2002 – 2005

"With whom My hand will be established;
My arm also will strengthen him."
Psalm 89:21

The first two years as a church, we came together to sacrifice and believe for our building. As soon as that adventure of faith was over, we went into the Afghanistan crisis, spending 104 days praying around the clock for our friends while also trying to handle the press and keep up with daily life and expectations.

For two and half years straight, we had been on the edge with God. Once Heather and Dayna were home safe, we were able to enjoy a season of calm. As we used our building to its full capacity, we turned our focus to strengthening the church and establishing the rhythms of community. God had placed so many dreams and desires in our hearts that we wanted to pursue.

So, for the next two years, we were blessed with a time to solidify our internal values, invest more in our urban ministries, and give more attention to developing our church-planting teams around the world.

Antioch Community Church – Internal Values
2002-2005

While we had made it a point in the first year as a church plant to teach and reiterate our values to our people, we continued over the next few years to strengthen and deepen our commitment to loving

God, living out Acts 2 community, and sharing the gospel. On every level of relationship and ministry, we focused on teaching our people how to live out these truths in their daily lives.

By the spring of 2005, we had seen each area of the church established with wonderful leadership. We did a survey to evaluate how the people were living out the different values of the Kingdom. The survey was anonymous in order for people to be as honest as possible. About 1,000 people filled it out, and the findings were both astounding and encouraging. The people were really rising up and taking hold of what God was doing in their lives.

Our first values question, and the most important to us, asked how often and how long people were spending time with Jesus each day. We found out that over sixty-five percent of our people were spending time with Jesus every day, seven days a week, and about sixty-five percent of these were spending more than an hour each day with Him. Of the rest of the people surveyed, roughly another thirty percent were spending time with Jesus 3-4 times a week in Bible study, prayer, and worship. When it was all said and done, there were only about two to three percent who were not spending any consistent time alone with the Lord. Our premise has always been that if we can get people with God, then their lives can be changed. It was a great encouragement to see this value being lived out.

The second value we asked people about was discipleship. We found that half of our people were being intentionally invested in. When it came to evangelism, sixty-seven percent of the adults and students said they had shared their faith with someone in Waco in the last six months and almost fifty percent of them had been on a short-term mission trip during their time with us. Wow, how encouraging. It was happening – the values were being lived out.

As more people visited Antioch, we wondered if they were getting connected with Lifegroups because we knew that if we could all live in community, then we could all learn to live out the simple values of the Kingdom. In the survey, we found that over 80 percent of the people were involved in Lifegroups. Of course, we desired that number to be closer to 100 percent, but we were still very encouraged

Another section of the survey asked people about the value of honoring God with our finances. We discovered that seventy-five percent of the church tithed (qualifying that as ten percent of their income to Antioch). When we asked if they gave to missions in addition to their tithe, again, seventy-five percent of them said they did. Wow, what a radical giving culture. People were abundantly sowing into the Kingdom.

We did not do this survey to boast about numbers but to see how well our people were getting and living out the vision of the church. After being established just a few years, we were so encouraged to see that our people were putting roots down, believing the vision, and living it out. In fact, one of the survey questions asked how many people felt they could articulate the values and vision of our church and ninety-six percent of them felt that they could do that.

These results really stirred our hearts to believe that our focus on the simple things of the Kingdom in the context of community could cause a whole people to embrace Christ's vision that He could be glorified through His church in the earth.

As we grew in the conviction that everyone is called by God to live out these values in whatever arena that God has them in, God began to open our eyes to the fact that ninety-nine percent of the world is not called to full-time vocational ministry but is involved in ministering in their workplace and neighborhood. Our job then, as church leadership, is to equip these folks so that they have everything they need to fully live out God's calling on their lives.

Some people might say, "I'm not a missionary, I'm just a businessman." Well, in God's Kingdom no one is "just a businessman." They are either called by God to business or they are not. If they are, then "Christ and the church" needs to be lived out in their business world. The same is true for those called to arts and entertainment, social work, education, construction, and every other field. Whatever God calls you to do is your place of influence and ministry.

We realized that if the church could really tap into the potential that lies in our people working in and influencing society, then we would walk into the greatest opportunity for world evangelization we have ever seen. As we continued to look at our values and how to see them implemented in every person's life, God was helping us to see how business could be missional, how educators had tremendous opportunity for impact, and how even our church-planting teams could function more holistically if the teams utilized the callings and gifts of individual members.

This revelation can shape the future of our ministry. Our ability to mobilize, equip, and empower men and women in their venues of service in their community has a lot to do with our effectiveness in reaching the world with the gospel.

At this point in 2007, there are 1,800 to 2,000 who gather weekly at Antioch. In a thousand different ways and expressions in their homes, neighborhoods, schools, and workplaces, our people are living out these values. Laura and I are constantly in awe at how God is moving among us. The stories of salvations, breakthroughs, and changed lives could fill a whole book on their own. We are honored to be a part of this family of faith called Antioch.

Antioch Community Church – Urban Ministry
2002-2005

As I have been saying all along, when people really take a hold of Jesus' values, when they don't just talk about it, but they walk them out every day, they cannot help but impact the world around them. This dynamic community of people at Antioch was beginning to look like Acts 2:42-47. Of course, we weren't getting it all right, but we were on the path towards seeing God do great things in and through us.

Those great things started in our own backyards. From the beginning, we put ourselves in the middle of the inner city so that we might live among people with a wide variety of needs, personally, socially, and economically. There are two models of community development: those who minister to the poor and those who live among the poor.

Since Antioch moved into the inner city in 1999, many adults and families from the church have moved into the neighborhood too. Laura and I and our family are a part of this group that moved into the neighborhood near our church. Our people have been tremendously effective in leading whole households to the Lord as well as praying regularly for the people who live on their block. As we went door-to-door, serving and loving the people, offering practical help, we saw a tremendous response.

Kim Cutler, Angela Adams, and Chas Hahn, along with many others, led out through the 1990s, giving their lives away for inner-city youth and for what would become our urban ministries. When we moved into the area, it took us a couple of years just to get established. Our guys worked hard loving the neighborhood and reaching out at every opportunity, but we were ready to make the urban ministry more significant.

When Ty Denney came back to lead the training school in 2000, he helped us expand our vision. We had people living in the neighborhood, we had ministries going on in homes, we had backyard Bible clubs, but it all needed to be pulled together so we could begin to make a higher impact. Under Ty's

Kim Cutler (center)

leadership, we saw the urban work begin to flourish and become more integrated into what we were doing as a church. Ty later became an elder before he and his wife Erica went with a team to plant a church in Los Angeles. Ty was not only my running buddy and dear friend but someone God used to help stir us in fresh and new areas.

Two of the most significant ministries started at this time were The Feast and STARS. The Feast is a meal that we serve at the church on Friday nights, welcoming the neighborhood in to love and serve them as well as finding ways to disciple them and connect them with a Lifegroup. STARS (Students Teaching and Reaching Students) is a mentoring program that pairs elementary and junior high kids with a mentor that tutors them in school subjects and invests spiritually in their lives.

With Lifegroups meeting in the neighborhood, people getting discipled, practical needs being met through The Feast and the children's ministry, Ty and Dean Lessman led the vision to start a drug rehabilitation and discipleship house for men. The Mercy House opened in 2005 as an 18-month residential, substance abuse recovery program. Each resident goes through a Biblically based 12-step program, is involved in work projects to serve the community, and receives teaching, counseling, and mentoring in both one-on-one and group settings. The program has been effective, and now we are working on opening a similar home for women.

Perhaps one of the most powerful testimonies to come out of the Mercy House is Wes. Wes was on drugs for 34 years; drugs destroyed his relationships, caused him to lose jobs, and almost killed him. Ruth Reese, Wes' sister, was a woman of prayer who interceded for Wes consistently for years. When Ruth died of cancer, it had a major effect on Wes. Four months after her death, he took all the dope he had in one shot, knowing it would either kill him or scare him enough to make a change.

God saved Wes' life that day. He went to church soon after, and while he was there, he encountered Jesus. He explains that during the altar call, he felt something like warm water pouring over him, and he was instantly changed. The desire for drugs was gone! Immediately, Wes bought into the idea of a changed life and moved into the Mercy House. Little by little, through spending time with Jesus, counseling and serving others, Wes was strengthened in his inner man.

Wes' decision to follow Jesus became all consuming. Before long, Wes began to open his heart to the nations of the world. When he would pray, the Lord would speak Tibet to his heart over and over. His desire to serve in China grew, and later that year, he had the opportunity to go on a short-term trip to China.

Kandy was already living in China and was the guide for Wes' team. Kandy had a similar background to Wes, having abused alcohol and drugs until God saved her at age 40. She worked two jobs to put herself through ATS night school and then moved to China to be a part of the church-planting team there.

When Wes met Kandy, he knew he wanted to spend the rest of his life with her. Kandy, too, felt that God had brought Wes into her life for marriage. Several months later, Wes proposed to Kandy at the Great Wall of China. These two plan on serving the nations together. God redeemed both of their pasts and brought them to a place where they can serve others together.

Wes and Kandy's story is an amazing testimony of God's grace, power, and love for His children. God takes darkness and converts it into light. No matter what failures we have in the past, God loves to give us a new start.

These few years of focused commitment to our neighbors and our city were awesome times of seeing God move in power. People were being saved, lives were being restored, families were being strengthened.

Today, God continues to add to this incredible urban ministries team under the leadership of Vincent Carpenter. Vincent and Tonja have continued to develop and expand on this base, and we are excited about their leading us into the future. I have great expectation that God will truly lead us to be the multi-cultural, multi-economic people He has called us to be. Because of those who give their lives daily to the broken and poor around us, God is blessing the work of our hands and for that we are forever grateful.

Antioch Ministries International
2002-2005

We were caring for our workers on the field and holding overseas conferences, but we wanted to develop more intentional ways of caring for our church-planting teams. If you birth something, you need to care for it. In a family, you don't birth a child and then ignore it until adulthood. Because we function out of a family concept, we are committed to caring for our people like parents are committed to caring for their children.

When Kevin Johnson took over leadership in the international area in 2003, he began to shape what we now call the Church-Planting Mobilization Team (CPMT). Under Kevin's leadership, this team took ownership of the ongoing training and development of our people on the field, and they also committed to serve and care for them.

In trying to train, equip, and serve our church-planting teams, we discovered that there are three major areas where people need to be facilitated. The first is strategy – our teams and team leaders need ongoing and continual refinement when trying to learn how best to reach the people groups they serve. The second area is pastoral care – our people need feedback, love, and someone to watch over their hearts as they are on the difficult journey of planting churches all over the world. Third, our teams need administrative help – someone on this side of the world to help them navigate logistical issues that can sometimes hinder the work they are trying to do.

To facilitate all these needs, we developed systems of regional managers, along with volunteers who raise support to serve our guys on the field. Jennifer Smyer, with great zeal, passion, and skill developed a team training process to help our people become more effective in their synergy of working together. This training allowed our teams to be much more powerful. We also became committed to visit each church plant once a year and to host a biannual international retreat where all of our missionaries gather for ministry, equipping, and fellowship.

Kevin and the CPMT were instrumental in bringing all of this together for our church-planting teams, and I know that our people overseas are so grateful for all he and the CPMT have done to help and support them. Kevin has been a faithful friend and brother to this whole movement. He has served in just about every position that we have other than the children's pastor. As a student himself, he worked with the youth. Then he led and pastored in Ulan-Ude while developing a training school there. When he came back, he helped start the ATS night school and took over our young adult ministry during our last couple of years at Highland and our first couple of years as Antioch. He then led our family ministries until he switched positions with Danny Mulkey to become our international director in 2003.

Kevin is a purist. His heart has always been to do everything with excellence and abandonment. His conscientiousness for detail, as well as his pioneering spirit, has allowed him to lead us in many areas of training, development, and leadership. Kevin, like so many of our leaders and team members on the field, is a man that I would trust with my whole life. Because of his love for Jesus and desire for holiness and purity, he is always challenging, stirring, and encouraging me to be all that God has called me to be.

Another important area of field care that we grew in during this time came in the area of counseling. With our people spread all over the globe, living in some of the most difficult circumstances, there is always someone dealing with a crisis or going through a difficult time. Whether it is conflict within the team or civil war in the country, stress on the field can take its toll if it is not addressed and ministered to.

God gave Bill and Rachel Gorman vision to do on-field care for our missionaries. They moved to Wiesbaden, Germany and set up the Haven, a place for people to come and be cared for, nurtured, built up, and strengthened. After the Afghan crisis, after a bombing in northeast Africa, after the war in Lebanon, our workers went to Bill and Rachel to receive pastoral care and counseling. Those wiped out by the challenges and struggles on the field now have a much more accessible place to go to be renewed and refreshed.

Following is a testimony from one of our teams on the field of how the Haven played an important role in their time of need:

For our family and team, living and serving in northeast Africa among unreached Muslims has been an exciting and a challenging journey. We have seen God move in many ways, yet all the while persevering in a developing nation plagued with poverty, war and an oppressive Islamic society. At different times, we faced trials where we sought an out-of-country break for needed rest and pastoral care. We are thankful that the Haven team situated in Germany has been that hospitable refuge of loving care. After one of these Haven getaways, a veteran missionary in our northeast Africa nation gave me heartfelt encouragement, 'I'm so glad to see you guys back!' My veteran missionary friend continued saying that in his 20 years of ministry in Africa, our nation was the hardest he had lived in. With tears, he continued saying that he has seen so many people leave the field because of not getting needed rest or care. We are so thankful we had the Haven that could facilitate our rest, pastoral care, and refreshment to return to our pioneering field.

The Haven has already been effective and will continue to grow in the years to come. Loving and caring for one another as a family helps us to see counseling and on-field assistance as a long-term need and priority. We want our people to have a place to come home to when ministry gets too stressful or if they experience challenges and hurts that are hindering their service or walk with Jesus. We are so blessed to have people in our midst who are giving their lives to restore, renew, comfort, and care for us.

As God continued to expand our work around the world among the poor and the projects that go along with all that is happening overseas, we really needed to look for more organized opportunities for people to invest financially. We never wanted to do "development" because our heart was not to become a normal Christian machine when it comes to fund-raising. We knew that if we ever went there, we had to have the right person in place to lead us.

Well, just as God has brought along the right people at the right time all through the years, He did it again with this need. As we were praying through how to handle some different projects, Pat and Tanya Murphy came into our church. Earlier in the book, Pat shared his story of how his daughter had been transformed and how he and Tanya were drawn to us.

When I explained to Pat what we were looking for in development, I told him that our ultimate goal would not be to raise money but instead to disciple people who have abundant resources. He would be free to dive into their lives, even if it meant we would not always receive income as a result. Ultimately we wanted to see people's lives changed, and as a result, their heart for giving. If that happened, then we would have an opportunity to have our needs met as well. Pat took the job in July 2004. Little did we know that just six months later, we would dive into the largest aid project we had ever done and would need major financial assistance to pull it off. God brought Pat into our midst at just the right time.

At the same time, the CPMT had been working on a plan for us to respond quickly to emergency situations around the world. We knew that somehow God wanted to provide church-planting opportunities through such crises. Little did we know that at the end of 2004, with the devastation of the tsunami in Southeast Asia we would find ourselves drawn into an emergency immediately.

When Robert Herber began to gather people for our initial response to the tsunami in Sri Lanka, we were able to implement his thoughts quickly and get everyone mobilized within just days. It was amazing to see how the church was able to mobilize, empower, implement, and connect to a long-term vision so quickly since all of the pieces were in place.

In the years between the Afghanistan crisis and the Southeast Asia emergency, Antioch was able to put down deeper roots and establish some much needed rhythms within our own community. People were strengthened, families were established, and godly men and women were leading each area of ministry. There was health, vitality, and strength.

As always, God was not strengthening us simply for ourselves.

Chapter 15

Destruction to Restoration 2005-2006

*"O God, restore us
And cause Your face to shine upon us,
and we will be saved."
Psalm 80:3*

Sadly, life is full of personal tragedies and international catastrophes. How we respond to these many times determines our destiny. Our desire as a church is to respond with the grace and love of God in these most difficult situations. We can't always explain why things happen the way they do, but we do know that God's love, peace, and grace are available when we step into the lives of others, with the love of God, to help in tangible ways.

This has always been who we are, a people willing to show up and get involved in the world around us. And when we do, we trust God to be Himself, pouring our mercy, grace, love, and help to the practical needs and heart of man.

It is with this attitude that we ran towards the devastation of the tsunami of 2004, and we are so thankful that we did. Countless lives have been touched as hurting people were loved, cared for, and restored.

Antioch Community Church – When Tragedy Strikes
December 2004 – January 2005

It was the day after Christmas, December 26, 2004. Our family was at Laura's mother's home in Houston when I began seeing reports on the tsunami that hit Southeast Asia. At first, the damage seemed somewhat minimal, but as more information came in, we began to realize that it was one of the greatest tragedies in world history.

We were immediately moved to prayer, asking God what we should do in response. Robert Herber, our college pastor, was also deeply stirred. He called me from vacation and said, "I am willing to lead out a team immediately for Sri Lanka and Indonesia if we can get one together. Are you up for my gathering that team?"

I knew I would not be back in Waco for a couple of days, but I said, "Sure, man, if you can get the people together." Within 24 hours, 23 people signed up.

Laura and I prayed about whether we should go with the team, but felt we were not supposed to go at that time. We thought that it might be an opportunity for our 15-year-old daughter, Abby, though. She had been asking us about serving one of our church plants, so when this chance to go came up, we asked her to pray about going. Within a few moments, Abby was thrilled, excited, and planning to go.

Though it was an emotional decision for us, sending our daughter overseas for the first time without us, not knowing what she would encounter in that devastating situation, we knew that she was in great hands with our friends. We had known for years that when it was time for her to go, she would be well taken care of. More than anything though, we knew that God's calling on her life was more important than our own need to protect and comfort her. He would sustain her.

Laura and I stayed behind, thrilled to support the exciting work God was doing through the body of Christ at Antioch. Over the next month, we sent 75 people, but turned away 200 more who were ready and willing to go. As soon as word got out that teams were going, people began giving their time, talents, and resources to help them leave as soon as possible. Volunteers worked feverishly around the clock, gathering supplies, loading boxes, making arrangements, doing whatever was necessary to get our teams ready. People sacrificially gave more than $200,000 to help the teams respond to this crisis on the other side of the world. Immediately, people began crying out to God to work powerfully and change lives in Sri Lanka and Indonesia.

The first team of people left for Sri Lanka on January 1st. We sent a second wave to Indonesia on January 6th and then a third group to Sri Lanka on January 10th.

In the face of tragedy, our people came alive. Watching them mobilize so quickly made me believe again that the way we were doing church really could be reproduced anywhere in the world.

Sri Lanka
January 2005

Robert Herber, Carl Gulley, and Jennifer Smyer led the initial team of 20 volunteers to Sri Lanka. They ministered in two areas and saw God move in great power among the people there. Since I was not there personally, I asked Robert to share some of what they saw God do.

After getting a beachhead in the south, a small group of us broke off from the rest of the team to respond to God's voice to go out to the east. Before we left the south, though, a woman on our team told me, 'Robert, you are going to meet a young Christian man, but your tendency is going to be to underestimate him. The Spirit is saying don't underestimate him. He will open doors for you.'

Starting off the trip proved to be a challenge. We had made very important relationships in the south, but we knew no one in the east. Even as we tried to get drivers to take us there, no one would go because they were too scared. They feared a group called the Tamil Tigers who were hijacking transportation passing through the area. We finally got some van drivers that would go. One walked up to me and said, 'Everyone dies sometime; I will go.'

Before we started driving, we asked God where He wanted us to go. Carl, a team leader, and Sohani, our Sri Lankan translator, came up to me with words from the Lord at different times. Carl said he felt like we needed to go to a town called Kalmunai. Sohani said she felt like we were supposed to go to some town that starts with 'kal.' They had no idea that the other had sensed the same thing from God. Believing this was a word from the Lord, we started towards this city.

When we got there, it looked like a ghost town. The U.N. and world press were the only people there besides us. The only place to stay was a hotel where we ended up sleeping on the floor with a crew of U.N. relief workers.

The next morning, God gave me a vision of a guy in a maroon shirt. We headed out, praying and asking God to speak to us because we had no idea what to do. Driving toward the coast, we were continually asking, 'Holy Spirit do we go left or right?' Finally, we came upon an Assembly of God church, the only building standing among blocks of rubble. I felt like we should stop. As we walked toward the church, a guy in a maroon shirt walked up to us and gave us a big smile, revealing his missing front tooth. His name was Ravi, and he was a believer!

Ravi had been saved from the tsunami because he was at the church service when the tsunami hit his town. He said he wanted to help us, so he hopped into the car and started leading us around. We were amazed, knowing that he was both the man that I had seen in my vision that morning and also the young Christian whom God had spoken about through my team member back in the south.

Ravi took us into a refugee camp with hundreds of people all of whom had lost their homes in the tsunami. As we looked around, we were overwhelmed with the need. I think Carl's quote to a newspaper explained perfectly how we felt: 'On one hand we are totally ill equipped, but on the other hand we are totally well equipped.' It was true! While we had no idea what to do and had no experience doing relief work, we knew Isaiah 61:1 says, 'The Spirit of the Lord God is upon me, because the Lord has anointed me to bring good news to the afflicted; He has sent me to bind up the brokenhearted, to proclaim liberty to captives and freedom to prisoners.' We were equipped because His Spirit was on us!

So, we gathered the children in the camp and started playing with them. The whole refugee camp gathered around and everyone began laughing and having fun. Eric and Jady, two team members, started cleaning wounds as if they had been doing it their whole lives. Carl ran to a nearby market and bought a large supply of food for the people.

While we were serving them, a man approached me and asked for my help. He said that he had deep lacerations in his intestines and was in great pain. I told him that we didn't have any medicine to give him, but that we would pray for him in the name of Jesus. We started praying for him, and I put my hand on his stomach. After praying for him for a long time, his sides began to shake. I felt my hand getting really hot, and his eyes started to get big. He smiled, and when we stopped praying, he said that he was completely healed. I told him that God could heal his body, but He really wanted to change his life.

The man said, 'I accept!' I explained to him he couldn't accept yet; I needed to share with him what he was accepting. But the man was so touched by God's love that he was eager to embrace Him. While I was sharing the gospel with him, he kept repeating, 'I accept; I accept; I accept!' His excitement began to draw a crowd. I told him to tell the other people about what God just did for him. As he told people what had happened, a line formed of people who wanted to be healed.

The next guy in line came to us with a hand so swollen that he couldn't move it. When the tsunami hit, a car had crushed it. The man who had just been healed and I started praying for him. We prayed for a long time, and all of a sudden the swelling went down. We were able to see his knuckles! Then, people who weren't even believers started to lay their hands on him. It was awesome! His hand started moving back and forth, and he began to wiggle it. We continued praying for him, and Ravi, our friend in the maroon shirt, came up to him and said, 'Have faith, have faith.' This man's hand kept getting better and better. As we were praying for him, we got to lead him to the Lord.

Another guy came to us with a back problem. As we prayed for him, he was healed too! Then a couple walked up to us. The wife had a horrible fever and headache. We laid hands on her and began to pray. As we were praying, she said that her headache was gone, and she gave her life to Jesus. We started praying for her, again, and all of a sudden the heat in her head was gone too. Everyone was amazed.

After this, a young man approached Ravi and asked if we could go to a room where his whole family was. We walked inside and found his sweet family sitting there. As we talked to them, we asked them if they knew Jesus. They had only heard of him. As we shared the gospel, the whole family gave their lives to Christ. I told Ravi that this would be his new Lifegroup to lead.

Over the next week we were able to lead many more people to the Lord. We teamed up with the Assembly of God church and were able to knit many into their congregation. The pastor said he had never seen so many people come to the Lord. I, too, had been in Sri Lanka before and had never seen so many people responsive to Jesus. It was clear that this was an hour when God was moving. God had come in a time of crisis to show His great love and power.

Indonesia
January 2005

Another crisis response team went to Indonesia under the leadership of Ty Denney and Marty and Susan Peters. Their experience was much more adventurous than the Sri Lanka teams, as these 13 risked their lives to share the love of Jesus in a devastated village in Banda Aceh. Here is Susan's account.

We organized a medical team of doctors, nurses, and helpers to respond to the crisis in Indonesia. Most of the team members were normal church people, but they had all led Lifegroup, shared their faith, loved people, and been on an overseas trip before. They were mature believers who could handle the stress.

In Banda Aceh, we met friends who worked in that part of the world and were fluent in the language. It had been one week since the tsunami, and the government was clamping down on westerners going deep into Aceh to help the people. That part of Aceh had been closed to westerners for five years.

Jim Yost, a 25-year veteran missionary to Indonesia told us to take this small fishing boat along the coast to a town called Teunom. So, all of our team, 13 from Waco and 13 Indonesians, got on the boat. It was over 100 degrees while we sat tied to the dock for about three hours while the captain waited for more paying customers. As we rocked back and forth, we all got sicker and sicker. We had already driven through wreckage, bodies, and all kinds of horror. Sitting in that smoldering heat getting seasick was challenging for all of us.

The boat was made of wood with only a very small covered area for our luggage and the captain. The team sat on the floor with the sides of the boat only about three feet high. Very soon after we left, everyone was throwing up overboard. We went through two Monsoon rains with extremely high waves. We were terrified.

After eight hours of cold rain, seasickness, and fear, it got dark. We finally convinced the captain to SOS a navy ship. The Indonesian ship had already rescued other boats and was so huge next to our little boat. They threw a rope ladder over the side that went down maybe 30 feet to us. I thought, 'How are our people going to jump from a rocking boat two to three feet over the ocean onto a rope and climb up so high being as sick as we are?'

Just then in the dark we heard a splash and, 'Man overboard!' We all prayed and tried to see what to do to help. The captain grabbed the one small life preserver on the boat and jumped in to save an Indonesian who could not swim. At that point, I seriously thought we might need to abort our mission.

The captain of the Indonesian military ship turned out to be a Christian and gave us a room to sleep in and a good breakfast. Everyone felt better in the morning and after worshipping and praying together, the peace of God came on us and everyone was fine to continue.

We got back on our boat and only had to go 15 minutes straight across to the nearest town. There was already a medical team there serving the people. One of our guys had an outrageous idea of asking the U.S. military helicopters that drop shipments for a lift to Teunom. We put three at a time on helicopters as they made their drops for the rest of the day, and eventually we all arrived in Teunom, seven days after leaving Waco.

The town was completely destroyed, and there was a strong stench of dead bodies. We found out that most of the people had fled to a nearby village and only came during the day to go through their things because at night rebels came looking for food and would kill anyone around. We spent that night in a rustic military outpost and finally arrived at the village of Tanah Anou to serve the next morning.

The people in Tanah Anou welcomed us warmly. We set up our tents and medical clinic. Hundreds lined up every day as we listened to their stories, cried with them, treated them and gave them medicine. When we asked if we could pray for them in the name of Jesus, everyone wanted us to.

My husband and a couple of others played with the children every day. They had lost their parents, siblings, teachers, homes, and school. They had suffered so much. We had soccer balls, crayons, and bubbles to help us love on the kids. Just to play with them and listen to their stories was part of their medicine.

This proved to be the most perilous trip any of us could have anticipated. But on the boat, the military ship, the helicopter, at every incredible challenge, the team never got angry. They never lashed out or said, 'How did you get us into this?' They all trusted God because they had surrendered their lives genuinely and deeply to Jesus. They remained quiet, sober, and prayerful. We were a united team intent on honoring our King, each other, and giving our lives and whatever skill we had to hurting people, not holding on to our own comforts, security, or even our lives.

Not one person on our team during that entire ordeal said one word about quitting. None of them complained about it being too hard. Their hearts were always, 'What is the next step?'

Sri Lanka
January 2005

At the same time our teams were serving in Sri Lanka, a *New York Times* reporter was going through the IDP camps (Internally Displaced Peoples) to report on the conditions. When he got to our camp and observed what was going on, he was upset to find out that we were sharing the gospel and that Buddhists were coming to know Christ. According to him, it was not right to give aid and share the gospel. He found some other Christian groups that only gave aid and did not share the gospel to support him.

During an interview with this reporter, I asked him what kind of work he had observed our team doing in Sri Lanka. He said, "Of all the camps, it is the best practical work going on. They are caring for the people, meeting their medical, emotional and educational needs."

I said, "What's the problem then?"

"The problem is that you are sharing the gospel while you do it."

"Well, then," I responded, "we have a philosophical difference."

He said, "Yes, we do, and people need to hear about it."

That Saturday morning, on the front page of the *New York Times*, there was a picture of some of our guys playing with kids in Sri Lanka with a caption that read: "Mix of Quake Aid and Preaching Stirs Concern." In the article, the reporter laid out a divisive point, counterpoint argument with other Christian groups who didn't agree with us. He even misquoted some people we know and love.

The same article was printed Sunday morning in Sri-Lanka. Our people were supposed to meet the following day with the Prime Minister's brother to sign off on some land they had promised to give us to help rebuild a village. Kevin Johnson was meeting with anyone we thought might possibly be offended by the article to set things right. Not knowing what to expect on Monday morning with the release of the article and the response of the press, they went into the Prime Minister's brother's office and said, "Obviously you have read the article. It is not all accurate. Would you like to talk about it?"

He responded, "It seems like that is between you and the other Christians. I'm a Buddhist, and I think you are doing great work. Let's go ahead and make this deal."

Unbelievers can often see straight through western ideology to the heart. Our heart is to be ourselves. I had told this reporter, as I have often told other groups, "When you love Jesus, you share who you are. You never make anyone convert by giving him or her aid and expecting something in return. We give everything freely, but we cannot *not* share who we are. We cannot *not* share the message of eternal life. If another tsunami had come weeks later and we had not shared the message of eternal life found in Jesus Christ, more people would have died and lived in a Christ-less eternity. It is a have-to to share the gospel...it is who we are."

Morakatiara, Sri Lanka
Restoration Village
2005-2006

Before the teams ever left Waco, we communicated to them that they should do whatever was needed to serve the people and show them Christ. If there were orphans, we should take them in. If there were wounded, we should help restore their bodies. Whatever they encountered, we wanted to be able to meet people's practical needs in the name of Jesus.

The village the team served in southern Sri Lanka was a small fishing community named Morakatiara. Half of the people had died in the tsunami, and half of the village was destroyed. Our team saw a great need for housing and counseling, but most of all, a great need for Jesus.

(L-R) Pat Murphy, the Prime Minister of Sri Lanka, Jennifer Smyer

As the team served in Morakatiara, they fell in love with the people. As they asked God what He wanted to do in this village, He placed a vision in Jennifer Smyer's and others' hearts to do more than help with the initial aid. I asked Jennifer to share in her own words what God spoke and how He brought it all to pass.

When the destructive wave crashed the coastline of Sri Lanka on December 26, 2004, Antioch Community Church felt God's passion to display Himself in that hour. An emergency relief team was sent to Sri Lanka to be His hands, practically serving the people there with tenderness and comfort.

God led our steps to Morakatiara, a small fishing village in the southern part of Sri Lanka. This fishing village was ninety-eight percent Buddhist, with more than 450 precious people dealing with the loss of children, loved ones, and their entire fishing community. As I walked the perimeter of this village and saw the men and women suffering such a natural loss, I asked God, 'What do You want to do in this hour with these people?'

I felt God say to me so clearly, 'Jennifer, if you will build practical, physical homes for them, I will make homes for them in heaven. Put a stake down in the ground. I'm giving you an opportunity to put your foot in the door, and I will bring My glory to this nation.'

The dream began to take shape among us: As a church, what if we built physical homes for these families and saw their community restored? What if we saw men and women working again and their hearts comforted by the love of God? We realized that through this practical, hands-on work, we could see the Kingdom of God established.

In my mind's eye, I could see a picture of this community living in restored homes. I could see children playing in the street, men working in gardens and women hanging clothes on the clothesline. But, more than that, I could see new believers professing Jesus as Lord, saying, 'God allowed a tsunami to come to our village, but somehow through that, He came and revealed Himself to us. We've given our lives to Him, and we will never be the same.'

After a brief conversation with Jimmy on the phone, he spoke with the elders, and we all felt a mutual sense that this was in fact the leadership of God for this time. That put me and the team I was leading on an incredible journey of securing land for the people on which we could build these new homes.

God gave me a tenacious heart for this fishing village. Their government could easily have overlooked them, but God certainly had not overlooked them. In a frantic rush to acquire land, Pat Murphy, Director of Financial Development at Antioch, and I raced around the island to find out where the Prime Minister was allotting this land. In our first meeting with the Prime Minister, God allowed us to petition his heart for these people. At first, he tried to discourage us from securing the land, but through persistence and God's favor, he finally agreed to give us 29 acres.

This meeting not only established our relationship with the Prime Minister but also with his brother, his right-hand man. On multiple occasions, I talked with the Prime Minister's brother. During one particular visit, he asked me, 'Jennifer, what do the people think of me and the Prime Minister?'

God had prepared me with His heart for that moment. I replied, 'Sir, they believe that you are men who understand where they come from, for you, too, came from a poor village.'

He said, 'Sometimes I don't know what to do.'

Right then, God reminded me of the story of Joseph, who was placed in an hour of power for God's glory. I said to him, 'Sir, God has placed you in this position for this time. I encourage you to ask God to show you how to lead these people. In times like this, it is easy to be distracted by money and fame, but I encourage you to use your position for the people's good.' In that moment, I could see the Spirit of God register in his eyes, and I could feel His conviction in the room.

God opened other amazing doors during this journey as well, such as meeting the Prime Minister's wife and having lunch with her in their home. Every time we were able to meet with this family, they would ask, 'Why do you want to fight for our people?'

We always responded, "The reason we are here is because Jesus has placed us here. He is fighting for your people. He wants His love to shine in this hour of destruction."

In the following month, God provided in miraculous ways. We worked with villagers to clear all of the land. Some monks and other spiritual forces did not welcome the presence of God, and thus opposed us, but we were not deterred. By God's grace, our team was present daily in the lives of this fishing village, caring for the children, running a temporary school, and physically meeting the needs of the people the best we could.

Meanwhile, our whole church was getting behind this project back home. They raised money and sent out multiple short-term teams to Sri Lanka to help in our efforts. Over 200 people from our church and other churches came to serve in this village. Finally, more than $1.3 million came in to see this vision come to completion!

The most amazing testimonies from this project, though, came directly from the villagers themselves. One man and his wife would lay their baby down every night by a candle and then pull out their Bible, which they had never had before. Sitting together on their floor mats, they would read stories of the Good News. One night, God spoke to this man's heart with a dream: He was in a deep pit with darkness all around him when suddenly a bright light came and a figure stood before him and said, 'I am the way, the truth and the life.' This villager and his family are currently involved in the local church that is being raised up there. He went to a church-planting movement conference and is on fire with the love of God, strongly desiring to spread the gospel!

Another villager came to our team asking, 'What must I do to be saved?' He heard the good news and then received Christ as Lord. Now, he is sharing with his wife and family and teaching the good news to his brother-in-law through the words of the Bible.

One older fisherman testified during the early days after the tsunami: "Jennifer, many people have come and gone. But your people have come and everyday loved our children. They have played with our children, offered them school and been tender with our hearts at this time. In my culture, we hang a picture of Buddha on the wall to worship him. This makes me want to buy a picture of your God, hang Him on the wall and worship him." There are countless stories of how people are being touched by the word of God as we share the gospel and practically serve them with our lives.

Today, there is a long-term team living among the people and establishing a church with hope that it will turn into a church-planting movement. The villagers involved in the church are growing in God and are becoming true fishers of men. They long for the good news to spread throughout the village into the entire island nation of Sri Lanka.

We named the village 'Restoration Village,' which came from a study I did on the word 'restore.' Two years before the tsunami hit, I had experienced a tsunami of the heart. I went through a broken engagement after moving back from being on a church-plant team in North Africa. During those rebuilding years that followed, God spoke to me about the word 'restore' which means 'to bring back home, as if something were lost and then found again; to bring back to its original state of being.'

Restoration Village is a beautiful picture of true restoration, where men who were created by God to worship Him are now being restored in relationship with Him and into the village they were originally intended to worship Jesus in. This prayer and dream is coming alive. God truly is the One who restores.

The mission of Restoration Village has ultimately been about the body of Christ coming together. Jennifer was right; the whole church got behind this vision and gave themselves to it. Teachers stayed up all night writing curriculum for the kids who didn't have a school. Construction workers went back and forth, planning and building the town. Business people negotiated contracts and managed financial records. Medical personnel cared for wounds and needs. Counselors ministered to children struggling with the trauma. Many great men and women were giving their lives so generously for this project.

Through the process, some incredible stories of sacrifice surfaced as well. One engaged couple, instead of getting wedding gifts, asked people to give to an account in order to build homes in Sri Lanka.

Their sacrifice raised over $14,000. A sixteen-year-old girl asked people to give to the Sri Lankan cause instead of buying her birthday presents. More than $350 came in.

Antioch was not alone in the Restoration Village journey, though. People from all over the country and in some cases, all over the world, gave towards the project. A church in San Antonio gave $40,000. A businessman from Houston rallied support from his associates and raised over $50,000 to build the community center. A man living in Dubai, United Arab Emirates heard about it and sent money from the other side of the world.

More than $1.3 million came in over 18 months. We were able to completely rebuild Morakatiara debt free. There was never a time when we had to stop construction. Every time there was a need, God provided through the obedience and generosity of His children.

It was incredible to see people gather around a community on the other side of the world that was in such great need. Everyone stepped up and offered whatever they had, and in God's economy, when the body of Christ obediently gives what they have, it is always enough to accomplish His purposes. Once again, it had come back to being a simple people living out the values of the Kingdom, ready in season and out for whatever comes.

In this little fishing village in Sri Lanka, we watched beauty come out of ashes. We were not only able to meet their immediate needs in the wake of the crisis, but this community is back on its feet, on its way to functioning with a sustainable livelihood. A village of 85 homes has emerged with businesses and a developing community. Many families have come to Jesus, and there is a fellowship of believers in their midst now. Antioch has a long-term team serving there who has gathered this group of new believers and are worshipping as the church.

Once Restoration Village was complete, we asked some of the villagers what the journey had meant to them. Here are a few of their comments.

I believe after the tsunami, God gave us a new life and lifestyle. Before we thought in our minds, 'I want to live a better life.' Now we want it from our hearts. Now we know everyday that God is with us, and He will continue to help us.

My whole life has changed, and I'm so happy. I used to do very bad things, always smoking, always drunk. Now I want to go in the ways of Jesus. I feel totally different. I love Him in my heart. I believe in Jesus.

When we were in the depths of trouble we found out about Jesus. Now I know a lot of things about God, and now I pray to Him. The team told us to pray a lot. God gave us the power of the Holy Spirit to do everything we needed to do.

A testimony to Jesus has risen out of destruction. This was not just the restoration of a place but of a people. After church one Sunday, two villagers, Sisera and Ajith, along with one of our people there, wrote a worship song in the local language. These beautiful words capture their hearts of devotion and gratitude to Jesus for saving them in the midst of grief and loss.

Jesu hamadama obata adorei
(Jesus' love is always, all the time everyday)
Jesu hamadama oba samagai
(Jesus' love is always, staying here with us)
Lovata pipunu mala obei
(Like a flower, a sweet aroma)
Obe suwada api langai
(A lasting fragrance that will always be)
Jesu hari hondi
(Jesus, You are so good)
Jesu hari hondi
(Jesus, You are so good)
Jesu, Jesu
(Jesus, Jesus)
Jesu, Jesu
(Jesus, Jesus)

As I saw Restoration Village unfold, it really did make me realize that the local church just being the church allowed us to mobilize quickly to see people's lives changed. The mundane acts that we sometimes get lost in are really the building blocks that set us up for the great deeds of God.

Just a few months later, we had opportunities to respond to Hurricanes Katrina and Rita as well as the devastating earthquakes in Pakistan. God was continuing to expand us to be a people who were ready, in season and out, to serve the poor and to preach the gospel.

As I shared earlier, Archimedes once said, "Give me but one firm spot on which to stand, and I will move the earth." For 20 years, God has been establishing us, rooting us deeper, so that whether he calls us to share Christ in Waco or respond immediately to crisis situations around the world, we are ready to obey. We are His church, and it is through His church that He will reveal Himself to the world and draw all men to Himself.

Chapter 16

Yesterday to Tomorrow

"Jesus Christ is the same yesterday and today and forever."
Hebrews 13:8

In 1998, Floyd McClung, a dear friend and mentor, invited me to speak at a three-week intensive leadership school at the YWAM base in southern Colorado. As I looked around the room, I saw several significant leaders from different parts of the world that I had either heard of or known. It was a little intimidating, being that I was in my early 30s at the time, and I wondered how they would receive me as I spoke about having a passion for Jesus and His purposes on the earth.

Before I got up to speak, a man in the back raised his hand and asked to say something. He had been involved in a Muslim city where an Antioch team also served. He said, "Before Jimmy speaks, I want to say that what he is about to share with us works. Of all the teams I've seen come through our city, the team from Waco has been the best. When they arrived, they knew what they were supposed to do, and they hit the ground running. They wanted to reach people, so they shared Christ consistently. They discipled people and gathered them house-to-house. As they invested in them, we began to see the life of Christ reproduced in our city. When they had problems and came to us for counsel, they always spent time fasting and praying over those decisions. They have been teachable, open, and broken. But more than anything, we have enjoyed being with them because of their heart for worship and their love for Jesus. Before Jimmy speaks, I just wanted to say that the fruit in his people is real."

Nothing anyone could have said would have touched my heart deeper. For you see, Antioch is not about me and Laura, but it is about a whole family of people reproducing the life of Christ year after year, generation after generation so that all can hear and know.

There are still 2.1 billion people who have not heard the gospel and had a chance to respond. There are over 10,000 people-groups that do not have a life-giving Acts 2 gathering that is reproducing itself. When people discuss the best way to reach the whole world for Christ, the answer always seems clear to us: the church. God wants to be known in all the earth. He wants to rightly distribute Himself so that all can hear and all can know. The way He has chosen to do that is through the church.

We follow in the footsteps of thousands who have gone before us, but it is our time, it is our hour to see the coming of the Lord, to be a part of God's dream of answering His heart's cry.

People That Make a Difference

At Antioch, we really believe that the church of this generation can rise up to take the gospel to the ends of the earth. But we recognize that it won't just happen. We have to be the people of God, focused on obediently accomplishing His purposes. The question we constantly wrestle with is what kind of people actually make up the kind of church that will truly take the gospel to all nations?

We in the church should simply be people who learn from Jesus, make His values our own, and then reproduce those values everywhere we go. We must become what I call value carriers: people who take seriously who God is and how He wants us to live. Then, we give ourselves to walking it out and teaching others how to walk it out as well.

In Acts 4:13, nonbelievers saw that the apostles were not educated men, but "were amazed, and began to recognize them as having been with Jesus." Isn't that great? We want people to be growing in Christ-likeness and in the values of the Kingdom, so that when they gather from house to house, there is life there, a sense of awe. At Antioch, we believe that we are to equip the saints to do the work of the ministry by living out the values of the Kingdom.

There is no 20/80 rule in the church. Everybody should be in 100 percent and discipling those coming behind us to be involved 100 percent too. The North American church has gotten comfortable with relegating evangelism and discipleship to a few staff members, paying them to do the work we have all been called to. Full time ministers are not the only ones called by God to carry His values and live them out. As a pastor and leader, I am not satisfied until everyone in the church is engaging the basic values of the Kingdom.

At Antioch, we have clarified our values around three biblical truths: loving God, loving each other, and loving the lost. We believe that as these are simply lived out in community, we cannot help but bear fruit and see lives changed.

Value #1 – Love God

People need to be daily before God, seeking Him in a devotional life. No one has ever impacted the world around him or her for the glory of God without God.

A survey of thousands of small group leaders around the world determined that the main contributing factor to someone's ability to reproduce a cell group was his or her devotional life. Neither their culture, personal gifting, economic status, nor personality mattered much in their success. Those who multiplied consistently spent one to two hours in Bible study and prayer every day. Those who spent less than an hour multiplied but at a slower rate. Those who were not consistent in their own devotional life never multiplied groups. Jesus said, "I am the vine, you are the branches; he who abides in Me and I in him, he bears much fruit, for apart from Me you can do nothing" (John 15:5).

I cannot live without God. I say that out of deep fear and trembling. If I do not spend time in prayer and the Word every day, I do not function. I used to jokingly say, "If I miss a day, I get a little ornery. If I miss two days, I get mean. If I miss three days, I can commit just about any sin under the sun." While I used to say this just to prove a point, today I believe it to the core of my being. I don't have to eat. I don't have to sleep. I don't have to have a job or friends. But I have to have God.

Most of us do not feel we need God that much. If you are not compelled to be in God's presence by need, then be there by choice. My need wasn't so great when I started. I just had an ambition to be all that God wanted me to be. So, by choice I made decisions to try to learn in the journey. And as that journey went on, God helped me by making it a need. If we as a church are not meeting with God, meditating on and digesting His truth, we will be weak and anemic and that glorious church we are called to be will never be seen.

Just after my experience of seeing the power of God in Papua New Guinea, I was invited to lunch at Robert Ewing's house. Robert had been healed of stuttering as a 19-year-old and called to an apostolic ministry. He had students over to his house and told stories of God's work around the world. The unique thing about Robert was that to be in his presence was like being in the presence of the Lord. He was a 60-year-old single man who had chosen to wholly and completely belong to God.

Sometimes I couldn't grasp Robert's deep teaching, but there was something about his intimacy with God that drew me to him. I asked him, "Robert, how do you love Jesus so much? How do you live such a pure life and carry the presence of the Lord so wonderfully?"

Robert replied, "First of all Jimmy, you need to know that it is not me, but God working in me. For the last thirty years, I have started off my days by meditating on Scripture about the cross." He shared with me out of Isaiah 53, Hebrews 9 and 10, and Psalm 103. Robert told me, "I meditate on the cross every day and I identify with it. I roll off my concerns and anxieties into the person of Christ, and then I go into my day and I walk with the Lord. At the end of the day, I come to the cross again and I unburden the hurts and struggles of the day. I wake up in the cross and I sleep in the cross. That is how you live free in love. That is how you remain pure and holy before God."

That truth transformed my life. Christianity should not be wrapped up in religious exercises and principles, but in the person of Jesus Christ. I began to meditate daily on passages about God Almighty, the person of Jesus, and the Holy Spirit. It is still my habit today, 22 years later, to live and sleep in the cross on a daily basis. That journey has allowed me to experience freedom, joy, and grace through the trials and struggles. More than anything, it has kept me centered in a world that pulls me in a hundred different directions.

At Antioch, we teach this to be the ultimate pursuit of life. Christ must be the One consuming us, and out of that we do His bidding for His glory. We have found that intimacy with God is the hinge on which every issue in life turns. If we are connecting wholeheartedly with God, then we are able to live in His presence and accomplish what He has created us to do. Without Him, we are truly nothing.

Robert described it this way: the person of Christ must always be first in our lives; the purposes of Christ should be the natural outflow of that devotion; the projects of Christ are the practical expression. Person, then purpose, then projects. If they ever get out of order, then we will miss the heart of God along the way.

So, to keep Jesus first in our lives, we have asked our people to be committed to seek God in the Word, worship, and prayer as the first thing they do every morning. We believe that doing this first keeps us in love with Jesus, able to work from a place of great grace and fueled with the strength, energy, wisdom, and counsel we need to continue on in all that God has for us to do.

What is thrilling and exciting about this value is not just seeing our own people engaging God and being transformed though. As we have gone to the nations of the world, we have passed this value on to those we have led to Christ and discipled. National leaders are now leading their own people to seek God first in the mornings. When we gather with them, it is so awesome to see them spend hours at the beginning of their day praying and in the Word. This simple truth has changed our lives, and it continues to change lives all over the world.

Value #2 – Love Each Other

Around Antioch, we often ask the question, "Whom are you investing in?" Just as we have been invested in, we should invest in others so that God can reproduce life among us. While we are structured in cell groups, outside of that, people meet in twos and threes for discipleship that empower the Lifegroup and the church. No one is left out or excused from this expectation. We ask everyone to invest in one, two, or three people in such a way that they too are investing in others. One of our core values is that discipleship must happen, and it must reproduce.

Because this has been our focus from the beginning, we now have twenty years of disciple makers in our midst. There are church-planting teams who went through college together asking, "Where will we plant a church and how will it look?" Today, those groups of discipled students are serving as disciple-making communities around the world.

We believe that every believer should be committed to discipleship so that the Kingdom can invade his or her sphere of influence. Every politician needs somebody discipling him or her. If they are discipled rightly, then Kingdom values will be lived out in their office. Every businessperson, health care professional, educator, parent, and so on, needs to be discipled. When the values of the Kingdom are imparted, the whole of society will be affected.

Over 20 years ago we began the simple process of investing in men and women's lives with the expectation that they would do the same. We have seen generation after generation of people who, by investing in each others lives, are bearing fruit all over the world.

You never know what will become of the people you invest in. In 1997, we gathered in Mongolia for a retreat with our people and other believers who were serving in various nations. As I looked around the room, I saw the effectiveness of discipleship right before my eyes. A freshman at Baylor had shared Christ with my brother, David. David gave his life to Jesus and eventually led me to Christ. God gave me a heart for discipleship, and I was able to invest in many people, two specifically who were in that room: Bret, the leader of the church plant in Mongolia, and Kurt, the leader in Afghanistan. Kurt went on to invest in Colby, our church plant leader in Uzbekistan. Bret invested in Lyle, the church plant leader in Irkutsk. Then, I saw Colby and Lyle's disciples at the conference, as well as other church planters and nationals they had invested in. This story is played out literally hundreds of times throughout our movement and around the world as people have the opportunity to see with their eyes the fruit of discipleship and how it reproduces for the glory of God in the earth.

With more than 200 laborers spread out around the world, these lines of discipleship continue to multiply and touch countless lives. What I saw in Mongolia was just a microcosm of what God is doing through discipleship. There are hundreds of other lines of discipleship relationships that are impacting generations and nations.

The discipleship process really does work. God can take one life and multiply it to the unreached of the earth.

When discipleship is at the core of your relationships, life-giving community happens. Community for community sake is a dead-end street. In the upcoming generation, there is a major interest in community, but we need to make sure there is a purpose driving us. The people of Antioch are knit at the hip and the heart because we are joined together for a purpose, not for the purpose of each other but for the purposes and values of the Kingdom for the glory of God.

Jesus said, "Go and make disciples, teaching them to observe all that I command you..." (Matthew 28:19). We are driven by discipleship and that is why we consistently evaluate and ask one another, "Whom are you intentionally investing in and how are they reproducing the Kingdom out of what you are giving them?"

Value #3 – Love the Lost

The gospel is the power of God unto salvation. It is what sets people free. No matter how much good work we do, no matter how many different ideas we have about how to most effectively share the gospel, ultimately the gospel has power in and of itself to save. It is our desire to share the gospel in every way God makes possible to us.

I love our people because they share Christ everywhere they go. Around Waco, I regularly run into people whom someone from Antioch shared with. A waitress once approached me, and asked if I was the guy that spoke on Sunday mornings at Antioch. I told her I was, and then she told me her story.

A group of people from Antioch sat at her table one day and asked if they could pray for her. She was touched by their offer and allowed them to pray. When they left, they gave her a good tip and she was even more impressed. Then, another group of Antioch people sat at her table who not only prayed for her but invited her to Lifegroup. She went and had a good time. They shared with her, but she didn't make a decision for Christ that night. On Sunday morning, she came to the service and listened to the message. At the end of my talk, I asked if there was anyone there who needed Jesus. She raised her hand and prayed to accept Christ that morning.

"I just want to thank you for having people that pray for others," she said.

Yeah! This thing works. Our people are out in the city handing out tracts, praying for the lost, and sharing the gospel. Even some of our young mothers found a way to actively pursue loving the lost. They had grown tired of thinking they couldn't do anything for the Kingdom because they were at home all day with their little children, so they got together and prayed. Then, they started going together to places like parks where one mom could watch all the kids, and the other moms could share the gospel. These women saw people saved and others added to Lifegroups. These women put practical feet to their commitment to evangelism and found a way to make it happen. When we sow, we reap; When we do not sow, we do not reap.

I've heard people say that evangelism is not their calling. My understanding of Scripture is that sharing the gospel is everyone's calling. This is an awesome calling because as we share Christ with others, we *will* see lives changed and transformed. We all get to be a part of God's grace coming to the lost and saving them from sin and hell.

One Sunday, at the end of church, a single mom came up to me with her little boy in her arms. She told me that she worked with a girl from Antioch named Susan. They had become friends over time, and Susan had encouraged her and prayed for her consistently. While this young woman had no interest in the things of God, she found great comfort through life's struggles and challenges as Susan counseled, encouraged, and helped her.

Eventually, after many invitations, she went with Susan to a Lifegroup. Her own admission to me was that it was a little weird being there, but because of her friendship with Susan, she continued to go for several weeks. More and more, she found herself wanting to know God, which eventually led to her coming to Sunday services.

She told me, "I was actually really scared to come here, and I sat in the very back. After a couple of weeks, as I heard you sharing, I was deeply drawn. I got a CD of one of the messages and listened to it while I was driving to work a few weeks ago. You talked about God's love for us and our need to know Him. I found myself crying uncontrollably, and I pulled off to the side of the road and gave my heart and life to Jesus. The last few weeks have been wonderful and life changing as I have found people to walk with and to love me."

This young woman went on, "The reason I told you that story is that I wanted to introduce you to my little son Ryan. I wanted to let you know that because of your people and this message of the gospel, his destiny will be different. He also will be a man of God."

Right there, I could have gone to heaven and been happy. The process works. A community of people loved and cared for a young woman and the destiny of generations has been changed.

Love God. Love each other. Love the lost. Do you think these values aren't worth living out? Do you think it isn't worth laying it all down so that you can see lives changed? This is worth giving our lives for. There is no cost too great for all to hear and know, for all to see Jesus glorified. If we love Jesus and are obsessed with Him, if we love the church and have biblical conviction, then what else can we do but give our all?

Jesus knew that we were too complex to gather in too many thoughts, so He said that all the commandments could be wrapped up in loving God with all our heart, soul, mind, and strength and loving our neighbor as yourself. My prayer is that we will never lose these simple responses to God, and that as a people, we will be known for reproducing these Kingdom values in the uttermost parts of the earth.

Fruitful but Fragile

A couple of times a year, our leadership gathers to pray through vision and direction for the upcoming year. We spend time seeking God together and talking through implementation.

In 2004, as I was asking God about this upcoming time together, He spoke to me this simple phrase: *we are fruitful, but fragile*. I realized that in seeing God work in incredible ways over the years, we had become part of a movement. We were no longer just a church that plants churches, but a movement of people with like hearts and minds, with similar values that were touching people all around the world. God was blessing us with much fruit. But, though we were fruitful, we were also fragile.

We are fragile on two levels. First, we are fragile in the sense that we have focused our lives and ministries around our intimate, day-today walk with Jesus. If at any time we lose that sensitivity, that daily personal devotion, that worship and honor of Him in every aspect of our lives, we could quickly fall apart. If there is anything that has kept us on track, it is seeking Him daily, listening to Him and responding to Him in every way.

The second thing that makes us fragile is that we have committed ourselves to relationships. We have built a relational network around the world that is both wonderful and difficult. As we invest wholeheartedly in our people's lives in Waco, we are constantly sending them off to serve around the world and then welcoming new people in. It is hard at times to keep up with everything and everybody. God admonishes us over and over again to love one another, forgive one another, restore one another, and speak truth to one another. All the "one another" commands of Scripture need to be in operation in our midst.

When we commit ourselves to relational ministry, there are always conflicts to resolve, people to help, misunderstandings to clarify, and teams to develop. Sometimes it seems like it would be easier to set up a structure of hiring and firing people, but God hasn't called us to that kind of life. He has called us to a type of organic life that will cost us everything, causing us to continue to grow in love and be changed by the grace of God. This life-on-life discipleship and ministry has made us very fruitful, but also very fragile.

Hopefully, throughout this book, you have captured the essence of what we are all about. In a statement: we are in it for Him, and we are in it for them.

We want to love, honor, and glorify Jesus, not just in the big things, but in every little thing, listening and responding to Him. When people come to us and celebrate what is happening around us, we can truly say that all glory goes to God because we have simply listened and responded to Him.

We are also in it for them. When the Bible says to love our neighbors as ourselves, we see that our calling is wrapped up in serving others. For us to get all of our inheritance in God, we have to be about other people getting their inheritance, too. There is no one person who can change the world, but a team of people who effectively see the glory of God in their lives can. It truly is about Him and them. Whenever we lose sight of either, we miss out on what God has for us.

The Gulley's are a wonderful family that has impacted our whole movement because they have truly been in it "for Him and for them." Laurie Gulley is an intercessor and a mom of all moms. Ed Gulley is a man of resolve and conviction, desiring God to get all glory in all things. They raised five boys to love God and others. Carl and

The Gulley Boys (L-R) Stephen, James Mark, Jeffrey, Jonathan, Carl

Blair Gulley have been some of our major leaders, serving as our youth pastors since the beginning of the church plant and now are directing our college ministry. James Mark and Maria Gulley have been our worship & arts leaders from the beginning of the church plant and have led us in developing the whole worship& arts area. Jonathan and his wife, Amy, lead our church plant in Wheaton, Illinois. Steven and his wife, Neelie, are part of the Wheaton church plant where Steven serves as the worship leader, faithfully and powerfully seeing that church reproduce the life of God.

Jeffrey, the youngest son, was also a passionate man but is no longer with us. He passed away in 2005 when he was just 20 years old. With Jeffrey's death, we watched as a family who loved one another so passionately poured out their hearts to God and found Him as their source. If there is anything that has revealed God's heart to me, it was walking with the Gulley's in their season of grief. The Gulley family is symbolic of all of Antioch, and many times they have been the igniters and value carriers for what we are all about.

Carl Gulley, after his trip to Sri Lanka in 2005, wrote a poem that beautifully captures and reveals our hearts to be "in it for Him and for them." The message and passion of this piece communicates so powerfully who we are that I cannot think of a better way to conclude our story. I pray that the Holy Spirit will move and change you to become all He intended you to be through your relationship with Him in Jesus Christ.

Otherness

Otherness. *That's what we're all about. Not trying to be like anyone or anything else. Just Jesus. It makes us look like aliens. Foreigners in a distant land.* **We stick out.** *And humbly so. Why? Because the way we love is unusual. Our words bring tears of laughter and solace. Our music and dance are fueled by a different drummer –and a better One at that. The fruit? A different song. A different value system. Not pushing the edge of sin and hell. Not OK with status quo. A place where beneficial vs. permissible is clearly understood. And no one even wants the boundary line. We would much rather lunge out to the Kingdom's cutting edge...which is heaven's arms. Sitting on His lap is fine with me. His heart beat rhythmically puts me at rest. Not apathetic slumber that leads to poverty.* **But deep love that thrusts us to Nineveh.** *Macedonians are still calling. And Ethiopians are still asking for someone to come and help them understand. And how do we know this?*

For we look into a different pair of eyes. Not just the window to His soul. But a magnifying glass of theirs. Look again: His tears aren't clear- and they don't taste like salt. They're colorful banners of the nations... and taste like the blood that was shed for them. A tear trickles down and I see Sri Lanka. Another hangs in the corner of His eye and deep inside it I see a Sudanese lady worshipping over the family that just abandoned her. Here comes three more: **Canada, France, Mexico.** *As He wipes His eyes, I see the colors of* **Morocco, Russia, Scotland, and China** *on the palms of His hands. And where do those tears go? Stored in a bottle. Not just 'a' bottle; but 'The' bottle. The one that has held the cries of the saints of Germany. The one that held the deep secrets of* **Thailand's orphans, America's addicts, and Indonesia's widows**. *The groans from North Korea's underground church. And South Korea's prayer mountain. All in the bottle. Waiting for me to open my hands so He can pour them out. Why would He trust us with these treasures? These precious children of His? Because He calls us family. And He can trust us.* **Because we've seen the**

246

*otherness of God. **And long for more**. For if You, God, were the same as the rest, You wouldn't be holy. And my unholiness craves Your holiness. Your cleansing. **You**. In the process, we have become 'other.' And the importance of that? So many stories being told. Vying for my affections. **My passions. My heart**.*

*But I refuse to be caught up in the small stories that seem brilliant at the moment, but soon become faded glory. I desire to be taken into His story. Into Your great plot for me and mankind. So I leap into the chariot of fire and ask for humility and courage to leave it all behind: **NO MATTER THE COST!** Because You deserve it. And they need it. Because I love You. And they need You. And the Spirit and the Bride are still crying out, '**Come, Lord Jesus**' And You will. You always do.*

Staff Pictures

International Staff Conference 2006

Russia/Mongolia Regional Conference 2007

Headquarters Leadership Team 2007

Antioch Board of Advisors 2008
(Front L-R) Darrell & Margie Atwood, Ron & Janine Parrish,
Joe Ewen, Charles Davis (Back L-R) Jamey Miller,
Floyd McClung

Acknowledgements

Throughout this book many people have been mentioned with thankfulness and love. There is no way to list all the stories and the people that have made us who we are. These few acknowledgements are one more attempt to thank and express gratitude for the many. This actually has been the most difficult part of the book for me. I love and am thankful for so many and want everyone to know they are valued and loved. If your name does not appear in print know that your love and impact is written on our hearts.

Thank you to the Antioch Community Church Family

Your love, support, and lifestyle of giving your lives, gifts and resources here in our local community empowers all that we do here and around the world. I want to say a special thank you to the early pioneer families that jumped in with us. Though I am not able to mention everyone by name, your impact on us all continues until today.

To our Board of Advisors

Floyd & Sally McClung, Ron & Janine Parrish, Joe & Yvonne Ewen, Darrell & Margie Atwood, Charles & Frances Davis, Jamey & Kim Miller

You truly have been, and continue to be, fathers and mothers in the faith to all of us. Thank you for not only being our heroes but our helpers in all things. We love you.

To our Elders and their families
Jeff & Dorothy Abshire, Kevin & Stacy Johnson, Danny & Kathy Mulkey, and our honorary elders, Gus and Clare Hunter

Thank you for your consistent and dedicated love for Laura and me and for the people of Antioch. You have always put God's Kingdom first and others before yourselves, therefore God is honored by your lives.

To the Elders of the past and their families
Ty and Erica Denney, Ben and Ruth Loring, Kely and Jennifer Braswell

Thank you for your love, consistency, and faithfulness. We continue to cheer you on in all the work that God has called you to do.

To the Elders at Highland Baptist Church led by Barry Camp and Mark Wible
Thank you Barry, Martha, Mark, and Laurie. Thank you for loving us, being patient with us and leading us. Thank you for your continual support. There is no way we would be where we are without you in our lives. I look forward to many years of fellowship and friendship in the future.

To our current Pastoral Team and their families
Hannah & Devon Jonklaas, Shawn & Connie Dunn, Carl & Blair Gulley, Fred & Becca Nelson, Vincent & Tonja Carpenter, Danny & Kathy Mulkey, James Mark & Maria Gulley, Nate & Jamie Bobbett, Joe & Jessica Padilla, Shoan & Michelle Holley, Susan & Marty Peters, Penny & Ron Allison, Vicki Smyer, Drew & Bethany Steadman, Kelly & Chris Woods, Donny & Bryanna Martin, Robert & Heather Fuller, Pat & Tanya Murphy, Joan & Terry Hobbs

Antioch Community Church is what it is because of your consistent love and faithfulness to fulfill the will of God at every turn. Thank you for being so trustworthy and faithful.

To our current Administrative Team
Jeff Abshire, Shawn Griesemer, Angela Kubeczka, Jacob Critz, Keegan Rogers, Chris Woods, Mary Greenwald, Ethan Mulkey, Sherri Lessman, Monica Vardeman, Caleb Gallifant, Allison McBrayer, Laura Storm, Melissa Hammond, Sherrie Eyth, Donna Stewart, Blanton Lewis, Joseph Burdick, Justin Boland, Catherine Bower, Betty Lewis, Joel Strickland, Tommy Burns, Jessie Harris, Mike Heron, Laura Willits, Chris Laredo

Thank you for your consistent love, diligence, and service. I know that we could never be what we are called to be without you and your loving, servant hearts and your incredible competence. You are not only our right arm but you are our left tackle.

I want to say a special thank you to Dawn Manoleas for 15 years of loving, serving and caring for so many of us. Dawn, you have always been a faithful friend and have stood by not only my side but by our side. I don't know how many literally thousands of hours that have gone on behind the scenes that some people will never know. I know and will be forever grateful.

Thank you Pam and Talmage Minter for your love, integrity, and 1000's of hours of prayer. Pam your faithfulness has been an example of love to us all.

Thank you Lisa Daily for pioneering with us. Your faith to step out made a way for the many who have followed.

To Mary Greenwald: God sent you "for such a time as this". Thank you for your love, faithfulness, prayers, and continual care. You not only represent me but all of us with joy, love and life. You truly are a perfect fit.

And to Ruth Reese: Dear Ruth, you are now in Heaven. I just had to say thank you for being a friend that sticks closer than a brother. Thank you for your intercession and your service to all of us through the years. You continue to live in our hearts and we can't wait to see you face to face.

To our current CPMT Leaders and Volunteers
Kevin Johnson, Penny Allison, Shawn Griesemer, Angela Kubeczka, Ethan Mulkey, Becky Lockhart, Bruce & Carol Mazzare, Heather Bonney, Jennifer Smyer, Keegan Rogers, Kerry Ethridge, Todd Meek, Rachel Svrchek, Brian & Ashley Bundy

How could we serve our people around the world without you? Thank you, thank you, thank you for being the servants of all, so that His Kingdom can come all over the world.

To our current Urban Staff
Vincent & Tonja Carpenter, Dean & Sherri Lessman, Kami Suttle, Courtney Burdick, Nereida Beccara, Beth Whittington, Stephanie Harnden, Charles Pink

Your tireless commitment to love and serve our friends in the inner city is changing lives day by day. Your willingness to sacrifice financially and every other way does not go unnoticed. Thank you, thank you, thank you for everything that you do.

To our current AMI workers all over the world, laboring among the unreached.
Martha, Jim, Pat, David, Stacy, Wes, Kandy, Kelly, Misha, Stephanie, Faith, Bret, Jackie, Freda, Joshua, Sagaana, Jeff, Winae, Russell, Carla, Robert, Liza, Aric, Juleigh, Elizabeth, Bill, Andrea, Rich, Diane, Fred, Kathy, Lexia, Rudy, Emily, Samantha, MJ, Hayley, Nick, Stephanie, Treavor, Alina, Kat, Glen, Michele, Colby, Jennifer, Chris, Blair, Mark, Dayna, Jeremy, Mark, Anne, Zach, Christina, Allison, Clayton, Jessica, Susan, Oscar, Tim, Janice, Peggy, Marcus, Becky, Chris, Rebekah, Micah, Cara, Trey, Leigh Anne, Robert, Jim, Janelle, Blake, Marci, Mindy, John, Jamie, Clint, Rachel, Karissa, Jeanette, J.D., Erin, Paul, Jonathan, Nicole, Debra, Chas, Claudia, Greg, Sharon, Jason, Kyle, Melissa, Pete, Vikki, Kurt, Karen, Petrus, Lisle, Nicole, Scott, Jocelyn, Byron, Liz

Though we cannot mention your last names (for your security and those whom you are serving) you are heroes to all of us. Thank you for your love, example, and for giving your lives for the unreached of the earth.

Berlin, Germany
Van & Kelly Vandegriff, Noel & Amy Tarter, William & Sheila Whittenberg, Shannon Rogers, Stephanie Johnson, Sarah Clark
Mainz, Germany
Pete & Jennifer Leininger, Carrie Homburg, Jennifer Robbins
Wiesbaden, Germany
Bill & Rachel Gorman, Scott & Jenni Robinson, Kim Carroll
Sheffield, England
Daniel & Jeannie McGinnis, Stephen & Cheri McElroy, Autumn Davis, Todd & Lauren Roberts
Seville, Spain
Clayton & Jessica Thompson, Susan Whitlatch, Oscar Torres

Way to go Europe! Your investment in a post modern world, I believe with all my heart, will bring us back to a reality of the life of God. Thanks for all that you are and all that you do.

To our US Church Planters
Belton, Texas
Tad & Sherry Smith and the leadership staff
Boston, Massachusetts
Sean & Laura Richmond, Jeff & Sarah Bianchi, and leadership staff
Dallas, Texas
Jordan & Christy Ogden and leadership staff
Knoxville, Tennessee
Kely & Jennifer Braswell and Jarrod & Jennifer Justice
Los Angeles, California
Ty & Erica Denney, Sarah Bodie, Natalie Camper, Emily Reynolds, Angela Adams
Portland, Oregon
Billy & Teresa Sieh, Jason & Ashley Kennedy, Daniel & Lesley Roby, and leadership staff

Seattle, Washington
Jady & Liz Griffin, Erika Kraus, Brian Eastland, Kristina Bradford
San Diego, California
Robert & Stefanie Herber, Jonathan & Suzanne Lair, Kendall & Shelly Laughlin, Kirk & Lisa McCown
Wheaton, Illinois
Jonathan & Amy Gulley, Chris & Libby Deleenheer, Stephen & Neelie Gulley, Will Wilshusen

May God bring revival to our nation again. May each of you be a catalyst for seeing fresh movements established all over the United States and the world. We love you and are so grateful for you.

Antioch Training Schools -
Staff and Leaders of the past and present –
Nate & Jamie Bobbett, Danny & Kathy Mulkey, Joe & Jessica Padilla, Shoan & Michelle Holley, Ty & Erica Denney, Tad & Sherry Smith, Kely & Jennifer Braswell, Jeff Bianchi, Kevin Johnson, Dorothy Abshire, John & Kelly Atkinson, Andrew & Carrie Bach, Stephanie Bateman, Audrey Berry, Don Birchum, Heather Bonney, Lexia, Raegan Carlson, Bill Gorman, Carl Gulley, Tim Head, Stefanie Herber, Carrie Homburg, Kyle & Melissa, David Karnes, Pete & Vikki, Heidi Kraus, Colby, Pete Leininger, Mark & Anne, Heather McAnear, Julie McBrayer, Chris, Barry McCuistion, Stephen McElroy, Lauren Nelson, Amy Parker, Laura Perez, Byron, Nathan & Elise Syer, John Storm, Laura Summersett, Amy Tarter, Clayton & Jessica Thompson, Allison, Pam Minter, James & Adriana Walker, Brandon Wilson, Leisa Wiseman, Grant & Rachel Wortman, Suzanne Wyatt, Lynn Youngblood, and anyone else we may have left out - you are loved and appreciated!

Thank you for equipping the men and women of God for changing the world.

To all our Financial Supporters
You truly have been partners in the gospel. Your inheritance is full because of your love and sacrifice through the years. Thank you for storing up your treasures in heaven.

Friends & Family

I want to say a special thank you to Mark & Andrea Owen, Marty & Susan Peters, Danny & Melissa Wible, and all of your children. Thank you for choosing us as friends to walk with in this journey together so that our children will fully surpass us in all that God has called them to be.

This story would not be complete without thanking our families. Thank you for your continual love and support. Thank you to our parents; Wendell and Marie Seibert and Grace Mielke, and in loving memory of Stanley Mielke. And to our brothers and sisters: John Seibert, David Seibert, Ann Steinbrecher, Greg Mielke, David Mielke, and their families.

And to the thousands of people who have come through our midst through the years who we have not been able to mention by name, every one of you has added to our lives. Many of you have contributed in ways that will change us forever. We are unable to fully express our gratitude and all that is in our hearts, but we are thankful that God sees all and knows all.

13830801R00137

Made in the USA
Charleston, SC
03 August 2012